D1491677

BAT
&
PAD

BAT
&
PAD

WRITINGS ON AUSTRALIAN CRICKET
1804-1984

COMPILED BY
PAT MULLINS & PHILIP DERRIMAN

WITH A FOREWORD BY
BOB HAWKE

Oxford   New York
OXFORD UNIVERSITY PRESS

Oxford University Press, Walton Street, Oxford OX2 6DP

Oxford New York Toronto
Delhi Bombay Calcutta Madras Karachi
Kuala Lumpur Singapore Hong Kong Tokyo
Nairobi Dar es Salaam Cape Town
Melbourne Auckland

and associated companies in
Beirut Berlin Ibadan Nicosia

Oxford is a trade mark of Oxford University Press

First published 1984 by Oxford University Press, Melbourne
Reprinted 1986

Bat & pad : writings on Australian cricket
1804–1984.
1. Cricket—Australia—History
I. Mullins, Pat   II. Derriman, Philip
796.35' 8' 0944   GV928.A8
ISBN 0-19-554518-4

Printed in Great Britain by
Billing & Sons Ltd,
Worcester

CONTENTS

For
Bernard and Pat,
an Englishman
and an Irishman,
both pioneers

FOREWORD

OF ALL GREAT OUTDOOR GAMES, I SUPPOSE THERE IS NONE WHICH HAS attracted writers, good and bad, as much as cricket. The frequent richness of personality of the game's outstanding players, the demands it makes on character as well as talent, its gamut of performance from the heroic to the humiliating, and its great scope, perhaps only rivalled by golf, for the ridiculous — all these qualities make cricket as stimulating to think, talk and write about as it is to play and watch.

The game has changed remarkably in recent years, particularly in its commercial organization, but this book serves to remind us of the broad thread of continuity which has survived for well over a century in Australian cricket. For example, the argument — heard most vociferously in this country during the 'Bodyline' tour but still very much alive in the era of Lillee and 'Thommo' and the current great West Indies attack — that the game suffers from an excess of bouncers, finds eloquent and admirably concise expression in Anon's poem, 'Bump', of 1898:

> Hit him — body, head or wicket —
> 'Tis the soul of Modern Cricket.

For those of us who were inclined to regard sledging as a peculiarly contemporary phenomenon, it comes as a surprise to see it here precisely described and roundly condemned by the Sydney *Commercial Journal* — in 1838!

The general tone of English reporting on cricket tours of Australia over the last 100 years is superbly established by W.G. Grace's extended whinge about the preparation of the wicket at Stawell in 1873, as well as his comments on the flies and the condition of the road to Warrnambool (to be a little fairer, W.G.'s account of the touring party's journey into country Victoria, returning by 'small coastal steamer' to Melbourne, is a vivid piece of sporting and social history).

An insight into the tensions and stresses to which our modern Test selectors are no doubt prone is provided by the official report, published here, by the Secretary of the Cricket Board of Control, of a fight between the great Clem Hill and Peter McAlister at an Australian selectors' meeting in Sydney in 1912:

McAlister: At all events, I reckon I am a better skipper than either Trumper, Armstrong or yourself.

Hill: You have been looking for a punch in the jaw all night and I will give you one.

Among the great pleasures of this book are the generous and perceptive appreciations by former great Australian players of their great contemporaries — Noble and Hill on Trumper, Oldfield on Gregory and McDonald, O'Reilly on Bradman, Fingleton on Bradman and (ribs probably aching with each word) Larwood, Davidson on Miller, Benaud on Davidson.

There are splendid contributions by some of the finest writers on cricket — Arthur Mailey, Jack Fingleton, Bob Simpson (all as proficient behind the typewriter as out in the middle), Ray Robinson, Neville Cardus, John Arlott, Denzil Batchelor and Michael Parkinson — as well as interesting offerings by writers more renowned in other fields of literature: 'Banjo' Patterson, C.J. Dennis, Bob Ellis, Adrian McGregor, Blanche d'Alpuget (in a piece of prose which almost does justice to the innings it describes), John Masefield, J.M. Barrie and Terence Rattigan. A.A. Milne's ruthless defence of bodyline hardly seems to come from the same world as Christopher Robin and Winnie the Pooh.

It is also fascinating to read written contributions by personalities more associated with the spoken word. 'Yabba', on the form shown here, was probably more devastating with the tongue than the pen. Kate Fitzpatrick, with whom I recall sharing a most enjoyable television appearance with Jack Fingleton some years ago, provides an unexpected insight into Greg Chappell's batting grip.

Pat Mullins and Philip Derriman have performed a great service in bringing together this delightful anthology. It will bring pleasure to cricket followers not only in Australia but wherever the game is played and loved.

BOB HAWKE
Canberra, 1984

INTRODUCTION

Cricket is a summer game for the player and the observer, but a winter game for the reader and thinker who sits by his fireside and evokes unperishable memories.

SIR ROBERT MENZIES

COMPILING A CRICKET ANTHOLOGY IS NECESSARILY A TRICKY UNDER-taking, given the vast amount of material from which the compiler may choose. The anthologist must survey the material available and then include or discard on the basis of whether each item is interesting, novel, humorous, historical or rare enough — at least as it seems to him. Each anthology should therefore differ from all the others, for each is, in reality, an expression of the anthologist's personal taste. It is certainly to be hoped that this anthology differs from those that have appeared previously.

Our intention has been, first, to use mainly material that has not been anthologized before, and this is true of probably 90 per cent of the items in the book. In fact, the bulk of the contents are reproduced here for the first time since their original appearance in print. In one or two cases, they have not appeared anywhere in print before.

Our intention was also to use where possible the work of celebrated writers, whether or not they were cricket writers. Hence, the presence in the following pages of pieces by authors and poets such as A.B. Paterson, C.J. Dennis, George Essex Evans, John Masefield, Terence Rattigan and J.M. Barrie.

Above all, our intention was to use material of quality, with the result, we hope, that this may be considered a broadsheet anthology, not a tabloid one.

It hardly needs to be pointed out, too, that this is an anthology of writing about Australian cricket, not an anthology of cricket writing by Australians. The difference is important, because it means that the best of the English writers qualify for inclusion. In fact, the following pages probably contain more set pieces, as distinct from news reports, by English writers than by Australian, and for that no apology is necessary. England's cricket literature, we Australians might as well admit, is a good deal richer than our own. There are several reasons why this is so, and one of the most important of them has to do with the tradition of sports journalism in each country. Australian newspapers, by and large, have been prepared to settle for sports reporting, while English newspapers have aspired to sports writing. Australian newspapers have rarely required of their cricket writers more than a factual account of a day's cricket; English newspapers have expected something more in the nature of an essay. The significance of this is that a big majority of England's finest cricket writers over the years have been newspapermen to begin with.

Some of Australia's best-known cricket writers were tradesmen journalists, too, including Ray Robinson, Richie Benaud and Jack Fingleton, the last of whom was quick to remind anyone in doubt about the matter that he was a journalist (although not, it seems, a cricket writer) several years before he made a name for himself in cricket. In Australia, however, many noted cricket writers, more proportionally than in England, have been former cricketers. Some of them — Monty Noble and Bill O'Reilly, for instance — have written with great flair, but the literary skill of many others has not matched their skill at cricket. Where former players appear as authors in this book it is because of the worth of their writing, not their reputation on the field.

When Oxford University Press asked me to gather material for an Australian cricket anthology, I turned for help to Pat Mullins, a family friend who happens to own Australia's biggest and best private cricket library. Might he, as a favour, agree to contribute an odd deserving item? He did agree, and proceeded to contribute so generously that I was able to withdraw immediately into the background and allow him to take over.

Pat Mullins is one of the most distinguished figures, off the field, in Australian cricket. Born in Townsville in 1923, he is the son of a hotel-keeper, also named Pat, who with his brother Mick ran a hotel in Tully widely known as Pat and Mick's. For many years it was one of the landmarks of North Queensland. Pat Mullins was no more than a moderately good cricketer himself, but from the age of nine he had a passionate interest in the game, which even at that time manifested itself in an urge to collect cricket literature and memorabilia. He began collecting in earnest in 1946, about the time he graduated as a lawyer, and, apart from a period in the late 1950s and early 1960s when his interest flagged, he has been collecting ever since. His library now contains more than 8,000 books and a huge accumulation of cricket magazines, many of them genuinely rare, stacked from floor to ceiling around the four walls of his study. The library is one of the treasures of the cricket world, and it is no wonder that over the years a huge number of students of the game, Sir Donald Bradman among them, has called at the Mullins home to dip into it. One of the best things about this book is that it will allow many others to dip into it, too.

PHILIP DERRIMAN
Sydney, 1984

In Days
of Old

FAIR WEATHER FOR CRICKET

This is the oldest known reference to the game in Australia
(THE *SYDNEY GAZETTE*, JANUARY 8, 1804)

THE late intense weather has been very favorable to the amateurs of Cricket, who have scarcely lost a day for the last month. The frequent immoderate heats might have been considered inimical to the amusement, but were productive of very opposite consequences, as the state of the atmosphere might always regulate the portion of exercise necessary to the ends this laborious diversion was originally intended to answer.

A MANLY GAME

The report of a challenge match between soldiers and Sydney civilians on February 26, 1830
(THE *AUSTRALIAN*)

SATURDAY'S (it was really Friday's) trial of this manly and healthful sport passed off with éclat, to both sides. . . Early in the day the soldiers had considerably the advantage, and it was thought for a long time would have beat the native cricketers hollow. There were several hundreds of spectators till between three and four p.m., when the number increased — the native lads, cheered on by the presence of their relatives and companions, the soldiers by several of their officers and numbers of comrades. One of the best players among the soldiers received an unlucky salute on the nose with a ball, which laid him flat. Another player on the opposite side was nearly deprived of respiration by the ball which took him in the middle; but no other accidents occurred to vary the hilarity of the contest.

THE PREVAILING AMUSEMENT

(THE *SYDNEY GAZETTE*, 1832)

CRICKET is now the prevailing amusement of the day. Let no man henceforth set up for a sporting character whose name is not enrolled among the "gentlemen cricketers" of Sydney. Let no adoring swain hereafter think to "dangle at a lady's apron string," or

— feast upon the smiles
From partial beauty won,

unless he can boast of excellence in handling a bat, or sending up a ball — the former will reject his company, the latter his addresses. Hyde Park is now almost daily graced by the aspiring youth of Sydney practising their favourite recreation, and respectable females looking on to enliven the scene. A new club has been formed in addition to the one before existing, and we expect that New South Wales will soon be able to boast players that might bear away the palm of victory even at Lord's.

The Melbourne Cricket Club's First Match
Played on November 22, 1838, in William Street against a team of soldiers
(THE *PORT PHILLIP GAZETTE*, DECEMBER 1, 1838. QUOTED IN KEITH DUNSTAN'S *THE PADDOCK THAT GREW*, MELBOURNE, 1974)

PLEASURE and recreation are absolutely necessary to relieve our minds and bodies from too constant attention and labour with truly gratified feelings there. Did we not witness the gentlemen of the district assemble last Saturday week on the beautiful pleasure grounds around this fast rising town, to bring into practice one of the most elegant and manly sports that can be enjoyed? Yes, it was pleasurable to witness those whose mental and enterprising minds had turned this, but short time since wilderness, into a busy emporium of traffic, relinquishing for a time their occupations and writings. These efforts to establish sports such as these.

During the week arrangements had been made by the gentlemen civilians of the district to play a match at cricket again at the military. Captain Smyth, with the enthusiasm natural to him, and desirous of forwarding everything either really beneficial or of useful amusement, was joined by many of those who had retired from the Services, but whose hearts are still with it, mustered on the ground a company with which they would have attempted a more stirring contest.

It was a heartening sight to witness from an adjacent hill the ground as it was laid out. Camps pitched, banners tastefully arranged, and all the enlivening smiles of beauty that would have graced a far-famed tournament of other time, formed a scene which we trust often again to witness.

At 12 o'clock precisely, a signal called the players to their post, when the game commenced, the Military taking the first innings. We have not the particulars of the game before us and can therefore but briefly notice those who particularly distinguished themselves.

After a duration of some hours, it concluded by a triumph on the part of the civilians.

Mr Powlett, Mr D. G. McArthur's bowling and Mr Russell's batting attracted universal applause.

On the whole, the game was played with an esprit de corps, a judgment and an activity that a first-rate club in England might be proud of.

SLEDGING IN 1838

From a report of a match between two Sydney clubs, Australian and Union, on February 7, 1838
(THE *COMMERCIAL JOURNAL*)

WE have no objection to a little *humorous* chaff, either in the field or out of it, but we certainly condemn that low slang and insulting remarks, so often resorted to by the Australians — it is much to their discredit.

A REMINISCENCE BY MR HILLIARD

Born in 1826, Harry Hilliard played in the first match between New South Wales and Victoria in 1856
(*CRICKET*, 1894)

"THE batting and bowling are a great deal better than they were in my time, but I won't admit that you can field any better than we could. The wickets are better, and the bowling is a great deal more tricky than it was. They bowl with the 'head' as the saying is. But making allowances for the fielding ground, I say that we used to field quite as well in my time as they do now. The other day someone was talking to me about the splendid fielding, and I said, 'So it ought to be; they play in a parlour now.' But look at the grounds we had to field on. Why, the first match we played in Victoria in 1856 was on this ground, and there wasn't a bit of grass on it. We all played with our boots off. Some in naked feet and some kept their stockings on. You didn't know where the ball was coming at you then, and you had to watch for it. But even then if you missed a catch the bowler would be almost inclined to give you a smack over the ear.

"Talking about bowling, I mind once when the Victorians were making between two and three hundred in their second innings, because our men could not bowl straight. It was all underhand bowling, too. You see Gilbert, our captain, would keep himself on all day bowling, no matter how they were pasting him. And he tried all the others at the other end, but they couldn't get any nearer the wicket than he could. Why, Tommy Wills hit one out into the Richmond Paddock there, and they made 8 runs for it. It took two men to throw it back. So I got sick of that, and at the end of the over I collared the ball. 'What are you going to do with that?' said Gilbert. 'I'm going on to bowl,' I says. 'Who told you so?' says he. 'I'm going on to bowl, anyhow,' I says; 'there's not one of you can go near the wickets, and I'm going to put 'em in some straight ones.' I did bowl, and I sent in some straight underhand ones and soon made a separation.

"It was Captain Ward first taught us (round-arm bowling) in Sydney; but it was Gid. Elliott, of Victoria, who taught us best. We did not know much about it then, and he mowed us down. There was one match where we only wanted 16 runs to win, and it cost us seven wickets to get them. There was great excitement, I can tell you. But there wasn't much difference between bowling and throwing for a good bit. I remember one match where it was all throwing, so I thought. Tommy Wills and Wardill (a brother of Major Wardill) threw for Victoria, and we had two men to throw for us — one of them was a black fellow, Twopenny we used to call him, and he was a good thrower. But they got more particular after a time."

Coaching the Colonials

By William Caffyn, a leading English professional who toured Australia in 1863–64 and stayed on to coach
(FROM HIS *SEVENTY-ONE NOT OUT*, LONDON, 1899)

When I left England with Parr's team nothing was further from my thoughts than that I should stay in Australia. While I was at Melbourne an offer was made to me by the executive of the Melbourne Club that I should remain with them for two years — with the option of an extra twelve months — at a salary of £300 a year, as coach and general instructor of cricket to the members. After some little natural hesitation, I closed with them on the terms stated. I did a good deal of bowling at the club members, and soon succeeded in improving the play of many of them. The system I worked on was never to try and make all bat alike. If a man was a hitter, I tried to make him hit with as great safety as was possible; and if, on the other hand, another player was naturally a "stone-wall" batter, I encouraged him in this style of play. Of course I was careful not to induce either batsman to carry out his particular style of play too far. After a time, at the suggestion of some of the members themselves, I myself would take the bat and give an exhibition of batting at the net. There were no side nets in those days, so we were obliged to have several fielders. I used to bat for an hour at a time with three bowlers at me, and found it very hard work under the intensely hot sun, especially when there was a hot wind blowing at the same time. A crowd of people would stand and look on while I was batting, and they would cheer me lustily whenever I made a good hit. I never saw such painstaking cricketers as the Australians were in those days, and it was most interesting work teaching then when one could see the way they improved. The progress they had made at cricket was very noticeable to me when I visited the Antipodes with the second English team after a lapse of a couple of years, and this improvement became still more apparent two years later still. Some of the younger players used, I could see, to try and copy my own style of batting to the letter, and I had to caution them against doing this in *every* particular. For instance, in playing back I never used to move my right foot, and all my pupils endeavoured to play back in the same way, some of them tucking themselves up and becoming very helpless in consequence. I could soon perceive that some of them were able to be much more effective in their back play by stepping nearer the wicket in making the stroke; and whenever I found this to be the case I used to advise their adopting the custom, always taking care to check the fault of drawing away wide of the stumps. There was a fixed belief in Australia in those days that it was bad form to move the right foot at all when defending the wicket; and when I had proved to many of them that it was often advantageous for some batsmen to do so when playing back, they, perhaps not unnaturally, asked me if the same foot might not also be moved when playing *forward*. This idea, of course, I had to negative very strongly. The chief difficulty I had at first in teaching them batting was to keep the ball down in cutting, and for a long time they were at a loss to understand how I was able to do this so successfully myself. I endeavoured to impress it on them that one of the chief essentials to

successful cutting was the *timing* of the ball accurately. I used to get the
bowlers to bowl ball after ball to me to cut, in order to show them how
the stroke should be made. I was able to cut very close to the stumps in
those days, and in imitating me in this particular several batsmen used
often to try and cut a ball which was dead on the wicket — an attempt
which generally resulted in disaster. As a rule, they learnt to do the
forward cut, with the left leg advanced, much more quickly than they
were able to master the late cut. Although they were aware that the *right*
foot must necessarily be moved in order to make this latter stroke, still
they had become so imbued with the idea that the right foot should
never be moved for *defensive* purposes that they were often thinking of
this rule when an off-ball came which required cutting late, and were
not able to move the foot quick enough to make a late cut. Many of
them at the early period of which I write had seen comparatively little
first-class cricket, and as was only natural, through binding themselves
by hard-and-fast rules, they became somewhat automatic in their style
of batting — a fault which no one could possibly charge them with in
after-years.

They were delightful pupils for one to have to teach, even as far back
as "the sixties" — always willing to be shown a new stroke and quick to
do their best to retrieve an error, never taking offence at having their
faults pointed out, and never jealous of one another. When I remember
all this, it is not so much a matter of surprise to me to see what
Australian cricket has become to-day as perhaps may be the case with
some people.

Poor Tommy Wills

By W. J. Hammersley
(THE *SYDNEY MAIL*, 1883)

SINCE my last article appeared a friend has kindly lent me some records
of sport extending over many years and ranging from the turf to the
cooking of a kangaroo steamer, for which I observe he has four
different recipes. Amongst the cricket records a name frequently
appears to which I have once or twice alluded — a name connected with
cricket — that never will be forgotten, the name of a gentleman born in
New South Wales, the name of poor Tommy Wills. Thomas
Wentworth Wills, though a native, was educated at Rugby, and thence
went to Cambridge, for which University Eleven he played against

Oxford, but it was after my year, which was 1847. I have heard his right to play in the eleven questioned by an Oxford man, as he was only at Magdalen College (a very fast one in my day) for one term, and that he had taken his name off at the time. However, play he did, and then he came to Victoria in the same steamer with Sir Henry Barkly. I think I only played in one match with Wills at Kennington Oval, about 1853 or '54, and I knew little or nothing of him at home, as I had given up playing almost when he began. But here, of course, I knew him well, and a finer young fellow never donned the flannels than Tom Wills. He was a very peculiar man, rather taciturn, but very good-natured and a very general favourite. I knew his father and his mother well, the latter a most kind, affectionate mother to him, and I spent some pleasant days with Tommy on their estate at Point Henry, near Geelong, where we used to shoot ducks and quails. The old gentleman was a shrewd man of business and looked well after Tommy, and it may be remembered how he and all his party, some 14 or 15 persons, were killed by the blacks on his station, near Nogoa in Queensland. Tom Wills has frequently told me that he never trusted the natives, but always carried two six-shooters and often warned "the governor" to do the same, but the old man prided himself on being able to manage the blacks from his experience of them gained in Victoria, and said they would never harm him. But one night they slaughtered the whole party at the camp — women and all, including George Elliott, brother of Gid the cricketer. Wills told me that when the blacks first visited the camp, the party consisted of about 20 splendid men, headed by one of herculean proportions, all stark naked. The old man, after a parley, called the chief aside and gave him to understand that as there were women in the camp, they must wear some article of attire, and furnished the chief with a long roll of white calico, with instructions "how to dress". The party retired for the day, but next morning, to Tom Wills's intense amusement, they appeared "dressed," walking solemnly in file, but in a novel style. Each sable warrior had about two yards of calico to himself, but tied in front round the waist with the ends streaming behind in the breeze like the lappels of a dress coat! The old man had to administer a sharp rebuke to the chief, and to give him another lesson. It may be remembered what a fearful slaughter of the blacks took place after this massacre, but the particulars as related to me are too sickening for recital. To give even a brief record of Tom Wills' cricketing career would take too much space, suffice it to say he played in every important match for years, and generally acted as "skipper," for which position he was A1. He could bowl in all shapes — fast, slow, medium and he could throw, too, so neatly and cleverly that few umpires were down on him. With an ugly style of batting he could stop the best bowling and get runs, too, and no one who had once seen his peculiarly ugly style of play would ever forget it. He was secretary of the Melbourne Cricket Club for one season, and when he left office everything was in a muddle — club papers, books, cricket-balls, cricket guides, Zingari flannels, cigars, "spiked" boots — everything one can conceive, stuffed together in the large tin box of the club. A most untidy mortal he was, and quite unfit for such work. The cricket field was his place, and I don't think Tommy ever gave a thought to anything but cricket in his life. I remember one practice match, just before an Intercolonial, he and several other players, including George Marshall and Gid Elliott, were very nearly killed by sunstroke. A hot wind blew with a blazing sun; and, as there were a lot of spectators, they did not like to retire, but at last Phoebus triumphed. I thought, really, it was all up with Tommy, as we put wet towels on his head as he lay stretched on the table in the pavilion. I have often thought that if Tommy had had the advantages that some of the players of the present day have he would have eclipsed many of them. His end was a sad one. He was attacked with softening of the brain, induced by his not taking that care of himself which he should have done, and gradually became irresponsible for his actions, and in a fit of frenzy stabbed himself in the left side with a pair of scissors he snatched from the table. He sleeps quietly in the cemetery at Heidelberg, about 8 miles from Melbourne.

Bush Cricket in Australia, 1873-74
By W. G. Grace
(FROM HIS 'W.G.': CRICKETING REMINISCENCES AND PERSONAL REFLECTIONS, LONDON, 1899)

On the Sunday — which we spent at Ballarat — we had our first experience of an Australian dust storm. A hot wind swept over the city, scorching everything up, and clouds of blinding dust whirled along the roads and streets. It was thoroughly unpleasant, as the whole town was in darkness while the storm raged. On this Sunday Humphrey met with an accident, which deprived us of his services in the two succeeding matches. He went for a drive into the bush country, and was thrown out of the trap, falling on the stump of a tree, and straining the muscles in his thigh.

Our troubles began in earnest when we turned our backs upon

Ballarat, and our faces towards Stawell, where we were to play our next match. The journey of 74 miles had to be made in an old-fashioned Cobb's coach over a rough bush track, quite undeserving of the name of road. At the outset there were difficulties to overcome. When they saw the vehicle in which they had to make the journey several members of the team flatly refused to take their seats, and were only, after much coaxing, prevailed upon to do so. We left Ballarat at 8.30 a.m. The first fifteen miles were through cultivated country, and the roads were tolerably decent, but for the remaining sixty miles we endured agonies. The horses laboured along up to their hocks in white dust, with which we were literally cloaked, so that we looked for all the world like so many millers as we sat on the jolting and rickety vehicle.

To break the monotony of the journey, two members of the team, who had guns with them, amused themselves, if not their comrades, by banging at the magpies and parrots as we went along. It seems rather cruel to kill the lively and entertaining parrot, but as they are as plentiful in Australia as sparrows are in London the offence was perhaps not very serious. The secretary of Stawell Cricket Club, and a few other cricket enthusiasts in the neighbourhood, came twenty miles from home to meet us at Ararat. Four miles off Stawell itself it seemed as if the whole town had turned out *en masse* to greet us. As we approached the crowd cheered wildly, and two brass bands struck up a welcoming strain. The horses in one of the waggonettes at once took fright, and overturned the vehicle. Luckily, though the trap was smashed to atoms, no one was injured. Stawell was reached at 8.30. We had been twelve hours on the road, travelling under the most uncomfortable conditions, but our reception made us forget the trials and troubles of the long drive.

At that time Stawell was a small, but rich, mining centre of about 8000 inhabitants, and on the following day most of the professionals in our team inspected the North Cross Reef Gold Mine, which was reputed to be the best paying mine in Victoria. My cousin, W. R. Gilbert, and I hired a buggy and drove about ten or twelve miles to a lagoon in the bush, where we had a fine day's sport with our guns. Gilbert and I were in hopes of bagging a kangaroo, but no such luck came our way that day.

Our match against twenty-two of Stawell began next morning, under conditions by no means inspiriting. The ground was in a deplorable condition. Here and there were small patches of grass, but the greater part was utterly devoid of any herbage. We were not surprised to hear that the field had only been ploughed up three months before, and that the grass had been sown in view of our visit. The wicket was execrable, but there was no help for it — we had travelled seventy miles through bush and dust to play the match, and there was no option but to play.

Of course the cricket was shockingly poor, and the match a ludicrous farce. How bad the ground really was may be judged from the fact that one slow ball actually stuck in the dust, and never reached the batsman. It was ridiculous to play on such a wicket, but we were in for it and went through with it. Jupp and I batted first, and adopted slogging tactics. There was really nothing else to do, but the result was that in seventy minutes we were all out for 43 runs. If all the catches we gave had been held our total would have been still smaller. We were not sorry when our innings ended, as the wicket was one of the class which I have described, as bringing all players, good and bad, down to one level. Our opponents, who were more accustomed to such wickets, kept us in the field for a couple of hours, and made 71. McIntyre did the bowling for us, taking nine wickets for 10 runs. It is scarcely worth while recording the progress of the play, though it should be stated that we were beaten by ten wickets. A plague of flies, which swept over the field while play was in progress, added to our discomfort in this remarkable match.

As the match finished in two days, a single wicket match between six of our professionals and twelve of the Stawell team was arranged for the third day. The wicket was worse, and the cricket more grotesque than ever. In response to the 29 made by the twelve the six English professionals scored 2 — made by McIntyre with one hit. I went off for some more shooting in the bush, along with one or two of the other members of the team, and we were not surprised, though we were amused, to hear on our return what had happened during the day. Some of the Stawell people apparently thought that our men did not try to do their best; but with the ground in such a state, it was almost astonishing that any runs were scored at all. If the ball was hit in the air it travelled all right, but if it was sent along the ground it could not possibly reach the boundary.

Another depressing drive across the bush country fell to our lot when we left Stawell for Warrnambool. We took it in two stages, journeying first to Ararat, where we spent the Sunday, and then proceeding to Warrnambool. On the Sunday the rain, which was very much wanted, fell in torrents, and when we started at 4.30 a.m. on Monday for our ninety-one miles drive we found the tracks in an appalling state. They were bad enough in all conscience when we traversed them *en route* to Stawell, but the rain had converted the dust into thick mud, in which the wheels sank almost to the axles.

Of all my travelling experiences that coach drive to Warrnambool was the most unpleasant. Rain fell pitilessly all the time, and we were soon drenched to the skin. The first thirty-one miles took five hours and a quarter, and though we changed horses now and again our progress was exasperatingly slow. On leaving Hexham, where we halted for dinner, we came to a slight incline. Here two of our horses jibbed, and refused to budge. B. B. Cooper (who made the runs against us at Melbourne, and distinguished himself by a pair of spectacles at Stawell), Lillywhite, Jupp, Southerton, McIntyre, and Humphrey stayed at Hexham to lighten the load. We managed to make the horses convey the rest of us to Warrnambool, which we reached at half-past eleven at night, after a ride of nineteen hours. We were wet through, and our cricket bags and portmanteaus were soaking. Notwithstanding the rain a large number of the people at Warrnambool, who expected us to arrive in the afternoon, had gone out to meet us, but as we made no appearance they assumed that our coaches had broken down.

But if we were not met on the road we were most hospitably received at the hotel, and I remember how thankful we were to find fires in our bedrooms. I had just gone to sleep when a bang at the door made me jump up. In answer to my inquiry I was told that some one wanted to speak to me. It was a reporter from one of the papers; but, as may be imagined, I did not think that midnight was the right hour for a man who had been travelling all day in the rain to encounter an interviewer. Though such journalistic enterprise deserved a better reward I did not receive the intruder with any kindly feeling, and turned him away with very little "copy."

After the bumping and jumping of the comfortless coach over muddy tracks and in persistent rain we were not in very fit condition for cricket, and our match against twenty-two of Warrnambool was not a brilliant display. Our opponents included B.B. Cooper, Allan, Wills, Gaggin and Conway, who throughout our tour followed us from place to place, and seemed prepared to regard themselves as representatives of any district in the Australian continent. The ground was sodden, and played slowly, which was perhaps a happy circumstance, as from its rough appearance it might have been dangerous to play upon if the wicket had been dry and fiery. It was incomparably superior to the wicket at Stawell, and the cricket partook less of the burlesque order. There was a very large company of spectators, a stand having been erected for the ladies, and a band was in attendance to enliven the proceedings. We lost the toss again, and the twenty-two, in their first innings, were dismissed for 68 runs. The last seven wickets fell for seven runs, Southerton doing the hat trick. It was in every respect a bowler's wicket, and our total of 104 was not, on the whole, a poor achievement. Jupp carried out his bat for 58 — one of the best innings he ever played. Allen's bowling was remarkably destructive, his record being 26 overs for 28 runs and six wickets. The wicket had improved by the second day, but Southerton and Lillywhite, who were in great form, were almost unplayable. Our fielding maintained a high level throughout, and we won the match by nine wickets — our first victory in Australia.

To fill out the time on the second day, Bush, Gilbert, my brother, and I played a single-wicket match against Ten of Warrnambool, but time was called before we arrived at any decisive result. On the third day another scratch match was arranged. The club authorities had, it appeared, let the selling of refreshments to a contractor, and in the agreement had used the words "for three days," instead of "for the match"; consequently they had to provide something for the third day. The six English professionals, along with five of the local cricketers, played a team of eighteen, who went in first, scored 88 before a wicket fell, and finally made 172. To this the eleven responded with 26, of which Greenwood contributed 16, while the other five Englishmen did not break their ducks. At Warrnambool we were occasioned some annoyance by the card-sharpers and professional gamblers, who swarmed on the ground, and plied their trade in complete disregard of the police, who seemed to have no power to suppress the nuisance.

The amateurs of the team amused themselves on the third day at Warrnambool by fishing and shooting. It was here that I had my introduction to kangaroo-hunting, which proved extremely interesting and not a little exciting. The way the stockmen ride when kangaroo-hunting was a revelation. Some of us stood aghast at the recklessness with which they dashed through the bush. I was much impressed with the bush ponies. They are extraordinarily clever creatures, and if you leave their heads alone they will go galloping across scrub and bracken, reaching up to their girth, and though fallen trees may be lying about in all directions they will pick their course with perfect certainty. The kangaroo is either hunted down with rough greyhounds, or ridden down by stockmen, who are so clever in the pursuit that they will gallop alongside a kangaroo till it is tired out, and then catch it by the tail without dismounting. The kangaroo has one deadly weapon of defence — a terrible claw on its hind foot, and the hunter must be careful not to get in front of the animal, or he may be ripped up. In some places kangaroos are driven into stockades, expressly made for the purpose, and there killed by the stockmen.

After a splendid day's sport in the bush we left Warrnambool, then a pretty seaside village, for Melbourne, making the sea voyage in one of the small coast steamers.

CRICKET AT COOKTOWN, 1879
By 'Leg Hit'
(A LETTER TO THE *QUEENSLANDER*, APRIL 19, 1879)

WE young people of North Queensland do at times things which would, I fear, make us appear ridiculous to the eyes of our Southern friends. For instance, Cricket under a tropical sun of 150 degrees. If they could see us indulging in the old English game under these distressing circumstances, I fear, they would be inclined to think "Much Cooktown hath made us mad"...

On Thursdays and Saturday afternoons in our part of the World, we close our places of business and devote the rest of the day to amusement at the TWO-MILE, our local resort. Nature has provided us a ground prettily situated and a good wicket — with a good rich growth of couch grass well eaten down by goats etc., skirted on one side by a tropical scrub rich in all different shades of green and here and there a friendly box-tree lends its shade to long leg and cover point. Here on the Northern Cricket field, we pass many a pleasant afternoon and although having no neighbours, with whom we might play a friendly game, still we arrange very interesting scratch matches ... and after refreshing the inner man at the Carrier's Arms, we return home in the sole public conveyance Cooktown boasts of, with good appetite and sunburnt faces...

AN INTERVIEW WITH THE DEMON BOWLER
(THE *PALL MALL BUDGET*, 1886)

"WHAT is the first duty of a bowler, Mr Spofforth?"

"To lead astray the batsman, to lead him astray by never allowing him to guess what is coming. So far as I am concerned I may send a very quick ball (I have never yet put all my strength into it), the next may be corresponding slow. Therein, I consider, lies any power I may have as a bowler — this ability to vary the pace from the very quick to the very slow. Then I try to deceive him by break and variety of pitch. If you know your batsman from previous meetings, a good bowler knows his weak points. I am speaking of the best known men in the world of cricket. When I am bowling against a batsman whose peculiarities I am not acquainted with, I generally gauge him by his style, and have his stock in three or four overs. I dare say a batsman would tell you the same thing about a bowler. We try to lead each other astray, but the batsman is generally the first to betray himself. Having penetrated the armour, then I go for him, tickling him and tempting him. He fancies he has got my gauge by one style of break. Then I try another, and suddenly revert to the first; or one puts, by the manner of holding the ball, a spin on that will not cause it to turn out of its course. The batsman may think by the action of the delivery that the ball will turn out of its course when it possibly finds it way to the wicket. But it is a difficult matter to explain. As I find a batsman is inclined to hit, to play back, or to play forward, so I tempt him, sometimes trying to 'beat the bat' — that is, going straight for his wicket, at others alluring him to hit so as to place the ball in the hands of one of the field. When do I consider myself unlucky? Well, when 'I beat the bat' — that is, pass the bat — and miss the wicket by an eighth of an inch. Then I feel angry. But every bowler knows these things. Personally I seldom go straight for bowling a man. I think Grace by far the best bat in the world. Some first-rate cricketers, after they have got twenty or thirty runs, will begin to slog. Grace never does this. He always means business. He is up to every move. In fact, he is very difficult to lead astray. I think Crossland is a faster bowler than myself. In my old days in Australia, long before I became known, a captain of a team would ask me to moderate my pace; but I used to use my own judgment, and did as I thought best. It was very disagreeable to be instructed how to bowl. But that is a thing of the past."

"You must practise much and keep your eye and hand in, and your body in training?"

"I never practise. I seldom play in Australia — half a dozen times a year, perhaps, and as I watch myself closely I always find when I come over here that I am seldom much good until after the fourth match. By that time I have got my muscles in trim and my eye in good order — (Mr Spofforth now looks like a typical athlete, eye clear and face ruddy and tanned) — the match the other day against Oxford was an exception. Then I am up to my best average to the end of the season. Of course one has good days and bad days, for which there is no accounting. To return to the matter of practising at cricket. To a certain extent it is good, of course, and material. But I have always found that I require the stimulus and excitement of a match to put me on my mettle. If I practise at a net in the usual way one is apt to become careless. One bowls perhaps to a man who objects to getting hurt ingloriously, and very naturally, though he thinks nothing of it in a big match. So I hold — please remember that this is only my own opinion — that practice, unless very thorough, very much in earnest, is not good, as it tends to become careless and slovenly, and teaches bad habits, which are with difficulty eradicated. You ask me about training. I take it that one of the beauties of cricket is that it requires none of the severe self-denial, the selection of particular diet in its practice. Personally I don't always have a pipe or a cigar in my mouth, but I smoke, nor am I a total abstainer. No, I never make any difference in my habits, and the constant training of the cricket ground is sufficient, at any rate, for men who are playing every day. Of course one wants wind and power of lasting, but a man never runs more than sixty or eighty yards at a time, and he has long spells in between. Those are my views. Do I ever feel nervous? I cannot say that I ever do. Excited? yes, on occasions."

"Do you ever try to frighten a batsman?"

"If a batsman is timid he is frightened long before I get at him. That's the worst of a powerful imagination. I certainly never go for a batsman with right down intent to frighten him. If he don't like my speed, that's his look-out, not mine."

"Supposing you wished to train a boy to become a bowler, what would you advise?"

"Bowl with the brains. Brains, I assure you, enter more largely into sport than is generally imagined. But to return to your question. I can only tell you my own experience. I may say that I learned to bowl as one learns to read. In the days of my tuition I was a great copyist. I was always changing from one style to another. I saw a particular kind of delivery, or a variety of pitch in another bowler. I watched him carefully, and then I did my best to imitate him. So it was with pace. In the early days of Australian cricket, and before the visits of English cricketers, no bowler had discovered how to break a ball. This was an art I found out for myself. Then it was only by dint of constant perseverance that I overcame prejudice. The critics and the press used to run me down. They likened me to a bull running at a gate. But I didn't care a jot. I weighed the criticisms in my mind and went on trying this, that, and the other. Somehow I generally got wickets, and that satisfied me. If I came off that was enough. I knew I couldn't be far out. They said I threw, and they were right. I did throw once, but when I found that out, after the difference had been explained to me (of course, that is a long time ago), I went to work and corrected it. Ah! it is not easy to make a name. I tried and tried again for years. If I bowled well they said it was luck; if I took wickets it was luck; my break was luck again or the wicket."

"A great bowler is born and not made, eh, Mr Spofforth? Great bowling is a heaven-born gift?"

"Not a bit of it. As I have said, you must use your brains if you have got any. No, I should say a bowler is made — he must be born, you know. You ask for my own experience. In my youthful days I had cricketing aspirations, and cricket in the colonies was at a low ebb. In those days, when I was very keen and very ambitious, I thought I should like to become a bowler, and really studied it as a problem. I used to think for myself how such and such a pitch, or such and such a speed, would affect a batsman. I used to propound mentally the most difficult combinations to overcome a batsman. Having thought of a certain style, as a billiard player might of a particular stroke, I went down to the ground to give it practical effect. An English professional player who was engaged by us, and who was in those somewhat remote days by the far the best bowler in Australia, used to go to the wickets and I used to try my new idea. He would then criticise. And thus I was constantly trying, first as a mental problem, then as a practical result. By this means I used to gauge myself for years."

"Will Australia continue to send us such cricketers as your famous team?"

"Cricketers, I think come in cycles. The best Australians now before the public were the best men six or eight years ago. I speak generally; of course every year brings new recruits, but, if you think my opinion is worth repeating, it is that there are interregnums in cricket."

Ted Evans
By A .B. ('Banjo') Paterson
(THE *SYDNEY MAIL*, 1932)

'Going back a long way into the mists of cricket memories one recalls the great identities of the past — men whose names are rarely heard nowadays, but who made cricket history in their time.

One such outstanding personality was "Ted" Evans, whose all-round cricketing ability was such that it procured him a job as inspector of selections.

When we heard, in the Yass district, that a cricketer was coming up to inspect our selections we wondered what sort of a man the authorities had sent us as arbitrator of our destinies.

Evans duly arrived, a fine, broad-shouldered fellow over six foot high and wearing a beard. The first thing was to get him a horse on which he could ride round the selections.

The station horses were put in the yard and a quiet old mount was selected for him, but his eye was taken by a very flash young horse that was trotting and snorting round the yard.

"I'd like that fellow," said Evans, "and I'd like to take a gun and do some shooting". We said that there were very few others that would attempt to carry a gun on that horse, but Evans said that he could manage him all right and he turned out to be a first-class horseman.

Then he astounded us by picking up a rifle and killing a kangaroo that was going past at full speed — a feat only attempted by very good professional kangaroo shooters.

The ducks were in thousands and he stopped them right and left barrels of his shotgun.

Truth to tell, his inspections were somewhat casual for when shown some miles of fence running up a steep hill he would say, "Oh it looks all right: let's get back to the creek. There's a big mob of ducks just gone down there." Evidently the keen eye that made him a crack slip-fieldsman was also useful along the sights of a gun.'

A LAND OF SNOBS AND YAHOOS

This letter, allegedly written by W. G. Grace to a friend during his first visit to Australia in 1873-74, was almost certainly the creation of an Australian journalist. It was reproduced in several Australian newspapers during Grace's second visit, 1891-92, and Grace was widely believed to be its author.
(THE *REFEREE*, JANUARY, 1918)

"DEAR M. — With one foot on sea and one on shore, I send you a few farewell lines, as you are about the only man I care to say good-bye to in this country of snobs and yahoos. You will excuse me feeling a little bitter in regard to my colonial experience, for things were made very rough for us in almost every place we went to. To commence with, those infernal apologies for newspapers in Melbourne lost no opportunity of showing up the team, and let us have it all around. One feels the inconvenience of being a gentleman sometimes. I know I did, or there would have been rare pulling of noses on more than one occasion. My brother was within an ace of pitching into one of the Melbourne cricketing cads about the disputed ball in the last match there, but, fortunately, he thought better of it, as, you know, he is shortly to return, for weighty reasons, and, as he says, he had sixty thousand objections to getting his name mixed up as a bruiser of colonials . . . The papers puzzled themselves all along to account for the actions of the team, but none of them got hold of the right end of the stick. To commence with, the professionals were sulky with me for making them travel second-class from home at the last minute. It is true I led them to believe up to the morning of sailing from Southampton that they would go in the saloon — but what else could I do? If I hadn't humbugged them they might have refused to go when it was too late to fill their places. I had great difficulty, indeed, in making up a team at all. Dicky Daft, Stow, and others I would have picked as professionals wouldn't come, and most of the good gentlemen players had their backs up through sundry rows with me on the Marylebone ground, so I did the best I could — got Southerton, Lillywhite, and Jupp, and filled the team up with second-raters. Bush got me out of the wicket-keeping difficulty, and I trusted to luck and big scores by myself, 'G.F.,' and Jupp to pull through. One thing sold us — the accounts of colonial cricket given us before we started by my brother, 'E.M.', George Parr, Idison, and others were quite out. The colonials must have improved wonderfully since the last English team was out. Our scratch crew did well, I maintain, all things considered . . . I quietly packed them second-class, and chanced it. They were sulky from the day they started. . . They shall pay for it when we get back, if my influence has any effect with the clubs engaging them. However, as I had pecuniary interest in the affair I was obliged to keep sweet with them so long as they played when required. I must admit that our gentlemen players had a very scabby fag-end; but, after all, we pulled through respectably, and I have the money, which is the only thing I wanted; for, to tell the truth, I care so little for colonial opinion that you may publish this letter if you like. It will show the cads what I think of them. A good deal was said about my stopping away from the lunch at various places. My reason was that I didn't want to fraternise with the tinkers, tailors, and snobs who are the great guns in your cricket world. To take their money was a fair thing in return for work done, but to hobnob with a lot of scum was a different thing. Fancy the chance of a greasy butcher in his travels walking up to me some day at Lord's with. 'How d' ye do, Mr Grace? I lunched with you in Australia.' My dear fellow, so far as I can see, colonial society is low — shockingly low. You have plenty of money, no doubt, but your gentlemen are yet unborn. I suppose, including yourself, I met about three during the whole of my trip. As to the promoters, they worked like demons to hide the split in our camp, but I heartily despised them, and put them in the hole nicely in the Adelaide match. And now, good-bye. I don't expect a very pleasant voyage home, for we are at daggers drawn among ourselves, and there will be a fight or two before it is all over. As to Australia itself, it is a fine country, but wants steeping for 24 hours in the sea to rid it of the human vermin crawling over it. So, with kind regards to yourself, and hearty contempt for the cads, bullies, and fools who exist among you in profusion, I am, dear M., yours truly, W.G. GRACE."

BONNOR'S TALL TALES
A newspaper report

To know the old giant hitter George Bonnor was to like him, and many were the tales he told of his own prowess at all games by flood and field. According to the mighty smiter he was the best boxer, best runner, best footballer, the biggest hitter, the best singer, and the longest cricket ball-thrower ever born in New South Wales. Who, among those who heard him relate the story, will every forget the pathos with which he told of one of his bush wanderings. He had gone out from the town of Orange right into the heart of the bush. He reluctantly and modestly admitted that on this particular occasion he was in such wonderful voice that he brought tears into his own eyes. It was a beautiful spring day, and yielding to the balmy influence of his surroundings he sat down on a log and poured out his soul in song.

As he sang on and forgot all about the time he was surprised to see that the sky had suddenly become black. Fearful of being caught in one of those terrible Orange thunderstorms Bon jumped up in alarm, only to discover that what he had imagined were black and threatening rain clouds were millions upon millions of birds who had darkened the sky for miles round as they hovered in the air listening spellbound to the sweet songster below.

On another occasion there was an argument as to who was the fastest bowler that ever lived. Many names were fancied, the late Fred Spofforth amongst the number, when Bonnor modestly claimed that he was at least five yards faster than Spofforth. Some of the old timers like

Jack Blackham and Sammy Jones would get up in disgust when the man from Orange was on his favourite subject of introspection but the colts encouraged him. And he concluded by saying that he had performed a cricketing feat unique in the annals of the game. "I was the fastest bowler that ever lived," he said, "and so great was my pace that in a match at Orange, after sending down one of my fastest deliveries, which I knew would be snicked in the slips, as I bowled for it, I ran down the pitch, chased the ball after it had been played, and caught it at deep first slip. I could not do it always; but that day I could do anything." And one must admit it was a unique feat.

BONNOR AND DR JOHNSON
(THE *REFEREE*)

MR Augustine Birrell, Q.C., M.P., lectured on Dr Johnson at the London Institute. Some time ago he (the lecturer) met at a supper of the Johnson Club, in Fleet-street, two guests. One was an Irish patriot, who had languished in gaol during a recent political *régime*. He had asked the Governor of the prison for some book to read — not the Bible — and the Governor gave him 'Boswell's Life.' The patriot immediately forgot all about his country's woes and his prison dress, and spent his period of incarceration joyfully. He was now no longer a 'patriot', but he remained a Boswellian. The other guest was Bonnor, the Australian cricketing giant. He declared he had never heard of Johnson till that evening, whereupon somebody was rude enough to titter. The huge cricketer got up and said: 'And, what is more, I come from a great country, where you can ride a horse at sixty miles a day for three months and never meet a soul who has heard of Dr Johnson either. But I can say this much, that if I weren't Bonnor, the cricketer, I should like to have been Dr Johnson.' At this retort a solemn conviction seized his (Mr Birrell's) soul that had the doctor been resurrected in the flesh that night he would have preferred the talk of the Australian cricketer to that of any of the Fleet-street critics gathered round the supper table.

BONNOR'S GREAT THROW, 1882

By Charles Beal, manager of the 1882 Australian team in England
(THE *REFEREE*, NOVEMBER, 1914)

SOON after leaving Malta an army officer was talking about throwing the cricket ball 100 yards. Bonnor, in his usual grandiloquent way, said: "100 yards! 100 yards! Why, I could jerk it!" And so he could. After a little talk, it culminated in a wager of £100 that Bonnor would not throw 115yds or more with the first throw, and on the first day he landed on English shores. I remember Bonnor coming down on board ship and telling me he had made the wager. Old Caleb Peacock, of Adelaide, was stakeholder. We got to Plymouth, and it was a fine day, so Bonnor, Murdoch, Tom Garrett, and myself got off the boat, the others going on. We tried to get a 5¼oz ball, but could not get any lighter than 5½oz. Before finally agreeing to the ground we went to several places, including The Hoe, but that was down hill — all right for Bonnor, but it did not suit the other party. Then we went to the Racecourse, but that was slippery, and, of course, did not suit us, so at last we arrived at the Barracks in Plymouth. As it was gravel, and there was no wind, all agreed that the conditions were fair. We got hold of the quartermaster — he happened to have a record in the army, for he had thrown 107 yards, I think. When we told him what the event was he became deeply interested. Bonnor got the quartermaster to put a pile of newspapers down as a target, about two feet high, at a distance of 120 yards, to aim at. He was going to throw without taking his waistcoat off. It showed you the cool belief he had in his powers. I insisted on his stripping to the singlet, though he didn't like the idea. He was toying with the ball. "A man of my inches not being able to throw this little thing 115 yards!" Well, he threw 119 yards 7 inches, and won the wager. I remember the old quartermaster begged for the ball, and we gave it to him. He never dreamt that anyone could throw so far, and he wanted the ball as a souvenir. You ought to have seen "Bon.," the centre of admiration at Plymouth Barracks after that throw. It was a pretty good throw, seeing that Bonnor had been six weeks on board ship.

'W.G.' The Talker
By M. A. Noble

Dr W.G. Grace, who is more familiarly known amongst cricketers as "W.G.," naturally forces himself upon the mind as pre-eminent amongst cricketers. I well remember the first occasion on which I figured against "W.G." It was at the Crystal Palace, and the first game played by the 1899 Australian team. Just before leaving the pavilion to take my place at the batting crease "Hughie" Trumble came to me and warned me about "W.G.'s" talking propensities. He said: "When you go in take care 'W.G.' doesn't talk you out. If he says anything, don't answer him, as he has a knack of getting young players bustled if he can only succeed in getting them talking." I replied, "All right, Hughie; I won't take any notice of him whatever." In I marched, and survived the first over. Sure enough up came the Doctor, and saluted me with the remark, "Good day, young fellow." I replied, "Good day," and walked away. At the end of the succeeding over 'W.G.' resumed operations with another salutation, which I studiously ignored. The conversation was continued by the old gentleman for several overs without receiving any encouragement from me, and I have often wondered since what "W.G." really thought of me.

After batting for some time I thought it would not matter much then, as I felt confident after remaining at the wickets thus long, and was not afraid of the Doctor's talk, being content to go out if "W.G." succeeded in upsetting my equilibrium by his chatter. Next time he approached me I replied to his inquiries, and from that time conversed freely. I am sure now that "W.G.'s" object was to encourage rather than bustle me. This is a fair example of Hugh Trumble's "leg-pulling," at which he is a pastmaster.

Murdoch's Death
By 'Felix'
(THE *AUSTRALASIAN*, FEBRUARY 25, 1911)

The famous cricketer, W.L. Murdoch, died on Saturday afternoon, at about 5 o'clock, in Dr W. Moore's private hospital. When I entered the M.C.C. pavilion shortly before noon I greeted him while he was chatting pleasantly with C. McLeod and Harry Rush. In a few minutes I left to get round to my old spot beneath the tree. Coming back in the afternoon I had not been long seated in the balcony when the veteran scorer, J. Taylor, brought the sad news that the famous cricketer had been suddenly stricken by apoplexy in the M.C.C. committee-room, and that, in an unconscious condition, he had been taken to a private hospital. In the pavilion Dr Ramsay Mailer, Dr Dyring, Dr Leary and Dr Horne did what they could to restore him, but their efforts were of no avail. He had luncheon with the M.C.C. committee, and was sitting next to Major Morkham. Just after luncheon he put his hand to his forehead, and the Major said, 'What's the matter?' 'Neuralgia, I think; I have a pain here.' These were the last words uttered by the grand old champion. He sank back unconscious, and remained so until the end came. In the history of Australian cricket no sadder shock has ever been experienced than that we all felt when the sad news came back from the hospital that the great old warrior had gone to his account.

OLD CRICKETERS

By A. B. ('Banjo') Paterson, in a radio talk
(FROM HIS *SONG OF THE PEN: COMPLETE WORKS 1901-41*,
SYDNEY, 1983)

AMONG other "first" things which have come my way was the first Australian eleven. Living away up in the bush as a boy, I followed the doings of the cricketers with rapt admiration, just as hundreds of other Australian boys were doing all over the country. Our cricketers were underdogs, if you understand what I mean, and not even the most optimistic of us believed that they would ever be able to play England on level terms: and all over the country there raged family arguments over the tea cups — we of the younger generation supporting our men as best we could, while the English- and Scottish-born heads of families adopted a tolerant and patronising attitude, very hard to bear. When I went down to school in Sydney, I was crammed with facts about cricketers and at last I had the satisfaction of meeting them in the flesh.

Things you see when your eyes are young always look bigger and better to you than the things you see when your eyes are old. I was watching the last test match here the other day and Grimmett was skittling the Africans wholesale. I noticed an old fellow sitting near me and he was shuffling about in his seat very upset about something: and at last he turned to me and he said, "He can't bowl".

I said, "Who can't bowl?"

He said, "This Grimmett".

I said, "Grimmett can't bowl? What's wrong with him?"

"Ah," he said, "George Bonnor would have hit him over the pavilion."

And I suppose that old man's grandson was sitting down by the side of the fence worshipping Grimmett.

Bonnor was a very picturesque personality. He was about six feet two high, a beautifully built man who could run a hundred yards in ten and a quarter seconds. He played a good game of billiards and he could throw a cricket ball a hundred and twenty yards. Bonnor despised all bowlers and while he was in he never scored less than a run a minute off his own bat.

Were there truly giants in those days? Well, after thinking things over for sixty years or so, I believe that there were. So far as I can remember, the first Australian team only took eleven men to England and they played right through a heavy list of matches without any reserves at all. Nowadays we send to them and they send to us fifteen or sixteen players, and there are always three or four of them on the sick or injured list. What is the reason for it? Were the boys of the old brigade tougher than our present champions? It would seem so and the reason may be, in default of anything better, that there was no golf, no lawn tennis and no surfing, so that the youngsters from their earliest days played nothing but cricket.

With this constant cricketing they got so tough that they could stand anything in the way of strain, just as the inhabitants of Java can stand the job of wading all day in the swamps planting rice, and the Egyptians have grown so used to burdens that any average Egyptian can carry as many bags of chaff as you can pack on him. It is all a matter of getting used to it, and our people were used to cricket.

I remember Dave Gregory, the captain of the first Australian eleven, black-bearded, high-shouldered, remarkably like the English captain Grace and with a good deal of Grace's invincible self-confidence. We hear a lot about temperament nowadays but neither Grace nor Gregory was afflicted with any temperament, not so that you could notice it. Spofforth, the demon bowler, six feet of wire and whipcord, was a one-idea man. If a ship were sinking under him, his last words would be of cricket. I have seen Spofforth on more than one occasion break a stump, and if he had bowled body-line he would have exterminated the opposition. Charley Bannerman was the nob of the Muscovite mob in the batting line. Not a tall man, he seemed to have the knack of getting balls bowled on the off, and would cut ball after ball to the fence without giving a chance. They don't seem able to do it nowadays, but why bring that up?

Poor old Charley Bannerman! There should be a statue to him on every cricket ground in Australia: but he never looked after his money and when the crowd had done with him I have seen him holding a bag for a kindly bookmaker at Randwick. Just think of it! At one time the idol of thousands, making money for cricket but none for himself, and winding up holding a bag for a bookmaker! His brother Alex Bannerman was the very reverse of Charley; he would take no risks in batting nor any risks with his money. He had a job in the Government printing office and when the touring teams got hard up, as they generally did, Alex was always able to finance them till pay day. He was a dyed-in-the-wool stone waller, or rather we thought he was until an English player named Scotton came along and made four runs in two hours. I don't know why we let him live.

Boyle of Victoria was another star bowler of that first team, but we in Sydney had little time for any Victorians and we reckoned that the English teams got themselves out to Boyle's bowling. He was the Bill O'Reilly of the day and only for his unfortunate domicile we would have made him a hero. We waived all objections in the case of Jack Blackham, the Victorian wicketkeeper. Blackham had that indefinable quality known as personality. With his battle-scarred fingers twisted like an eagle's claws he stood up to Spofforth's fast bowling without a backstop: he was no batsman, but he was what the American baseballers call a pinch hitter. If runs were badly wanted, he would get them somehow. Billy Murdoch, a debonair young solicitor, went away as Blackham's wicketkeeping understudy, afterwards to bloom as one of Australia's greatest batsmen. Then there was Tom Garrett, little more than a boy when the first team went away. An all-rounder, he could bat, bowl, and field anywhere: and he had such a good time in England that (as he afterwards confided to me) it took him a couple of years to pay off the trip.

Palmer was another great bowler. I umpired a match once as a schoolboy in which Palmer bowled, and he was coming in from the leg or from the off eighteen inches and keeping his length all the time.

Such were the first Australian eleven: most of them had beards but there was not a teetotaller nor a temperamental man among them. One of the great old-timers was Ted Evans, "Teddy the shepherd", a member of a western pastoral family. Evans cast up at our home in Illalong in the guise of Government Inspector of conditional purchases. The first question he asked on his arrival was whether there were any wild ducks about, and he settled down to three or four days' good duck shooting, inspecting conditional purchases at a distance from the back of a horse. When we mustered the horses for the first day's shooting, he picked out the flashest thing in the yard and rode it, carrying a gun on it, like the bushranger he was. Not that all our men were all-rounders, by any means. One can hardly believe it, but "Affy" Jarvis the South Australian wicketkeeper, when he first visited England had never even driven a horse; and when a lady admirer called to take him for a drive with a bang-up dogcart, a tiger at the back and a flash quadruped in the shafts, he was nonplussed when she asked him to drive. All the team were watching him from the windows, so he climbed to the seat and picked up the reins. The horse started off with a terrific bound and "Affy" gave it such a haul in the mouth that it reared straight up on end, which so terrified our hero that he shoved the reins into the hands of the tiger and fled back into the hotel. Hell hath no fury like the scorn of a woman.

I met many of these celebrities at the cricket ground of the Gladesville Mental Hospital, where Mr E.M. Betts, the superintendent, used to entertain visitors on lunches of cold roast sucking pig and all the beer they wanted. These functions were very popular. I saw Palmer bowl there, breaking the ball a foot either way on the somewhat luxuriant grass. I saw Tom Garrett play there, undertaking to drink a long beer after every twenty runs on a very hot day. To quote the old "hill" chorus, they would never get him out, but after a fairly long innings he retired: and when his side took the field he refused to bowl at all and would only field if allowed to stand under the shade of a tree. English cricketers sometimes came there for their idea of a happy day, and once the great George Giffen was "rung in" on Mr Betts.

A team from an English warship were coming up and, as Giffen was at a loose end in Sydney, some genius woke up to the idea of ringing Giffen in on him as a sailor. In uniform he looked just like a "matlow" and only a few people knew that Giffen was in Sydney. When the naval team arrived, the warship captain called a sailor over and said, "We've brought George Giffen up with us, Mr Betts. You won't mind his playing, will you?"

Mr Betts looked the sailor over, thoughtfully.

"Well, of course I'd know he wasn't Giffen," he said. "He's a bit too fat, but by Jove he's like him. What's his name?"

"His name's George Giffen."

"Oh, I see! A namesake! I'm glad to meet you, Mr Giffen. You can play, and I hope you get some runs."

Too true, he got some runs. He hit so hard that point and mid-wicket deserted their positions and fielded out on the boundary. Then he hit one clean off the earth, or at any rate it was never found again, and Mr Betts sought the naval captain.

"Better call that man in," he said. "He may be George Giffen or he may not: but that wicketkeeper of ours is here for homicidal mania and I saw him reach over to pull a stump out of the ground. Don't try him too high, that's all, don't try him too high."

How Coningham got Warm
By C. T. B. Turner

In 1893, when the Australians were playing against eighteen of Blackpool, an amusing incident occurred during the local men's innings. Arthur Coningham was fielding in the "country." It was a cold, raw day, and the Australians were playing in their sweaters. The batting not being too brilliant or lively, the outfields had little to do, and the idea evidently struck Coningham that he would like to get warm, so he gathered some bits of sticks and grass, piled them up, and then asked one of the spectators for a match. Having obtained this, he set fire to the little pile of grass and commenced to warm his hands. It amused a section of the spectators, who applauded him, and one wag suggested he should go inside and get a couple of hot potatoes to put in his pocket.

The Prince of Stumpers
By L. O. S. Poidevin

Once a little Scotch boy, when asked to name the greatest wicket-keeper in the world, replied without a moment's hesitation, "Mr Gregor M'Gregor." That was typically patriotic. English opinion is somewhat divided on the matter, though up Lancashire way, at all events, the honour unhesitatingly goes to "Dick" Pilling, who was considered by his contemporaries as a marvel behind the sticks. To Australians, however, and to the vast majority of the cricketing fraternity the world over, there is only one "greatest ever," and that one "the prince of stumpers," John M'Carthy Blackham. His feats are now invested with the glamour of tradition, and not all the cleverness of Lilley, the assured ease of Sherwell, or the demonstrative efficiency of Strudwick combined can shift the well-fitting mantle of superlative greatness from the shoulders of the Australian pioneer. As the subject of my little appreciation, he needs no introduction here. Every follower of the game knows quite well that he kept wickets in the very first test match between England and Australia, though it may not be remembered that he caught three opponents and stumped one in that historic contest — and that only six extras (including leg-byes, no-balls, and wides) were recorded in the two innings.

My own first distinct recollection of Blackham, as an international player, finds a comparatively modern setting; indeed, it was in the last of his long list of Test matches; and curiously enough, it was his batting on that occasion that a boyish memory selected to pack away in its cricket storehouse. Need I say it was that sensational match in Sydney in 1894, the first test of Stoddart's first tour, which Australia lost after making 586 runs in the first innings — the record innings in Test cricket. The details of that innings are a vivid memory to me now, but the sharpest of them all is the recollection of the bearded warrior — the last active link with the unforgettable past — relentlessly driving home the advantage so magnificently and somewhat unexpectedly gained by heroes to be, in the middle of the innings. How he bustled his partners along between wickets, diligently gathering every available run, and stealing them occasionally from the weary fieldsmen! With what avidity and energy did he force the pace against the languid bowling of Richardson, Peel, and Briggs, tamed and tired out with the continuous toil of nearly two days! In his eagerness to punish he repeatedly ran several yards out of his ground to meet the innocently offending ball, and when at length Richardson bowled him he had made the highest score of his career (74) in Test cricket. His batting, however, has the least claim upon our remembrance; even so, it was characteristic. He was one of those batsmen of whom you did not anticipate great things, yet who nearly always stayed in when least expected, and made runs when they were most needed. We sometimes ramble round corners in our homes which we have neglected or ignored, and, fumbling therein, touch some forgotten thing which starts into music at the touch. Blackham was just the sort of batting instrument to surprise us in a similar way.

His wicket-keeping, of course, was of a different quality. He was a pioneer in modern methods. More than any one else, perhaps, he taught the value and importance of the wicket-keeper to his team — that he is the head, so to speak, upon which all the ends of the game are come. More than that, he himself was a genius. The wide returns, the hot half-volleys, the leg-balls, the gentle snicks — all were gathered with supremest skill, often at the risk of hands and legs, and with a most generous determination to make the best of a fieldsman's folly or a bowler's lapse. He set the standard of wicket-keeping, which he maintained through a long and honourable international career.

A WICKET-KEEPING REVOLUTION
By John Blackham
(THE *REFEREE*, 1915)

MY FATHER was an old wicket-keeper. He was a printer on 'The Age,' and there were frequent Press matches in which he took part. I was a little fellow then, attending school, and playing with Carlton II. In a game between Romsey and the Press they put me on to represent dad. We were playing on Albert Park, and I stood up to the wicket with a long-stop, and impressed Jack Conway, who was captain of South Melbourne, a crack footballer, and who became manager of the first Australian combination. Jack said to dad that I could play with the first South Melbourne team, and next season I was a clubmate of Jack, Frank Allan, and 'Mid.' I showed form, and retained my place. It was in the final against East Melbourne, in the famous 'century' match, that I actually did away with the long-stop. The match took place at the Jolimont ground, where the wicket was as fine as any I have played on. Lou Woolf, the well-known barrister, was long-stop, a position in which he was a champion. He said, 'I'm getting nothing to do, Jack,' and suggested he should field fine-leg, which he did. This was when the alteration was made. At first I did not like being deprived of the safety valve. It was a great surprise to them in England where they had a long-stop to fast and fast-medium bowlers. Then they followed our idea.

THE SYDNEY GROUND
By A. B. ('Banjo') Paterson, in a radio talk
(FROM HIS *SONG OF THE PEN: COMPLETE WORKS 1901–41,*
SYDNEY, 1983)

MEMORIES of cricketers, athletes, tennis players: they all centre round the Cricket Ground. Breathes there a man with soul so dead that he never heard of the Sydney Cricket Ground? In the very early days it was called the Civil and Military ground and there was a ground before it, known as the Albert Ground, somewhere at the back of Redfern and now built over. Amateur athletics, patronised by the best people, were the strong suit of the old Albert Ground, but I have little memory of it. Many a Saturday afternoon I paid my shilling and sat out on the hill at the Sydney Cricket Ground and, like poor old Johnny Coleman, "I happened to be there" on the occasion of the Lord Harris riot, which made the bodyline controversy of later years look like a goodwill gesture.

You see, we were playing Lord Harris's English eleven and things were going very badly for us. Billy Murdoch was our only hope and Billy was just getting set when the umpire gave him run out — a very close decision. I was sitting by the picket fence, just below where the scoring board is now, and of course we couldn't tell from there whether he was out or not, but we all started to hoot and a chap sitting near me said, "Come on, boys, we can't stand this", and he jumped in over the pickets. His feet had hardly touched the ground when there were a thousand men over the fence, all running for the centre of the ground. The Englishmen thought they were going to be murdered and some of them got round the umpire, and the others pulled the stumps out of the ground to defend their lives. I remember seeing a big Yorkshireman named Ulyett waving a stump at the crowd, so I side-stepped him. I was only a boy. When we got to the wicket, we didn't know what to do. Everybody was hooting and shouting and arguing and the people from the members' stand were crowding in to help the English. Nobody really interfered with the English players — we just hooted them off the ground, and then it struck us that if we didn't go back to our seats we wouldn't see any more play. So back we all went and that was the end of the great Lord Harris riot which gave Australia a bad name for years.

An English View of an English Defeat, 1877
(THE *DAILY NEWS*, LONDON, SEPTEMBER, 1877)

THE most painful news has reached England from one of our distant colonial domains. The eleven of Sydney and district has defeated the English team by two wickets. This is what our enemies have long been expecting; ever since the session of the Ionian Islands they have declared that a nation which gives up territory is in its decadence. Here indeed is a melancholy fulfilment of hostile prophecies. Up to this year England had at least led the world at cricket. An American or Australian twenty-two might play an English eleven with fair chance of not being very badly beaten; but to be defeated in a contest, man to man, by the natives of an island comparatively lately discovered — it is too much; and yet a well-known bust in the head-quarters of the game is not reported to have shed tears, nor has any other omen been observed at Lord's or the Oval. For all that, the sceptre has passed away, so to speak; the flag is struck. Fortune has abased the proud. It may console them to note that the English race is not degenerate, and that in that distant land, and on turf where late the blackfellow hurled his boomerang, a generation has arisen which can play the best bowlers of the time.

The Match That Made The Ashes
By G. F. McCleary
(FROM HIS *CRICKET WITH THE KANGAROO*, LONDON, 1950)

MANY good judges of cricket have held that the Australian team of 1882 was the strongest that ever visited England. Such was the opinion of W.G. Grace, A.G. Steel, and Alfred Shaw, and no better judges of cricket could be found anywhere. But many teams have come and gone since those great cricketers left us, and if they could have seen the team of 1948 their views might possibly have been modified. It is a question that can never be settled; but what is beyond controversy is that the Australian eleven that opposed England at the Oval in the historic Test Match on 28th and 29th August 1882 was one of the strongest that ever appeared on any cricket ground.

The team consisted of thirteen players, of whom seven — Murdoch (captain), A. Bannerman, Bonnor, Garrett, Jones, Massie, and Spofforth — came from New South Wales. Five were from Victoria — Blackham, Boyle, Horan, McDonnell, and Palmer — and one, Giffen, from South Australia. They sailed from Melbourne on 16th March and arrived at Plymouth on 3rd May. During the voyage, one of the passengers offered to bet Bonnor £100 that he would not at his first attempt after landing in England throw a cricket ball 115 yards. Immediately after landing, Bonnor won the bet on the parade ground of the Raglan Barracks by throwing the ball 119 yards 5 inches. He then backed himself for £200 to make the next throw 125 yards, but the bet was not accepted. During the interval between landing and the first match, which began on 15th May, most members of the team took part in club cricket in the London area.

The most formidable member of the team was Spofforth, at that time the finest bowler in the world. Boyle was almost as deadly, and Garrett and Palmer were also bowlers of the highest class. Blackham as a wicket-keeper has had certainly no superior, probably no equal, and Murdoch as a batsman was then second only to W.G. Grace. Giffen was a fine all-round cricketer, and in Massie, McDonnell, and Bonnor the team had three of the most daring of rapid scorers. Massie especially was a most attractive batsman to watch. He was a tall, good-looking man with a slim, graceful figure. Always on the offensive, he made good use of his wrists and hit with great power. In the team's first match, played against Oxford Unversity in bitterly cold weather, he made 206, the second 100 in under an hour, chiefly by a brilliant demonstration of off-side strokes. Unfortunately, his career in first-class cricket was brief; this was the only season in which he played in England. He was a Sydney man, and in some elements of his batsmanship he was not unlike another Sydney man, of later times — Victor Trumper. It is hardly necessary to say that the fielding of the team was in every respect superb.

The team that represented England in the Test Match, which was selected by Lord Harris, F. Burbidge, I.D. Walker, and V.E. Walker, was also exceptionally strong. The captain was A.N. Hornby, captain of Lancashire, a man of amazing vitality, eminent in many kinds of sport. On a cricket field he, like Kipling's Fuzzy Wuzzy, was "all hot sand and ginger". A captain of genius, he had the defects of his qualities. He was impetuous, and in changing his bowlers, and selecting the order of his batsmen's going in, his judgment was sometimes at fault. But in his power to keep up the tails of his men in times of trouble he has probably had few equals; in many a contest his incandescent energy and inspiring leadership snatched victory from what seemed inevitable defeat. With R.G. Barlow, one of the most patient of batsmen, very hard to dislodge, Hornby for many years went in first for Lancashire, and the pair stole innumerable short runs. He was a fine dashing batsman, and his wiles between the wickets moved his schoolfellows at Harrow to bestow upon him the nickname "Monkey", by which he was known throughout life. Both he and Barlow were immortalized by Francis Thompson in his famous poem *At Lord's,* with the haunting refrain:

O my Hornby and my Barlow long ago.

He did not, however, wear the red rose crested cap of which the poet sings, for he invariably played bare-headed.

The team naturally included W.G. Grace, then thirty-four years old. With universal assent he was called the "Champion", and, in later years, more familiarly and affectionately, the "Old Man". Alfred Lyttelton, who many years later became Secretary of State for the Colonies, was not only a fine batsman but one of the greatest of wicket-keepers; some good judges considered him almost as good as Blackham. C.T. Studd was the most successful English batsman of the year. Steel, Ulyett, and Barlow were all-rounders of the highest class. Peate was then the foremost English bowler; he had been remarkably successful with the English team in Australia during the previous winter. He was, however, not a good batsman, was, in fact, the only member of the eleven of whom this could be said; every other member could properly have been selected for a representative England team on his batting record alone.

The match began at ten minutes past twelve on Monday, 28th August. Rain had fallen heavily on the previous Saturday and again early on Monday morning, and the wicket was bad. A great crowd of spectators packed the ground when Massie and Alec Bannerman began Australia's first innings. It was an innings of repeated disaster. At five minutes to three the last Australian wicket fell, and no more than 63 runs had been scored. In none of the twenty-nine matches the Australians had already played that season had they scored so few runs in an innings. The English bowlers — Barlow, Peate, and Ulyett — were at their best, the most successful being Barlow, who took 5 wickets for 19 runs. But the wicket had suited them; and there were many in the expectant throng of spectators who wondered how it would suit Spofforth, the demon bowler.

It was a wicket after his own heart. It might have been made for him. As the first two English batsmen, Grace and Barlow, advanced to the wicket the Demon was the most striking object to be seen on the field. Tall — nearly six feet three inches in height — almost spectre-thin in build, with a lean and hungry look, he was a disconcerting figure for a nervous batsman to come up against. Grace and Barlow, however, were not batsmen of that type. They were tough and well seasoned cricketers. Nevertheless, the Champion had made 4 runs only when the Demon clean bowled him with a yorker; and with the total at 18 he had Barlow caught at point. George Ulyett came in. Skilful with both bat and ball, he was for many years a tower of strength in Yorkshire cricket, and his cheerful disposition had gained for him the name of "Happy Jack". He and A.P. Lucas raised the total to 56, accompanied by the plaudits of the excited and vociferous crowd. Then Ulyett was stumped off the Demon's bowling, and when the score reached Australia's total 6 wickets had fallen. Steel and Read came to the rescue, and the score was raised to 101 before the last wicket fell. It was a poor total for so strong a batting side, but it was 38 ahead of Australia's score. The Demon had taken 7 wickets for 46 runs.

So ended the first day of this historic match. There was heavy rain during the night and again in the morning, but at ten minutes past twelve play began. In Barlow's opinion the ground was unfit for play. He wrote:

Mr. Hornby was our captain, and he went out in my judgment a bit too soon on the second day. The ground was wet, and Peate and I could not stand, while the ball was like soap. I had to get the groundsman to fetch a spade to get the mud out of the bowling holes, so that I could fill them up the sawdust.

Bannerman and Massie opened Australia's second innings, and each played his own characteristic game. Bannerman at the wicket was patient and unadventurous. In vain did the English bowlers, men of infinite guile, tempt him with balls as seductive as the Erl-King's daughter to hit out. He did not hit out. He let the ball hit the bat. To use an expression popular now but unknown then, he "hung his bat out to dry". He made few runs, but he kept his end up, and that was what his side expected of him.

But Massie! Massie played the innings of a hero, such an innings as d'Artagnan might have played had he been as skilled with the bat as with the sword. He hit the English bowlers — first-class bowlers making the most of a bad wicket — with glorious wristy strokes all over the field. He took risks. To do the best for his side he had to take risks. With his score at 38 he mistimed a ball from Barnes and lifted it to Lucas at long-off. Lucas was one of the best of fielders, but all men however skilful make mistakes, and the catch was missed. The escape seemed to endow Massie with new power and in fifty-five minutes the score had reached 66, of which he had made 55. Then Steel, one of the wiliest of bowlers, delivered to him a ball that looked as if butter wouldn't melt in its mouth. Massie sprang at it, hit across at it, was bowled by it, and left the field amid a tumult of acclaim. A useful score of 29 was made by Murdoch, but the innings closed for 122. The Englishmen had to make no more than 85 runs to win. They were confident of victory. The side was enormously strong in batting down to the tenth man. True, the wicket was bad, but bad wickets were nothing new to this team. Grace and Ulyett, to mention no others, had each often made over 85 runs on a bad wicket. In C.T. Studd's account of the match he wrote:

The weather was cold. We sat in the Committee Room, and the windows were shut because of the cold. Except that such strange things happen in cricket, none dreamed we should be beaten.

In the ten minutes' interval before England's second innings began, the Australians discussed the prospect. They turned to Spofforth, as men in times of crisis turn to their strongest in will and deed. He was calm and confident. The match, he assured them, could and should be won. He had noted the condition of the wicket. He knew it was one on which he and his colleagues could do their deadliest. But victory would be hard to win; and it was in a spirit of grim determination that Australia's cricketers took the field for the decisive innings of this memorable contest.

To most of the spectators the match seemed as good as won. But there were some old stagers who were not so optimistic. They couldn't help thinking of a spring day four years earlier, when the Demon and his colleague, H.F. Boyle, had dismissed one of the strongest of M.C.C. elevens for 33 runs in the first innings and 19 in the second. They knew — and it was to be proved again years later on the Gallipoli beaches — that Australians are at their best when things look black.

But here, at a quarter-to-four (there was no tea interval in those virile days), are the bearded Champion and the English captain descending the pavilion steps. The Demon bowls from the Vauxhall end, and at the pavilion end is T.W. Garrett, who lived to welcome the England team of 1937 to Sydney. The score slowly mounts to 15, when Hornby is bowled by the Demon, and with the next ball Barlow also is bowled.

Two good wickets for 15! A bad start. Grace is joined by "Happy Jack" Ulyett, and in the next half-hour these two well-seasoned batsmen raise the score to 51. Only 35 to win and 8 wickets in hand! What do those croaking old stagers say to that? But the Demon, who from the beginning has been bowling with an infinite variety of pace, flight, length, and break — but never the slightest change in his action — is now at the pavilion end and sends down to Ulyett the extra fast ball he has always up his sleeve. "Happy Jack" mistimes it and is caught at the wicket. Lucas comes in. Two more runs are scored, when the crowd, with a thrill of horror, see Grace caught at mid-off from one of Boyle's insidious and illusory deliveries. Grace has made 32, the score is 53, and 4 wickets are down. Lyttelton comes in and at once hits Boyle for 4. Then follows a period of slow play, but the score creeps up. It reaches 60. We have only 25 to win and 6 wickets still in hand.

But, as the afternoon wears on, it is becoming evident that those 25 runs are going to be very hard to get. We have reached a stage in the match in which the batsmen seem unable to score. Twelve maiden overs are bowled in succession. Lucas is facing Spofforth and playing back to him ball after ball. Lyttelton is not scoring off Boyle, but he seems able to keep his end up; Boyle's box of tricks is becoming known to him. He is a master of the drive. Suppose he were to hit a few 4's? Not more than 25 runs are needed for Australia's defeat.

These considerations have not escaped the watchful eye and untiring brain of Spofforth. He has been studying Lyttelton's batsmanship, and is confident that he can get him out. He tells his captain so, and a stratagem is devised. Boyle delivers to Lucas a ball that almost cries aloud to be hit to mid-off. Lucas hits it to mid-off; Bannerman, who is fielding there, deliberately misfields it, and a single is scored. Lyttelton is now facing the Demon, who is bowling with the dark background of the pavilion behind him. Four more maidens are bowled, and then the Demon with a ball of perfect length and a breakback of some eight inches bowls down Lyttelton's middle and leg stumps. Steel comes in; the score is slowly taken up to 70, when the Demon with his invariable fast-bowler action sends Steel a slow break-back and follows it up in the direction of short mid-off. Steel plays forward, and is caught and bowled by the Demon's skinny right hand. Maurice Read comes in and receives two balls from the Demon. The first he with difficulty keeps out of his wicket; by the second he is clean bowled. Seven wickets are down and 15 runs are needed to win. William Barnes, a fine batsman, very popular with the cricket-loving public, takes Read's place and hits the Demon for 2. The next ball goes for 3 byes. Only 10 runs are needed to win; there are 3 wickets in hand, and two of England's best batsmen face the bowlers. Surely the crowd have no cause for apprehension!

But the last ball of the Demon's next over is fatal to Lucas. He plays it on to his feet; it makes for the wicket and comes up against the leg stump gently but with sufficient force just to dislodge the leg bail. Lucas departs and C.T. Studd takes the vacant place at the Vauxhall wicket.

A deathlike silence has descended upon the vast crowd as they watch, hushed and intent, the coming of the doomed batsmen to the place of sacrifice. The Demon's lean and hungry look grows leaner and hungrier with each successive over. From his last eleven overs 2 runs have been scored at a cost of 4 wickets. The huge gas-holders seem to glower with foreboding. One spectator bites through the handle of his umbrella without knowing it. Another is stricken with heart failure, collapses, and is carried from the ground — dead.

But at the wicket we still have C.T. Studd, the most successful English batsman of the year, a well-loved athlete, soon to begin a life of hardship, privation, and selfless devotion in the foreign mission field. In previous matches he has already scored a couple of centuries against this Australian team — one for Cambridge University and one for the M.C.C. With three good strokes he might win the match!

His predecessor at the Vauxhall wicket, Lucas, fell to the last ball of the Demon's over, and now Studd watches Boyle prepare to bowl the first ball of his over to Barnes at the opposite wicket. Boyle, one of the wiliest of bowlers, wears a beard. Bearded cricketers were not uncommon in those days . . . W.G. Grace, as everybody knows, had a beard of vast extent. At the present time, the appearance of a bearded player in first-class cricket would excite remark, but in the eighteen-eighties it was not so.

Barnes, who played Boyle's last over with confidence, is awaiting the first ball of this over. It is a malignant ball. It shoots up from the turf like an evil spirit ejected from the nether regions. It strikes Barnes's glove and rebounds to point, where it is well and truly held by Murdoch. Nine wickets are down, and still 9 runs are needed to avoid defeat.

But who is this with the purposeful aspect that strides to the vacant wicket? He is Edmund Peate, the great Yorkshire slow bowler; a consummate artist with the ball, a poor performer with the bat. He has been instructed to keep his end up and leave the scoring to Studd. He shows not the slightest sign of nervousness. His heart is as the heart of Richard Grenville upon another desperate occasion. He will bang these devildoms of Australia. He does. He bangs his first ball to square-leg for 2. Now we have only 8 runs to win. He survives his second ball, but it was a near thing, and as he prepares for his third he is full of an ill-timed confidence. He swings his bat for a mighty swipe — swings it "like a flail" it is recorded — he hears the ball crash into the stumps; and as the spectators carry Spofforth on their shoulders in triumph to the pavilion, the wires are flashing to the expectant throngs under the Southern Cross 12,000 miles away the news that Australia has won a glorious victory. The crowd is wild with enthusiasm. "The shouting and cheering that followed," wrote W.G. Grace, "I shall remember to my dying day." The Demon had taken 14 wickets for 90 runs. Studd has not received a ball. "Very sorry, gentlemen," says Peate to his sorrowing comrades, "but I could not trust Mr Studd."

Sixty-seven years ago! Yet in Australia's beautiful cities, and in the depths of her "outback", you may even now meet old men who thrill today with the memory of that August afternoon, when before the matchless bowling of the Demon the flower of English cricket became as stubble before the wind.

Why did Hornby send in Studd so late in England's second innings? It is still one of the unsolved mysteries of this extraordinary match. In Studd's own account of what took place he wrote:

We had made over 50 for 2 wickets . . . runs had come freely enough. Then came the time when the best English batsmen played over after over and never made a run. They got out, and Hornby on his own account began to alter the order of going in. He asked me if I minded and I said "No". Then things began to change and a procession began. Of course, Hornby told me he was holding me in reserve. So I went in eighth wicket down, and saw two wickets fall and myself never received a ball.

Other players who took part in the match left records of their impressions of it. R.G. Barlow, who had an unusually long experience of first-class cricket, first as player and later as umpire, wrote:

Of all the many matches in which I have played, the most exciting, without exception, was the Test Match England v. Australia in 1882 at the Oval. . . I shall never forget that match while I live. The excitement was indescribable, and the scene after the match something to remember for all time.

Some twenty-five years after the match, T. Horan, the well-known "Felix" of Australian journalism, contributed an account of it to the Melbourne *Australasian*, from which the following extract is taken:

That was the match in which for the final half-hour you could have heard a pin drop, while the celebrated batsmen, A.P. Lucas and Alfred Lyttelton, were together, and Spofforth and Boyle bowling at them as they had never bowled before . . . when the scorer's hand shook so that he wrote Peate's name exactly like "Geese", and when, in the wild tumult at the fall of the last wicket, the crowd in one tremendous roar cried "Bravo Australia" with a special cheer for Spofforth, who in that grand final bit of bowling took 4 wickets for 2 runs off forty-four balls against the cream of English batsmen. That was a match worth playing in, and I doubt whether there will ever be such another game for prolonged and terribly trying tension.

On 2nd September 1882, four days after the match, the *Sporting Times*, which was printed on pink paper and popularly known as the *Pink 'Un*, published the following obituary notice:

In Affectionate Remembrance
of
ENGLISH CRICKET
which died at the Oval
on
29th August 1882

Deeply lamented by a large circle of
Sorrowing Friends and Acquaintances
R.I.P.
N.B. — The body will be cremated, and the
Ashes taken to Australia

From this notice sprang the legend of the "Ashes", which has become
one of the most characteristic elements of the folk-lore of the British
Commonwealth.

The full score of the match follows:

The Ninth Test Match
At the Oval, 28th and 29th August 1882

AUSTRALIA

1st Innings		2nd Innings	
A C Bannerman c Grace b Peate	9	c Studd b Barnes	13
H H Massie b Ulyett	1	b Steel	55
W L Murdoch (captain) b Peate	13	run out	29
G J Bonnor b Barlow	1	b Ulyett	2
T Horan b Barlow	3	c Grace b Peate	2
G Giffen b Peate	2	c Grace b Peate	0
J M Blackham c Grace b Barlow	17	c Lyttelton b Peate	7
T W Garrett c Read b Peate	10	not out	2
H F Boyle b Barlow	2	b Steel	0
S P Jones c Barnes b Barlow	0	run out	6
F R Spofforth not out	4	b Peate	0
Extras	1		6
Total	63	Total	122

ENGLAND

2nd Innings		2nd Innings	
R G Barlow c Bannerman b Spofforth	11	b Spofforth	0
W G Grace b Spofforth	4	c Bannerman b Boyle	32
G Ulyett st Blackham b Spofforth	26	c Blackham b Spofforth	11
A P Lucas c Blackham b Boyle	9	b Spofforth	5
A Lyttleton c Blackham b Spofforth	2	b Spofforth	12
C T Studd b Spofforth	0	not out	0
J M Read not out	19	b Spofforth	0
W Barnes b Boyle	5	c Murdoch b Boyle	2
A G Steel b Garrett	14	c and b Spofforth	0
A N Hornby (captain) b Spofforth	2	b Spofforth	9
E Peate c Boyle b Spofforth	0	b Boyle	2
Extras	9		4
Total	101	Total	77

Spofforth took 14 wickets for 90 runs, Boyle 5 for 43, and Garrett 1 for 32. Peate was the most successful English bowler, taking 8 wickets for 71. Barlow took 5 for 46, Steel 2 for 15, Ulyett 2 for 21 and Barnes 1 for 15.

In the following winter, a strong, though hardly a representative, English team visited Australia with the Hon. Ivo Bligh (later Lord Darnley) as captain. The team included six other amateurs: C.F.H. Leslie, W. Read, A.G. Steel, C.T. and G.B. Studd, and E.F.S. Tylecote; and four professionals: R.G. Barlow, W. Barnes, W. Bates, and F. Morley. The main object of the visit was to play three Test Matches with the Australian team that had defeated England at the Oval, and of these England won two and Australia one. After the third match, a group of Melbourne ladies presented Bligh with a collection of ashes of burnt cricket stumps enclosed in a small gold urn, on which were inscribed these lines:

> When Ivo goes back with the Urn, the Urn,
> Studds, Steel, Read, and Tylecote return, return.
> The Welkin will ring loud,
> The great crowd will feel proud
> Seeing Barlow and Bates with the Urn, the Urn.

Lord Darnley bequeathed the urn with its contents to the Marylebone Cricket Club, and it now rests under a glass case in the Long Room at Lord's.

The Melbourne ladies, however, were premature in their presentation. Bligh did not win *the* Ashes. He was induced to play an England v. Australia match not included in the original list of fixtures, the Australia XI being specially selected on current form. Australia won this additional match by 4 wickets. The number of Test Matches played by Bligh's team was not three but four, and each side won two. The four Tests, therefore, made no change in the custody of *the* Ashes — the legendary Ashes that symbolize the supremacy in Anglo-Australian cricket. They remained in Australia.

BODYLINE

BODYLINE REMEMBERED
By Jack Fingleton, 1968

THE "Mods," I am afraid, so often find my generation boring when we dip into the past but you can't always ignore history when it has to do with the present.

At Lord's recently the International Cricket Conference issued some nebulous stuff asking all countries to ponder the curse of pad-play. At the same time, I was chatting with Harold Larwood at Trent Bridge and I couldn't help thinking that without Larwood there would not have been this prevalent pad-play.

Of necessity, it sends me back to 1932-33, a turbulent period that burst upon me as a youngster in his first Test series against England. And as one connects Larwood with pad-play, so it must be added that had there been no Bradman there would have been no bodyline. It was, in itself, a tribute to Bradman's greatness.

Bradman had made Test scores in England in 1930 of 131, 254, 334 and 232. There had been nothing like him before. He cut all bowlers to shreds. He was the greatest challenge English cricket had known and a dour, remorseless Scot named Douglas Jardine was given the job of bringing him to heel and, of all places, in Australia. Jardine was 130 years after his time. He should have gone to Australia in charge of a convict-hulk.

So many of that English team have told me subsequently that they abhorred bodyline and wanted nothing to do with it. But it was a deep plot which obviously had its genesis before the English team was chosen. In that side were four fast bowlers — Larwood, Voce, Bowes and Allen — and Bowes just previously had bowled bodyline against the great Jack Hobbs at The Oval. There was no sterner critic of this than Sir Pelham Warner who wrote that it prostituted the art of cricket and that if it were continued it would ruin the game. Warner said Bowes had to stop it immediately.

"Plum" Warner, as he was known, soon after was made manager of the team led by Jardine to Australia. There must have been many nights when he never slept a wink.

In simple terms bodyline was nothing more than playing the man and not the ball. It was conceived for Bradman and, with Larwood the perfect instrument, it cut Bradman down to comparative size. But, as Warner said, it wasn't cricket. The batman's first thought, against the thunderbolts of Larwood and Voce at his ribs and around his head, was of self-preservation.

Oldfield had a fractured skull; Woodfull was hit a nasty blow over the heart as so many others of us were. I can still recall the whistle of a bouncer from Larwood past my temple; I almost moved into it. Some Australians showed up in poor colours. Several didn't want to play; one champion indeed asked to be dropped. The mutterings were intense. No Australian as the series drew on passed a word with an Englishman.

Riding the storm — and crowd riots were often imminent with mounted police on call outside Adelaide Oval — was the imperious, unflappable Jardine. He saw his job and he did it, impervious to all, including Warner, who remained publicly mute on the tour.

But Warner was more worried even than the Australians. I saw a letter which he wrote subsequently in which he said, in a *cri de coeur:* "I could do nothing with Jardine. He hates the Australians. The mere sight of one upsets him. I pleaded with him to stop it, at least to ease it. He coldly ignored me."

G.O. (Gubby) Allen alone stood up to Jardine. The skipper told Allen he wanted him to bowl bodyline in the second Test. Allen, who was a very good fast bowler, refused. "Then," said Jardine, "You won't play." Fifteen minutes before the game began, Allen was still in his street clothes. "Why aren't you dressed, Gubby?" asked Jardine. It was the only time on the incredible tour that Jardine lost a point. But Allen was an amateur. Larwood, Voce and Bowes were pros who did as they were told.

In the fifth Test, Larwood broke a bone in his foot while bowling and Jardine wouldn't let him leave the field while Bradman was batting. When Bradman got out (to Verity), Jardine turned to his great fast bowler and said, "You can go off now, Larwood." And Bradman and Larwood, in silence, walked off the field together. Larwood never walked on to another Test field.

There was the day when Warner and Palairet, his assistant manager, came into our Adelaide dressing-room to commiserate with the stricken Woodfull. Woodfull, under medical attention, said to the two Englishmen: "I don't want to discuss it. There are two sides out there. One is playing cricket. The other isn't." Warner and Palairet left the Australian dressing room in acute distress.

Warner wrote in a book later, "Unfortunately, there was a member of the Australian team who was a journalist and next day the story was blazoned all over the front pages."

That was hard one at me. I was the only journalist in the two teams and I knew stories of that tour to make a newspaperman's pen drip with ink. But I kept quiet. The reporter who got the story told me years afterwards of how he made a rendezvous with one of our team the night of the incident and he was told all. The stigma stayed with me. I told Woodfull years later who the "culprit" was. "A pity," said Woodfull, "that cost you the 1934 tour of England."

It was, of course, a distressing business. It was immoral against Bradman but Jardine's mistake was in using the unrelenting bodyline attack of Larwood and Voce — Bowes lacked the intensity of the others — against all the Australians.

It took years to abate and some of the bruises never healed. Bradman and Jardine never made it up — as others of us did with both Jardine and Larwood. I sat in front of the two in the Leeds Press Box in 1953 where some odd person had seated them together. "Good morning, Mr Bradman," would say Jardine. "Good morning, Mr Jardine," would say Bradman, and that was it for the day until the evening farewell came along.

No Australian blamed Larwood, wonderful bowler that he was. As I talked with him it was beneath a graphic picture of him delivering the ball. It all came back again. The classical upright pose of the body, with every muscle and sinew coming into the delivery. It is one of the immortal pictures of cricket.

It was odd that he should settle in Australia. In 1948, George Duckworth asked me if I would visit Larwood in his little Blackpool shop in which he sold sweets and cigarettes — with no name over the door. Larwood was suspicious. He thought I was after a story. We induced him to come for a "sup of ale" and from that flowed a warm friendship which finished in him emigrating to Australia.

One Saturday in 1950 in Canberra I received a cable from him: "Leaving tomorrow with wife, five daughters and eldest daughter's fiancé stop can you find jobs and accommodation."

It was, at a time of housing shortage, a tall order, and it was an Australian Prime Minister, Ben Chifley, who helped Larwood most to settle. "I think," said Chifley, "that Larwood was too good for you chaps."

I told Larwood when he arrived he should come to Canberra and thank Mr Chifley. He was delighted to do so. I took him in and Larwood, in his thick Notts accent, thanked Mr Chifley. Chif, as he was known, looked in some amazement at me. "What did he say, Jack?" he asked. I interpreted. Then Mr Chifley, in his nasal Australian tones, said some nice words about Larwood, who looked at me. "What did he say?" asked Larwood. Again I interpreted.

Somebody asked Larwood at Trent Bridge whether he would like to return to England. "No bloody fear," said Lol, "I'm a bloody Australian now."

You see, then, how boring an old-time cricketer can become: I really set out to draw a parallel between Larwood's return to his homeland and MCC's edict of pad-play. If there hadn't been a Larwood, there would not have been a revision of the lbw rule allowing a decision to a ball pitched outside the off-stump.

This was a sop from Australia to help bury bodyline, to draw concentration away from the leg-stump. It led to a flood of offspin and seam-bowlers and this, over the years, had led in turn to the batsmen negating these theories by prodding the front pad at the ball.

Larwood was a shy man, a modest man, a great bowler — but what an effect he had, even to this day, upon cricket! Maybe, soon, to cure the ill of pad-play, cricket will revert to the old lbw rule. It would be the final and fitting tribute to him.

BODYLINE – IS IT CRICKET?
(THE *BRISBANE COURIER*, JANUARY 28, 1933)

THIS is not the game you taught us!
Is it cricket?
It has lost the charm it brought us!
Is it cricket?
On the dear old village green,
Where the vicar and the dean
Kept the bowling 'all serene':
That was cricket!

If you're 'short weight' in the mart
It's not 'cricket'!
If your business deals are 'smart' —
That's not 'cricket'!
Hanki panki is for fools,
It's not taught you in your schools
So expunge it from your Rules:
It's not cricket.

Age-long query of the Saxon!
Is it cricket?
See the bruises, there, our backs on:
Is it cricket?

No, this new fangled bumping
That has set Australia 'jumping'
And our batsmen's hearts a-thumping —
Isn't cricket.

LEO O'BRIEN, ONE OF THE OLD SCHOOL
By David Frith
(FROM WISDEN CRICKET MONTHLY, APRIL, 1983)

JUST when you think you can't stand any further resurrection of the 1932-33 Bodyline series, you bump into a chap like Leo O'Brien, who was not only a central character, but has something to say that hasn't been made public before. O'Brien, now a startlingly fit 75, not only played in the second and fifth Tests of that notorious series, but he was Australia's 12th man at Adelaide, when matters erupted. Woodfull was hit in the chest, Oldfield on the skull, and the crowd was close to invading the oval to do Lord knows what to the English players, Larwood and Jardine in particular.

Thereby hangs the most fascinating tale of all. We all know that England's virtuous manager went into the Australian dressing-room to commiserate with Woodfull as he received attention for the bruising. We all know of Woodfull's brusque response, and of Jack Fingleton's lifelong contention that he was 'framed' for leaking the comments to the Press. Leo O'Brien now tells it his way.

'The 12th man's job can be a busy one,' he says. 'I was on the field a lot in that match, and Vic Richardson kept wickets because Bertie got hit. Anyway, when Bill Woodfull got hit — or a while after — he came back into the dressing-room. I went in shortly after, and Woodie came out of the shower, towelling his head. "How are you, Bill?" I said. "Not too good," he said. "Bit rough out there."

'Then Warner and the assistant manager of the MCC team, fella named Palairet, came into the room. The rest of the Australians seemed frightened to come in!

'Anyhow, that's when Woodfull said there were two teams out there but only one was playing cricket. They both turned on their heels and walked out.

'Now the masseur who was there was stone deaf and wouldn't have heard a thing. Fingleton wasn't it that room. Nor was Bradman. I remember who was: there was Alan Kippax and Jack Ryder and Ernie

Jones, the old fast bowler — he was over 60 then, great big moustache. Ernie reckoned he could still, at his age, bowl faster than Larwood!'

Perhaps, dear reader, we are nearer to knowing how the story leaked. Perhaps.

O'Brien has a sportsman's crewcut — grey — and the flattened nose betokens 30-odd amateur bouts, of which only the last was lost. Such are his poise and stamina that he doesn't need to lean against the Hotel Australia bar even in a six-round beer-sipping session. He played 40 times for Victoria and five times for Australia, a courageous left-hander who could field brilliantly, as you'd expect from a senior league baseballer. Sixteen seasons of top Aussie Rules football and even a close challenge to the world skipping champion spell out an all-round sportsman to stand with the best of them. He was — is — incapable of a mean word; he seeks always to exude admiration for the true sport. His modesty is matched by his eagerness to put credit where it belongs.

For instance, he cannot understand the fashion of querying Bradman's genius: 'By far the best bat I've ever seen. In 234 matches he made 117 centuries — a hundred every second time he batted! And 93 of his centuries were chanceless before he reached three figures! He was also the most dangerous fieldsman I ever played against. Bill Ponsford said to me in my early days, "Don't run to him. If you do, we'll both finish at one end, and you'll be at the wrong end." '

O'Brien tells a good one about his Test debut, at Melbourne in the second of the Bodyline Tests: 'Woodie put the batting order up — Woodfull, Fingleton, O'Brien! Don was already putting his pads on! Woodie never said a word to me. He just relied on my nous — to take the shine off the ball. I got 10, run out. I'd just got out of the shower when Bradman came back in. He said he'd been bowled — didn't mention that he'd played on to Bowes. Very modest bloke.'

He says he used to talk to the Englishmen. And, on one auspicious occasion, one of them spoke to him: 'When Jardine reached his fifty at Adelaide he got a load of raspberries from the crowd. He turned to me — I was fielding at short leg — and he said, "I suppose I *was* a bit slow." '

'Len Darling was a good player. He used to stand up and hook Larwood square. There would have been no Bodyline without Larwood. There wasn't much you could duck. It came at your throat, really fast.'

He clears his throat often, and chuckles apologetically, as if to say, 'I shouldn't be burdening you with all this.' Another sip, another memory: 'We didn't wear thigh-pads, y'know. Just an old singlet stuffed down there.'

How close did Australia come to considering retaliation? 'No, that wasn't Billy Woodfull's cup of tea ... Vic Richardson would've though!' O'Brien toured South Africa three years afterwards under the leadership of Richardson, another superb all-rounder sportsman. 'Eddie Gilbert, the abo, was as fast as Larwood. Small fella. There was another at the settlement even faster, but he went bush when the scouts came along to see him.'

Did he harbour any ill-feeling over the lethal 'leg theory' off which he had made 61 brave runs in the final Test? He smiles and shakes his head. 'The Poms jumped on that word "unsportsmanlike" in our Board's cable. That's when they went on the back foot. Trouble is, they blame dead men these days. Joe Lyons, the Prime Minister; S.M. Bruce; Jimmy Thomas over in England. I dunno!'

Leo O'Brien has just played his 61st season of cricket, the game he loves so dearly. For over 50 of them he has played at least one match on the Melbourne Cricket Ground. It was there that his first-class career came to an end when he had to withdraw from a Test in 1936–37 because of a back injury.

Of nothing is he more proud than his coaching tours of India, Ceylon and Singapore in the early 1960s. 'Kapil Dev was coached by one of the coaches I trained!' O'Brien also taught turf culture over there.

Then there was the horse breeding and training — a 'bit of a hobby'. Bill Williamson rode one of his prize specimens to victory at Moonee Valley in a weight-for-age minor classic in the early 1950s.

His pipe had gone out, and he had to start thinking about making tracks home. Tomorrow he was going to pop over to see Fleetwood-Smith's widow. 'Chuck' had had been a classmate of his at school when the First World War ended.

A very nice man. One of the old school. I just hadn't the heart to ask him what he thought of the behaviour of some of today's Australian Test players.

LARWOOD THE WRECKER

Cyril Ritchard, appearing in Our Miss Gibbs *in Sydney during the summer of 1932–33, added this verse to his lines*

Now this new kind of cricket
Takes courage to stick it,
There's bruises and fractures galore,
After kissing their wives
And insuring their lives
Batsmen fearfully walk out to score.
With a prayer and a curse
They prepare for a hearse,
Undertakers look on with broad grins.
Oh, they'd be a lot calmer
In Ned Kelly's armour,
When Larwood the wrecker begins.

IN DEFENCE OF BODYLINE
By A. A. Milne
(A LETTER TO THE *TIMES*, JANUARY 20, 1933)

Now that it is officially announced that the bitter feeling already aroused by the colour of Mr Jardine's cap has been so intensified by the direction of Mr Larwood's bowling as to impair friendly relations between England and Australia, it is necessary that this new 'leg theory,' as it is called, should be considered, not only without heat, but also, if possible, with whatever of a sense of humour Test Matches can leave to a cricketer.

It seems funny, then, to one who did not serve his apprenticeship as a writer by playing for Australia that a few years ago we were all agreed that cricket was being 'killed' by 'mammoth scores' and 'Marathon matches', and that as soon as a means is devised of keeping scores down to a reasonable size cricket is 'killed' again. It seems comic to such a one that, after years of outcry against over-prepared wickets, a scream of horror should go up when a bowler proves that even such a wicket has no terrors for him. It is definitely the laugh of the year that, season after season, batsmen should break the hearts of bowlers by protecting their wickets with their persons, and that, when at last the bowler accepts the challenge and bowls at their persons, the outraged batsmen and ex-batsmen should shriek in chorus that he is not playing cricket.

These things seem funny: but there is, of course, a serious side to the Australian Board of Control's protest. This says that the English bowling has made 'protection of the body by the batsman the main consideration,' and if this were so there would be legitimate cause of complaint. But let us not forget that Mr McCabe, in his spare moments during the first Test Match, managed to collect 180 runs, and Mr Bradman, in the second, 100; each of them scoring (even though scoring was necessarily a minor consideration) four times as quickly as Mr Jardine, whose body (up to the cap) was held as sacred. Let us not forget that, if this new form of bowling is really as startlingly new as is implied, lesser batsmen than these two should at lease be given a chance of adapting themselves to it before the white flag is waved. But if modern batsmanship is really so unadventurous and unflexible that after three failures it announces itself beaten and calls for the laws to be altered, why, then, let the laws be altered; let everybody go on making runs, the artisan no less easily than the master; and let us admit frankly that the game is made for the batsmen only, and that it ceases to be cricket as soon as it can no longer be called 'a batsman's paradise.'

A LARWOOD COCKTAIL
By 'D. G. D.'
(AUSTRALIAN CRICKETER, MARCH, 1933)

"OUR MISS GIBBS," which began a season at "Her Majesty's" Theatre, Sydney, recently, differs greatly from the original, performed away back in 1911. In it we find much mention of cricket. Even Timothy Gibbs, the "coosin from Yorkshire," lays claim to being a neighbour of both Leyland and Sutcliffe. Even a verse of the far-famed "Yip-I-Addy-I-Ay" chorus is devoted to our Test stars. Perhaps the best joke, however, goes to "Hughie" (played by Cyril Ritchards), who asked his friend had he tasted the new Larwood cocktail. On being asked why it was so named, "Hughie" informed his friend in a very confidential manner: "Because it always goes to your head."

A Whining Digger

By J. C. Squire, on Australian complaints about bodyline
(THE *EVENING STANDARD*, JANUARY, 1933)

WHERE is that tough Australian grin?
    When comrades did you learn to faint?
    Can you not take without complaint
A dose of your own medicine?

Finish this futile brawl to-day.
    We won't believe the paradox,
    A whining Digger funking knocks,
Come on one up and two to play.

THE LARWOOD-BRADMAN DUEL
Anon.
(*AUSTRALIAN CRICKETER*, 1933)

BEFORE 1932-33

Larwoodus spied Bradmanus, and dashed across the main
    Ho Bradmanus, I have sought thee in many a hard fought game.
One of us two, O Bradmanus, henceforth will reign alone —
    So! Lay thou on for Australia, and I'll lay on for Home

BEFORE 1934

Said Bradmanus to Larwoodus as he flew across the main,
    Ho, Larwoodus, you have battered me in many a header game.
One of us two, O Larwoodus, will never more go home —
    I'll do my best with my cricket bat, and you can use your stone.

(With apologies to Macaulay)

JARDINE'S MEN V NEW SOUTH WALES
By 'Yabba', whose name appeared over a column in the Sunday Sun that summer

WELL, after four years waiting, I got a chance to see the Englishmen, and they got a chance to hear me.

Two days so far — Friday, bonser, Saturday, dead.

Friday was a real snifter day's cricket, watching Fingleton, and Saturday was a good snore-off waiting for the Englishmen to score.

Well, on Friday, when the one and only Don come on, the mob give him a cheer. Then for him to have the stiff luck to go out to that ball of Tate's that swung in very quick it seemed to me, well — to say the mob was disappointed is putting it mildly.

Then McCabe got going in his dashing style, and the mob enjoyed it.

As to the bowling, Tate is as good as ever.

Fingleton? Brilliant. The way he batted, getting belted like he was, was wonderful. He's one of my first selections for the Tests. If we don't encourage the young players, where will we get our next team for England? He's a brilliant field from any possy, as he showed yesterday, and another innings like that from him and they'll have the crowd waiting to get in.

Yesterday was dead. At first the mob barracked all right. They even barracked ME! Yes, as I came in, the mob sung out, " 'Ow's the wireless?" That got me stone mad. I'm not on the wireless. I only talk on the Hill.

Some of the mob counted Sutcliffe out, but as I explained, well, he's a professional man. It's his living.

Pataudi never looked like getting a score. The crowd were getting ready to count him out — but, as I explained — he was fighting for his possy in the Test. . . But he needn't have stopped there 25 minutes for four. He's not a professional like Sutcliffe — he's a Rajah, or something — cricket ain't his living.

And then, at five minutes to six, the umpires decided to draw the stumps; why, I don't know. I don't reckon it's ever been done before.

LEG THEORY AT SUNNYBROOK FARM
From a newspaper advertisement for the show, Rebecca of
Sunnybrook Farm

THERE's an Animal Test Match at Sunnybrook Farm;
And the Board of Control can't keep itself calm
For as soon as the centipede went in to bat,
A cow bowled leg theory and knocked ten legs flat.

Billy the Pig was next batsman in
Then the cow bowled a fast one which cracked on his chin
And a big lump of pig's cheek fell on the crease
So they bound the cow over to keep the piece.

Umpire Rebecca then took control
And no-balled the cow when he started to bowl;
So the ethics of cricket can suffer no harm
If we follow Rebecca of Sunnybrook Farm.

BRADMAN

DESTINY IN HIS HANDS
By H. S. Altham
(FROM *THE CRICKETER SPRING ANNUAL*, 1941)

'IN the many pictures that I have stored in my mind from the "burnt-out Junes" of forty years, there is none more dramatic or compelling than that of Bradman's small, serenely-moving figure in its big-peaked green cap coming out of the pavilion shadows into the sunshine, with the concentration, ardour and apprehension of surrounding thousands centred upon him, and the destiny of a Test Match in his hands.'

A CRACK BAT AT BOWRAL
Michael Page says in his biography of Sir Donald Bradman that these were the first words printed about Bradman's cricket career
(BY 'JOHN', *SMITH'S WEEKLY*, 1921)

SAW a curious thing at a junior cricket match at Bowral (New South Wales) recently. Don Bradman (crack bat) sent a ball over the boundary fence. It struck half a brick, rebounded onto a fence post, poised there for an appreciable time, and ran along the top of the palings the whole length of a panel of fencing before descending outside the boundary.

BRADMAN
By A. B. ('Banjo') Paterson, in a radio talk
(FROM HIS *SONG OF THE PEN: COLLECTED WORKS 1901-41*, SYDNEY, 1983)

I have to correct a mistake that I made the other day when talking about Australian cricketers. I said that George Bonnor was six feet two high, but I was only guessing at it. To my youthful eyes he looked about eight feet, but I didn't like to pitch it too strong so I said six feet two.

Now the Lamrocks, General Lamrock and his brother, who knew the Bonnors well, tell me with absolute certainty that George Bonnor was six feet eight high, and that he had a brother six feet ten, and another that was only six feet four. When the three of them used to talk down the street with the six foot four chap in the middle, people would say, 'Who's the little man with the two Bonnors?'

I'll tell you another thing that I forgot to say the other night. When George Bonnor was batting in a county match in England they put a lob bowler on a bowl, and when George came in this chap had only two balls to finish his over. As soon as the ball left the bowler's hand, Bonnor came skipping down the pitch to meet it on the full, six feet eight high he was, and covering as much ground at every jump as a kangaroo. He was nearly down at the other wicket when he met the ball and the umpire and the bowler thought that if he hit it at them, he would kill them. So they started to run round and round each other, each try to hide behind the other and pushing and cursing a treat. Well, George didn't hit it at them, but he hit it so hard that everybody lost sight of it for a minute. It was probably the biggest hit ever made on any cricket ground in the world and even then it was caught. Of course I wasn't there, but Charlie Bannerman was there and he told me about it and I always believed every word that Charlie Bannerman said. Charlie told me that this ball was caught by a chap fielding at deep third man in a match that was being played in another country altogether.

After that, there was another sensation. This lob bowler had to finish his over, and after his narrow escape he was badly rattled. The umpire was rattled too, and this is what happened. The lob bowler tried to pitch one wide out where Bonnor couldn't reach it, but in his excitement he dragged over the crease and the umpire called, 'No ball'. Then, when he saw how far out the ball was going, he didn't dream that Bonnor could reach it so he called 'Wide'. But Bonnor could reach anything and the next thing the umpire said was, 'No, by heavens he's hit it'. Then a fieldsman caught the ball and the umpire said, 'Well caught! Out.' Then he pulled himself together and said, 'Not out. Over.'

So his decision ran 'No ball, wide, no by heavens he's hit it, well caught, out, not out, over', all in one breath as you might say. I see that Woodfull had some trouble with the umpires in Melbourne the other day. I don't know how he'd have got on with this umpire.

And now to come down to the present day. A couple of years ago I was in a sports depot in Sydney and a wiry sunburnt young bush chap came in, and started looking over the goods. I've had so much to do with athletes I can generally pick a man fairly well, and I said to the salesman, 'That's a hard-looking young fellow and he's very light on his feet. I should say he had done some boxing or was accustomed to riding rough horses. They have to be pretty active for that game.'

So the salesman laughed and said, 'No, you're a bit out. But he's a somebody all the same.'

I said, 'Who is he?'

'Oh,' he said, 'that's Don Bradman, this new boy wonder cricketer they have just discovered.'

You see he was only Don Bradman, the Bowral boy then, and hadn't been to England. He's Mr. Bradman now, and many congratulations to him.

So the salesman brought the boy over — he seemed only a boy to me — and after we had exchanged a few remarks, Bradman went out. So then I asked the inevitable question: I said, 'How good is this fellow? Is he going to be as good as Trumper?'

Now, the salesman had been a first-class cricketer himself and he gave me what I consider a very clear summing up of the two men.

'Well,' he said, 'when Trumper got onto good wickets he developed a beautiful free style, like a golfer that plays a full swing with a good follow-through. He trusted the ball to come true off the wicket, and it if bumped, or shot, or kicked, he might be apt to get out. But this Bradman takes nothing on trust. Even after he has got onto good wickets, he won't trust the ball a foot, and he watches every ball till the last moment before he hits it. His eye is so good and his movements are so quick that he can hit a ball to the fence without any swing at all. That makes him look a bit rough in style compared with Trumper, and he hits across his wicket a lot. They say that's a fatal thing to do, but I never saw him miss one of them.'

So I said, 'You wouldn't remember W. G. Grace, can you remember Ranjitsinhji?'

'Yes,' he said, 'Ranji had a beautiful style, but he was a bit fond of playing to the gallery. If he'd liked to stonewall, they'd never have got him out, but he used to do exhibition shots — late cuts, and tricky little leg glances — and out he'd go. There's no exhibition shots about this Bradman.'

I said, 'How will he get on in England? Will he handle the English wickets?'

'Yes,' he said, 'don't you worry about him on English wickets. He'd play on a treacle wicket or on a corrugated iron wicket. He's used to kerosene tin wickets up there at Bowral. He'll never be the world's most artistic cricketer, but he'll be the world's hardest wicket to get.'

Well, it's not often that a prediction works out as well as that, is it?

LEEDS, 1930
By Neville Cardus
(THE *FIELD*, 1930)

THE first day's cricket at Leeds opened as ominously for England as for Australia. Jackson played too soon at an inswinger from Tate and was caught at forward short-leg. The jubilation of the crowed broke out quite voraciously as the score board announced Australia two for one wicket.

But those of us who had watched Larwood's first over were prepared for strong batsmanship, even though we did not for a moment anticipate an innings of 309 from a single player in a single afternoon.

The prophetic fact about Larwood's first over was that not a ball rose to a greater altitude than half-stump high. Clearly the wicket contained no fire at all; it was perfectly docile.

Bradman missed his first ball rather dangerously; then, despite his own and Australia's tentative beginning, he did not wait to play himself in.

But I must elaborate that statement, lest the impression be given of a Bradman who lived dangerously and impetuously.

Bradman at every part of his innings was as watchful as Woodfull himself; when a good-length ball came to him, after he had reached 200, he put his head down and over the line of the ball, and his bat was utterly canny, with the handle slightly in front of the blade.

When I say Bradman did not pause to play himself in, I mean that he did not, as most modern cricketers certainly do, decide *not* to hit a four, whatever the ball's length, until he had been at the wicket a long time. He began as though seeing the pitch and direction of the English attack with the eyes of a man whose score already stood at 150.

He began with a violent straight drive from Tate, but it was a defensive back shot. Then he knocked Larwood out of action by plundering eleven in an over, a drive through the covers, a square pull, a hit to leg, and a single to the off.

In fifty minutes he reached 50 out of 63 and then he had hit eight fours. Woodfull, at the other end, was as much forgotten by us, as much taken for granted, as Kreisler's accompanist.

Bradman never lifted a ball, never gave the faintest hint of a margin of human error. He was quick to see the overtossed and the short ball, and, more significant still, he was quick to see the ball which the bowler wanted him to hit. He never obliged!

His innings was unique in its perspicacity, its combined solidity and power, safety and speed.

He equalled the performance of Trumper and Macartney by scoring a century in a Test match before lunch on the first day of a Test match.

A remarkable fact of his innings which I have not yet seen pointed out anywhere, so far, is that he achieved his quickest rate of scoring in his first hour. He came to the wicket at twenty minutes to twelve and at twenty minutes to one he had made 70, including twelve boundaries.

Woodfull was out at three o'clock; the second Australian wicket made 192 in two hours, forty minutes, Bradman's share being 142. In the light of Bradman's brilliance, Woodfull had no objective reality for any of us save the scorers; but he was at his most obstinate. Yet, as a curiosity, it must be recorded that Bradman, despite the velocity, the range, and the energy of his cricket, seemed less likely than Woodfull to get out.

Kippax again played a suave innings and stayed with Bradman until after six o'clock. He was caught by Chapman when Australia's total was 423. The third wicket, held for two hours and three-quarters, was worth 229. Kippax's portion of 77 had the flavour of delicate culture.

At close of play, Bradman in five hours and three-quarters had hit 42 boundaries — showing us every stroke in batsmanship excepting the leg-glance; he had compiled 309, and Australia were 458 for three.

At one point of the historic afternoon, the score-board announced the glory of Bradman in these terms: *Australian Total*, 268; *Bradman*, 200.

Next morning, on a faster wicket, he was caught by Duckworth. In six hours, twenty-five minutes Bradman made 334, seldom hit a ball into the air, and gave no tangible hope to the field, with the exception of one hit to mid-on, off Richard Tyldesley, which might have been a catch had Tate got off the mark quickly enough.

This innings has caused something of a sensation in cricket. It has been described as the inauguration of a new era in batsmanship. And why? Bradman's innings was essentially orthodox; his strokes were all known to the game as far back as a quarter of a century ago.

Are we to acclaim him as sheer revelation because he uses his feet and possesses a rare range of strokes, and is capable of hitting very hard the sort of bowling which ties up the average county cricketer of these days, who seeks to bat from the crease?

Bradman's original contribution to batsmanship is not technical so much as temperamental. His strokes on Friday and Saturday might well have been photographed and used as illustrations to C. B. Fry's treatise on *Batsmanship*, written long ago. Bradman acts on Fry's principle — play back or drive.

Never is he to be seen lunging with his bat speculatively forward, and his right foot holding him back behind the crease. His stroke-play is clean, economic in energy — not an ounce wasted — but at bottom it is based upon a stance and footwork which allow him always to keep his head down and his eye on the ball. Where he differs from the great stroke-players of a quarter of a century ago is in the matter of his attitude to the game.

Whereas a batsman of the Trumper, Macartney, and the pre-war Hobbs class invariably went beyond his customary science and practised range of hits when he had reached, say, 150, Bradman brings to his longest innings the constant and unwavering mentality and vigilance of the modern record-breaker.

He is persistently playing every ball on its merits when his score is beyond 200, hitting the loose ball unmercifully, but never off his guard at the first hint of a serious challenge from the bowler.

Bradman never goes divinely mad, as Trumper and Hobbs did in the old days, when, having exhausted that part of their skill which was rational, they became like men possessed by romantic visions of wild and wonderful and new strokes in cricket. Bradman is not a romantic ever; he is perpetually a realist, with the oldest head a boy cricketer has carried on his shoulders since W. G. Grace.

A greater batsman — a phenomenal batsman for his age — yes! But a 'new era,' a creative force showing us arts never dreamed of before — this is nonsense. I might employ a Bradman as a beautiful example for a text book on the true and lasting principles of batsmanship. And the tone of it, the lessons and implications, would be quite conservative.

BRADMAN AT LORD'S, 1930
By Robert Lynd

IT was pleasant for those who were at Lord's on Saturday to read in Monday's Times that they had been the spectators of a day's play that would be famous in the history of cricket. Not that I had been in any doubt of this by the time Bradman had scored a hundred. But one's own certainties are worth little till they are confirmed by any expert. I do not think I am alone in being doubly confident of an opinion if I see it authoritatively endorsed in print. Hence, when I read The Times, it was like hearing a piece of good news to be told that I had been the witness of an historic event.

When Bradman came out of the pavilion with his bat you could have guessed that he was a man of genius even if you had never heard of him. Or, at least, you could have guessed that he had an individuality out of the common. There was character even in the set of his cap and in the way his collar was turned up. I see that one authority declares that Bradman is a craftsman rather than an artist, but though as a rule I bow to authority in such matters, no one will ever convince me that anyone but a great artist could afford such delight to the inexpert with his strokes.

Woodfull and Ponsford had withstood England; Bradman mastered it. And secure, conscious mastery of this kind is the crown of genius. By the time he had scored 50 I am sure that even the most ardent pro-English spectator in the ground would have been bitterly disappointed if he had gone out. Batting like this is something outside partisanship. It is a spectacle such as no one can expect to see often in a lifetime. Bowler after bowler was tried against him; he made most of them look ordinary and Woolley look comic. He exhausted the bowlers; he exhausted the fielders, whom he kept on a perpetual run; he exhausted himself so that, when Woodful was stumped, he sank over his bat like an oarsman who has collapsed after a race. But he did not exhaust the spectators. They forgot the heat of the day; they forgot to care who won. They asked for nothing better than that this should go on for ever. That Bradman had scored 155 not out when he fled to the pavilion at the end of the game with the spectators flying after him was a cause, not of despair, but of delight even to those who wanted England to win. They had seen a master in the hour of his inspiration. They had been the privileged spectators of an innings they knew in their hearts would live in the history of the game.

FIREWORKS AT BLACKHEATH
By *Irving Rosenwater*
(FROM HIS *SIR DONALD BRADMAN: A BIOGRAPHY*, LONDON 1978)

THE form Bradman was in around this period was astonishing even for him. On 2 November 1931 he actually scored 100 runs in the course of three overs, by means of ten 6s, nine 4s, a 2 and two singles. He was playing in an exhibition match at Blackheath, New South Wales (in the Blue Mountains, outside Sydney) for a combined Blue Mountains team against the Lithgow Pottery Cricket Club. The game was staged by the Blackheath Council to mark the official opening of their new ground and to test a new malthoid wicket being used for the first time in the Western Districts. The pitch resembled a thick linoleum floor and did away with the need for matting over the concrete beneath. Bradman, going in on the fall of an early wicket, revelled in it, and raced to 256 including 14 sixes and 29 fours. In the midst of his onslaught he hit 6, 6, 4, 2, 4, 4, 6, 1 off one over of off-breaks from Bill Black, thus retaining the strike. Off the next over, from Horrie Baker, a future Town Clerk of Lithgow, Bradman scored 40, with 6, 4, 4, 6, 6, 4, 6, 4. Black's next over was hit for 1, 6, 6, 1, 1, 4, 4, 6 — the first and fifth balls being hit for singles by O. Wendell Bill, the others by Bradman, who had thus scored 100 out of 102 in three overs. Black was promptly taken off after his two overs! At Blackheath to this day the fully-grown Monterey pines over which Don Bradman sent some of his leg-side sixes that day are still pointed out to visitors. Bradman hit 200 in boundaries alone that day in his 256, which must have been scored in an incredibly short time and it is a great pity that the innings appears not to have been timed.

One of the most delightful anecdotes of Bradman's career concerns that innings at Blackheath, which was actually the second time that season he had faced the slow to medium off-breaks of Bill Black. In the first match of Kippax's tour, on 12 September, Black was playing for Lithgow and surprisingly bowled Bradman for 52. The bowler's umpire, 'Gub' Kirkwood, called out excitedly: 'Bill, you've got him!' Umpires were apt to sacrifice something of their decorum when an event like this happened in a country town in the early 'thirties. And the ball that took the most prized wicket in Australia was mounted, inscribed, and presented to the bowler for proud and permanent retention in his home. Now to the anecdote. When Bradman was about 50 at Blackheath, the same fielding captain who had seen Black do his heroics at Lithgow threw the ball to Black in the hope he might do it again. 'I stood at the bowler's end', recalled Bill Black years later, 'and

while I placed my field Bradman was talking to the wicketkeeper, Leo
Waters. Later Leo told me this conversation took place.'

Bradman: 'What sort of bowler is this fellow?'

Waters: 'Don't you remember this bloke? He bowled you in the
exhibition match at Lithgow a few weeks ago and has been
boasting about it ever since at your expense.'

Two overs later Bill Black had to plead with his captain to be taken off,
nursing an analysis of 2-0-62-0.

BRADMAN 238

By 'S. E. N.'

(THE *SYDNEY MAIL*, NOVEMBER, 1932)

WHEN Bradman makes a score
Pavilions rock and hill-ites roar;
The man inside the scoring board,
Where all the waiting runs are stored,
He has no chance of feeling bored —
He wipes the sweat from out his eyes
And, rattling round the rollers, cries:
'Good lord! Another four!'
He has no time for taking pause,
He scarce has time to breathe, because
Don Bradman's out to score!
(Excuse that rhyme. I haven't time
To search for better ones when I'm
Absorbed in Bradman's score.)

When Bradman makes a score
The news flies to the city's core
By messenger and 'phone and wire;
It flashes all around like fire!
There's not a taxi waiting hire —
They flock in hundreds to the ground
Whene'er the news is going round
That Bradman's out to score.
And when they reach the S.C.G.
The first thing on the board they see
Is Bradman's fifty more,

And all are mad and glad, forsooth,
And old age e'en regains its youth
When Bradman makes a score!

When Bradman makes a score
His poetry and speed — oh, Lor'!
He picks a fast one from his toes
And like a shot for four it goes;
He says unto a full-toss, 'Hence!'
And gaily bangs it to the fence.
He snicks, and pulls, and cuts, and drives —
The field go racing for their lives
When Bradman makes a score!
And when at last the west'ring sun
Gives notice that the day is done,
And we have clapped until we're sore,
We homeward wend and talk it o'er.
Again, again, in tram and train,
How Bradman made his score.

THE KING OF ALL

By Oscar Asche, a leading Australian actor living in Britain
(A LETTER TO THE *DAILY TELEGRAPH*, NOVEMBER 7, 1931)

LORD Tennyson and Mr. Arthur Gilligan are both too young to draw comparisons between Bradman and Clem Hill and Victor Trumper. Hill was last here in 1905 and Trumper in 1909. They were both on the downward slope, and Lord Tennyson and Mr. Gilligan could only have been youngsters.

I saw Charles Bannerman make 165, retired hurt, in the first Test Match at Melbourne, March 1877. As I was only 5 years old at the time, I could not subscribe to the opinion, held by many old Australians, that he was the greatest bat Australia ever produced. But I saw both Hill and Trumper in their hey-day, and I saw Don Bradman here in '30.

He certainly did not give the impression of a seeker after publicity, though he quite rightly took advantage of the big fees offered him to write the story of his life, thereby incurring the displeasure of the autocratic Australian Board of Control. In fact he was very reserved, even amongst his comrades.

He had nearly every stroke except the lofted drive. It was because he kept nearly everything on the carpet and looked so safe that he was at times slightly boring to watch. As a run-getter he stands head and shoulders above all other Australian batsmen, and is, I think, only approached by Sutcliffe in this particular quality.

But close your eyes and dream back on the individual performances which have given you most pleasure and beauty of style, and the figures of Trumper and Macartney stand out clear from the fog of years.

So with English batsmen. There are bats one remembers having watched with greater enjoyment than Herbert Sutcliffe at his best, though none have equalled his record. Ranji, 'Tip' Foster, Spooner, Palairet, Woolley, George Gunn, all strike at the door of memory.

Bradman had his faults, which may get him into trouble when he has lost the schoolboy eye. There was one bat in the last Australian eleven who was more exhilarating to watch than the Don, and one who may prove his equal as a run-getter — McCabe.

After watching Bradman all through the summer of '30 I was guilty of the following doggerel:

> Not Ranji's grace, nor Trumper's trouncing shots,
> Nor Charles Macartney's footwork his, as yet;
> MacLaren still could teach the youngster lots,
> And Hobbs show him some strokes most bats forget.
> Yet ne'ertheless this youth of twenty-one
> Eclipse all that they have ever done.
> Six years ago a lad without a shirt,
> Playing the game upon a pitch of dirt,
> A sapling for a bat, a gutty ball,
> A tin-can wicket! Now the king of all!

LIGHTNING PERFECTION
By Margaret Hughes
(FROM HER *ALL ON A SUMMER'S DAY*, LONDON, 1953)

AT the Oval in 1934 I saw the lightning perfection of 'The Don' in action. Bradman and Ponsford encamped at that wicket, it seemed to an England supporter, for all time to come. Bradman's perfect timing drifts back to me now against a time-dimmed backcloth quite clearly, even to his advance from the pavilion to take his place at the crease. A prima donna could not have been a better judge of an entrance. Just a sufficient lapse of time to keep the crowd in suspense, a pause, and then while the air was taut with excitement out came that slight figure from the darkness behind to a huge burst of applause.

I can't understand why Bradman wasn't one of my early favourites. Perhaps it was because he was playing on the wrong side! He batted with a machine-like precision, his cover-drives as shots from rifles and his hooking so quick it was over in the flashing of an eye. I couldn't turn over in my mind again any of Bradman's shots, for they were gone practically before I had time to see them. He made a large number of runs. Perhaps he was the greatest of them all, but he could never oust Hammond from my mind for one single moment of the day.

'DON WON'T STAND FOR THIS'

Jack Fingleton's account of a match between a New South Wales Cricket Association side and a local side at Albury, September, 1933

'DUCKS' were in the air at Albury to-day. Ray Rowe, Stan McCabe, and myself were bundled out by the Alburians, and that, despite the fact that before the tour to-day not a single batsman had failed to get to double figures.

Furthermore, had a slip fieldsman been safer, Don Bradman would have made the trio of 'duckites' a quartette. Bowler Ruff might not have had any good feelings towards that particular slip fieldsman, but if Albury cricket enthusiasts do the right thing they will club together and erect a memorial to the man that missed Bradman before he had scored.

The miss enabled Don to go on and score a century that amazed the large crowd. It caused those of our side who have played a great deal of cricket with Bradman to declare that it was almost the most amazing innings they had ever seen the genius play.

I have the score book in front of me now, and to glance casually at the length of Bradman's score in it, one would never think that Don had made a century. Here is how the score book tells the tale:— 1, 1, 4, 4, 4, 4, 4, 4, 1, 2, 4, 2, 4, 4, 2, 1, 1, 4, 4, 1, 1, 1, 1, 4, 2, 2, 6, 4, 2, 1, 4, 4, 1, 4, 6, 4, 4.

Albury is a town of Australian Rules in the winter. The ground on which we played to-day is the principal Rules ground, and those who know anything about the size of the ground necessary for the Rules game will readily perceive how far Bradman's hits had to travel to reach the boundary.

So much for that particular aspect of Bradman's innings. Add to it a really good set of bowlers, a wicket that was of a very doubtful nature, and you have the material ingredients of a staggering display of batsmanship.

The first ball from Ruff to Bradman whistled around the worthy's ears, as there was unevenness in the pitch that enabled him to fly the ball nastily. It was off another flyer that Bradman was dropped in the slips.

'Don won't stand for this,' said one of our chaps, and he was right. From then onwards there flowed a succession of strokes that left everybody gasping.

The poor bowlers adopted such postures as to suggest they felt foolish. I have never seen Don put such power into his strokes. He seemed to throw every ounce of his lithe body into his movement, and such was his timing that the ball literally blazed its way to the fence. Two magnificent strokes cleared the pickets, and his boundaries blazed to all directions of the ground. Such genius is but seldom, if ever, witnessed by the average cricket follower. To-day Bradman gave Albury followers something they will talk about for the rest of their lives.

BATTING MUSIC
By Arthur Mailey, 1932

To me great batsmen are like great musicians. They have the same implements at their finger-tips, yet each is able to provide something different.

One blends a combination of tones and sounds into a light colourful melody, while another, with the same sounds, can produce a heavy, ponderous, unmelodious arrangement which, although not so tuneful, is equally as effective and interesting.

I thought this when I saw Woodfull and Bradman joined in a record-breaking partnership last Saturday. Bradman's batting had a fantastic, jazzy flavor about it while Woodfull's innings suggested a creation by Wagner by comparison.

One might almost say that there is an air of refinement about Woodfull's heavy work which is missing in his younger partner's batting. Both lack the artistry and grace of, say, Jackson or Kippax — neither of whom could be accused of introducing vulgar or coarse strokes.

Bradman's size is a handicap. It compels him to make cross-bat shots which, while they are effective, are not so beautiful to watch.

Woodfull plays the same ball with a bat as straight as possible, but he does not lift his bat sufficiently to get the terrific power in his strokes that Bradman does. Still, I think Woodfull places the ball better than does Bradman. He is more deliberate, more self-restrained (I do not wish to confuse self-restraint with confidence).

Bradman at times is unrestrained, but Woodfull never. Both have confidence of a different brand. Woodfull's confidence is of a modest nature, unlike Bradman's confidence annoys and irritates a bowler. He is what might be called arrogantly confident.

I think when Woodfull hits a third bowler to the boundary his heart is filled with pity and regret, while Bradman, under the same circumstances, would literally dance a highland fling on the bowler's grave.

Ponsford, the unmerciful, is like this. He and Don belong to the same school of thought: Ponsford started this business of amassing mammoth scores, and Bradman his disciple is putting the finishing touches on it.

First Duel
By Bill O'Reilly
(FROM HIS *CRICKET CONQUEST*, LONDON, 1949)

My first meeting with Don Bradman happened in the summer of 1924 when I was a student enrolled at the Sydney Teachers' College within the Sydney University. On my way home by train for summer vacation I passed through Bowral, a town situated about eighty miles south of Sydney and thirty miles from Wingello, the little town where my family lived. As the train stopped at Bowral I heard a voice calling out: 'Bill O'Reilly, get out, please.' I looked out to find the railway stationmaster from my home town diligently searching the train for me. When I called to him he excitedly informed me that the Wingello cricket team was playing Bowral on that afternoon and that I was selected to play. I told him that I had no cricket gear with me, but he smilingly observed that he had thought of all that before he had left home and that he had paid a hurried visit to my mother who, God bless her, had supplied all the necessary.

On leaving the train I was given a detailed account of a Bowral boy who had been showing excellent form with the bat and who was likely to supply such formidable opposition that the lads from my town thought that my services should be enlisted for the fray.

When the match began Bowral batted first. Having no theories about beating about the bush, my captain — appointed for seniority reasons rather than efficiency in the gentle art of manoeuvring a game into the right channels — gave me the ball to open hostilities. I quickly disposed of one of the opening batsmen and was interested to see the diminutive youngster coming to the wickets to carry on the fight. He looked to be no bigger than the bat, and probably because batting leg-guards were so heavy that he regarded them more as impediments than necessary equipment, he compromised by wearing one only — on his left leg, which he planted firmly down the wicket. Little did I know as I ran up to deliver my first ball to him that I was actually "opening hostilities" in what was to be a cricket lifetime's association.

The little fellow had several spots of luck early on. My slips-fieldsmen were not really classy. They had graduated to that position in the field mainly because they were short of a gallop and found any other position in the field called for more running than they were capable of giving. Strangely enough, this is not regarded as a serious handicap in country cricket at home. Two catches from Bradman were quite thoroughly carpeted by my slips-fieldsmen before he had reached 30. Having reached that score, he set about us with a will and employing his one attacking shot, a lofted on drive, he belted us round the countryside for the rest of the afternoon. He finished the day with 234 not out.

At that time his score was a terrible indignity to me. I just could not assimilate the knowledge that a pocket-sized schoolboy could have given me such a complete lacing. I spent the rest of the week which followed in trying to work out what it was that had gone wrong with my bowling to allow such an indignity to happen. In the years that have followed I have had many a wry smile as I bowled to the 'greatest run-getting machine the game has ever known' and remembered that there was a time when I believed that I had no future as a bowler because he had pasted me.

As luck sometimes has it, I got my revenge on the following Saturday afternoon. The match was resumed and Bradman continued his unfinished innings. With the very first ball that I bowled to him I knocked his 'house' over with one which came round his legs to hit the stumps. I cannot explain why it is that I still remember the incident. Probably there had been a lot of publicity about the school batting performance. Anyhow, I can still see the ball running round his legs, and the table turning. It came as no surprise to me whatever when I heard later that he had scored several phenomenally high scores in the local country competition.

Our next meeting occurred when we were both chosen to represent the N.S.W. second eleven against Victoria in the 1926–27 season. Hans Ebeling was another destined to play for Australia who took part in that match. He played for Victoria. My clearest memory of Bradman on that occasion was that he hardly spoke a word to anyone — a shy country boy playing his first important game in the city, and that he was out, stepping on to his wicket, hitting a boundary when his score was somewhere in the forties. I went on to selection in the N.S.W. Sheffield Shield team and Bradman went back to Bowral to await another chance.

When next we met again we were members of the N.S.W. team three years later. In the meantime I had been transferred to a remote country area by an Education Department which thought that I had been devoting too much of my time to cricket, and had spent three years far away from the watchful, or otherwise, eyes of the State selectors. During these three years Bradman had come to the city, quickly made his name, played for Australia against England in Australia, and had actually returned from a tour of England where his magnificent performances were such that they will live for ever. Many people have claimed some of the kudos for the meteoric rise of Bradman. You need believe none of them. Bradman had no more coaching than I did and that was the absolute minimum — none at all. He went for cricket as a duck goes for water.

There is no need to waste time on Bradman's records. They have been covered so often that the subject is likely to become boring. He bestrode the game during the twenty years that he took part in it and no other figure in it contemporaneously was worth a line of notice until the scribes had given Bradman his complete paragraph.

I have been tremendously sorry for Bradman throughout his career for the way in which he had had his private life ruined by the glaring limelight of unwanted publicity. If one were to ask him how often he has been able to go for a quiet walk anywhere, even in the depths of winter, without some earnest soul dwelling upon him to hold a confidential talk on cricket, the answer would surprise most people. It would not amaze me. He has had no private life in the last twenty years except that which he can commandeer by his own and his wife's obstinacy in keeping away from the prying eyes of supposed well-wishers. When Queen Juliana of Holland appealed to her people to let her have the freedom of the streets of The Hague without the boredom and annoyance of people 'earbashing,' I'll guarantee that Bradman sympathised with her wholeheartedly. I have seen him be recognised in Regent Street, London, and a crowd of people gathered in split seconds to have a good look at him. When the team is due to leave its hotel to go off to a Test match ground in either England or Australia, thousands of people congregate outside and block the traffic in their eagerness to see the 'Great Don.' That type of glory might appeal to the boy fresh from school, but to Bradman and any man who has been through the mill it is nauseating, to say the least.

Bradman has never been free from it since his first glorious trip to England. That explains why it is that I have always been extremely sorry for him. I wonder what would have happened to him, had he been one who frequented such places, if he had walked into an hotel bar to have a quiet spot. It would have taken him a season to have recovered from the enthusiastic pats on the back that would have been accorded him.

Don has captained Australia exceedingly well in four series of Tests against England. It has become popular with those who go for the 'build up' business to declare that he is the greatest captain that Australia had produced. I cannot stop to give any such assertion much thought. When a man begins to compare the differing arts of captaincy he is, in my opinion, boasting in a very subtle manner. It makes me laugh loudly to hear men who have never played under any Test captain loudly broadcasting their opinions about the relative merits of men who have held an honoured place in the game. I have played under three Test captains and I do not feel disposed to draw odious comparisons between them. Each one of them made a pronounced impression upon me and I respect each one of them immensely. But I do not listen when I hear them being compared. Bradman was a competent captain and he won most of the Tests which he controlled. What more do you want of a man? I insist, however, that I do not listen when I am surrounded by Bradman fans declaring that he is the greatest of all Australian captains.

In personality Bradman is essentially matter of fact. He is not one who can put up with a fool gladly. He takes life seriously. He is at times inclined to take himself too seriously. He possesses a keen, analytical brain. He weighs the pros and cons with delicate care before he forms his opinion. He is never likely to 'let his head go.' Apart from his amazing deeds as a cricketer he has nothing that any thoughtful and successful business man has. There is no sparkle in his personality or conversation. He is just a solid, honest-to-goodness personality who relies on nothing else but the open door given him by his world-wide fame to help him along the Popularity Path.

In England, in 1948, he skippered the most successful Australian team ever against an England which must have been at her lowest cricket ebb. He played the game hard and left nothing to chance. One of the incidents which will always stick in my mind to explain the adjective 'hard' being used in describing Bradman's captaincy occurred at Old Trafford, Manchester. Jack Ikin, who had been experiencing a season of dismally small scores, had struck it rather lucky in Lancashire's second innings of the match against Australia which had been Cyril Washbrook's benefit match. When Ikin reached 99 runs, Bradman introduced the new ball when there were no more than two or three overs to be bowled before the match fizzled out. Ikin was bowled by Lindwall and missed the hundred. I felt like going round to the dressing-room to apologise to the Lancashire left-hander. It would not have mattered one iota to the Australians or to their captain's reputation had Ikin, a man who makes his livelihood from cricket, scored that extra run and had the satisfaction of going home to the Ikin household to tell the family that his long departed batting ability had returned. But I have seen Bradman act otherwise. In 1938 Bill Edrich had no possible hope of scoring this thousand runs in May unless Bradman had given him his opportunity to do so by letting Middlesex have another knock at a time when there was no other reason than his thoughtfulness for Edrich. Bradman was a much tougher captain in 1948, however. Probably it was because he had the responsibility of showing a large number of fledglings in his team the real atmosphere of international cricket.

At the finish of his great career he was given a grant Testimonial Match in Melbourne from which he was handed the sum of £9,000, and a few days later the news broke that he had been knighted.

Bradman has become legendary in cricket lore already. Just as the deeds of Robin Hood surround the folk lore of medieval England, Bradman's amazing deeds on the cricket fields of the Empire will permeate the game of cricket as long as it is played. He has become an Empire figure. Australia alone cannot claim him. I venture a guess that after His Majesty the King and Winston Churchill, Bradman is the best known man in the British Empire. He deserves the popularity that has come to him and good luck to him, say I.

BRADMAN, 1948

By Neville Cardus

(FROM *THE 1948 AUSTRALIANS: A SPORTING RECORD* HANDBOOK)

D. G. BRADMAN — Born Aug. 27, 1908. He beggars description. Not since W. G. Grace has there been a batsman so masterful and prolific, except perhaps Ranjitsinhji, who if he had given his mind day by day to run-making as dutifully as W. G. and Bradman, might easily have rendered all records null and void, on good or bad wickets.

Bradman sums up the contemporary philosophy and economy; when you have reached a century you begin again. Concentration on every ball. Every ball is your first ball. And the possibility that you might get out is not in your mind for a moment; there is no room or time for such an irrelevance.

No writer of fiction for schoolboys would have dared to invent a Bradman for his hero; no author of the 'Cock House of Felsgath' would dream of making the school captain score a hundred, a double-hundred, in nearly every big match! He would even let him get a 'pair,' to lend an air of verisimilitude to an otherwise unlikely story.

Bradman played in his first Test match in 1928; since then he has scored one hundred 100's and thirty-seven 200's. It is safe to say that if, before any Test match, the English bowlers were asked if they would allow Bradman credit of a century *on condition he did not bat*, the offer would be unanimously accepted — on a dry turf.

He has yet to satisfy all critics that he is good on a 'sticky' pitch, or rather that he ever wishes to play seriously in conditions where the ball spins and performs unforeseen motions. I find it hard to believe that he could not, if he set himself to the task, play great cricket on a 'glue-pot'; his eye, his footwork, the main and general style of his stroke-play, are the signs of a born great batsman, in any and all weathers, here or overseas.

He received next to no coaching when he was a boy, and what instruction was given him he to-day says he had quickly to forget. Yet from the first he batted with the science and sophistication of the most experienced of his 'modern' contemporaries.

He did not begin, as even genius begins, when young, with the usual impetuous mistakes. He has never struck at the ball with his body too far away, has never driven 'with his arms.' Instinctively he began, an urchin defending a kerosene tin, at the point where Ranjitsinhji, after years of study and practice, had to leave off.

Bradman at once got to the line of the ball; at once he 'found where the ball was and went to it,' which was 'Ranji's' doctrine. No batsman has played closer to the ball than Bradman; his bat is like another limb, a third leg to stand on, or a third right wrist and forearm, alive, with eyes in the blade.

Curiously enough he sometimes seems to begin an innings conscious that there is an edge to his bat, even an oil hole. But rarely does the bowler see for long this evidence in him of mortal fallibility; he is a lion by instinct; he probably would find it hard work to get out — if he tried.

The perfection of his technique during his astounding innings of 309 in a day in the Leeds Test of 1930, gave me the idea of a short story, which I have not yet written.

MY STORY IS ...

A trapeze artist is betrayed in love. One night, while the tragedy is still breaking his heart, he hears that his beloved and her new lover are in the audience, so he decides to end his life, by hurling himself from the trapeze into the audience's midst, killing himself under her very eyes, in the tenth row of the stalls. At the right moment, when the music ceases for his most dangerous feat, he tries to fling himself from the rapidly swinging trapeze. But he cannot do it — simply cannot. His technique won't let him.

Likewise, I imagine, is Bradman as much in the grip of his superb machine as he is master of it.

But I have no patience for those who say that it is a machine and nothing else; the force of Bradman's mind and personality are to be felt in every stroke, offensive or defensive. He has never played a dull innings. He takes risks which would ruin most other great batsmen; but so versatile, so quick and flexible, is his method that the less than imaginative eye is deceived into thinking that efficiency has expelled nature.

As a fact, Bradman is a very human batsman, each stoke is informed and generated by the essence of him; shrewd, realistic, purposeful, confident. There is occasional humour, too, if you will watch intelligently. And gusto — who has ever hooked or pulled with more than Bradman's gusto?

As he has grown to middle-age he has curbed one or two of his more punitive instincts — which means that he is, on the whole, nowadays harder to get out — which is not, for a bowler, a very comforting thought. I would like his his sunset to be grand, with a 'Temeraire' redness, and sense of good haven reached and attained.

THE MOST REMARKABLE BATSMAN I KNEW

This article by Jack Fingleton first appeared in the June 1968 issue of
World Sports

I recently wrote to Sir Donald Bradman, seeking, for the purposes of this article, an opinion from him on the merits of modern cricketers. He surprised me with the depth and the generosity of his reply — ranging over Tilden, Lindrum, swimming, athletics, golf ('what about the implements used? Nicklaus would have been in great trouble trying to drive today's distances with a gutta-percha ball and a wooden shaft') and so on, down to cricket.

It was a fascinating letter which reminded me of his batting. His letter was precise and deep-thinking. He brought to bear the same analytical approach with which he first dissected all bowlers of his era and then proceeded to decimate them — the whole lot of them. Let me quote his pertinent thoughts on his own game (he has played golf and tennis to a high standard). Noting how the clock served as a guide in many other sports, Sir Donald says: 'A batsman in cricket is not competing against the clock and himself. His feats are subject to what his opponents are doing — a varying set of conditions and a myriad of things of complexity.'

He says his own career covered the smaller ball and larger stumps, and much of it was under the off-side lbw rule. All this favoured the bowler. This, he says, indicates that S. F. Barnes was a greater bowler than his figures suggest . . . 'and Trumper had to bat against Barnes — I didn't'. He proceeds with sound, thoughtful stuff: 'I think the modern era tends to have champions of other days thrown in its face, but the error is often committed of comparing only former champions with the rank-and-file of today. What about the rank-and-file of yesterday? For this reason, I often think the modern cricketer is unduly maligned. Are you concerned with style or effectiveness? As Cardus has written, the eagle is more beautiful to watch than a modern jet plane, but there is no doubt which is the faster. My view is that a champion of any era would have adapted himself to be a champion in any era. But, having said that, I've no idea how you sort out Dempsey, Louis or Clay".

But I must resist temptation and not be side-tracked. I have to write of Sir Donald himself and I do so with zest because I played a lot with and against him and I see him in bold perspective against many of the greats I knew: Hammond, Compton, Woolley, Duleepsinhji, Hutton, Cowdrey, Dexter, May (what a pity the two latter played for such a short span!), Worrell, Sobers, Weekes, Hazare, Amarnath (a lovely stroke-maker), Pataudi jnr, Nourse, Pollock, Ponsford, McCabe,

Kippax, Morris, Miller (up and down but certainly great on his up-days), Harvey, Simpson and one or two others who were great with infrequency. As a youngster, I played with two of the very greatest: John Berry Hobbs and Charles Macartney. I knew, too, Collins, Bardsley, Taylor, Andrews, Hendren and South Africa's Taylor.

One, then, covers a glittering field, yet I have not the slightest hesitation in saying that Don Bradman was the most remarkable batsman I knew. Moreover, there would not be one of his generation who would not acclaim him the same way. He bestrode the cricket world as nobody before or since has done. His consistency was incredible. Dr. Grace, who had to contend with indifferent pitches and J. B. Hobbs were also remarkable for their consistency, but Bradman stood alone. In all matches he scored 50,731 runs in 669 innings for an average of 90.27. In first-class matches alone, Bradman scored 28,067 runs in 338 innings for an average of 95.14, and in Test matches he made 6,996 runs in 80 innings for an average of 99.94. Those are staggering figures and it is pertinent that 63 of his 80 Test innings were played against the common enemy, England. It is to be stressed that he never played on the fruitful batting pitches of India, the West Indies, South Africa nor New Zealand.

Of the 211 centuries Bradman scored in all matches, 41 were double centuries, eight were treble centuries and one a quadruple. He is the only Australian to have made a century of first-class centuries. He came to bat in his final Test at the Oval in 1948 on the verge of averaging a century in all Tests, but capricious fate saw him out for a duck second ball to Eric Hollies. I think the ovation given him by the crowd and the players unnerved him. Figures tell the undisputed story of Bradman's greatness, yet they tell only one side of his tremendous capacity. One had to bat with him, bowl or field against him, or knowing the game see and analyse his technique to comprehend the revolutionary dominance he brought to the game. He was not, in the sense of Trumper, McCabe or May, a classical stroke-maker as one knows the term. He was of medium build, well-muscled and supple in the wrists, yet there were no pretty passes or deft glides (in the Duleepsinhji manner) to suggest that some magical wand was weaving its spell over the field.

Some bowlers, for instance, might think that they had won through to Macartney's stumps only to find, hey presto, a fiendish flick at the very last fraction of time that sent the ball screaming to the boundary. So, too, with Sobers, but not with Bradman. There was not a stroke in the game he could not play, but he was common-sense to his fingertips.

'Are you concerned with style or effectiveness?' asks Sir Donald of me. It is a good question. He was such a genius that he could well have indulged himself in the artistic flourishes of batting, but he was too much of a realist for that. He knew two basic things about bowlers: none likes to be met constantly with the full face of the bat; none likes to see what is ordinarily good-length bowling transposed into over-pitched stuff by twinkling footwork. His fundamental thinking and love of cricket were, if you like, basically sadistic. He loved the crash of the ball against the boundary-fence; he delighted in seeing the figures revolve against his name on the score-board; he loved to murder bowlers and make the opposing skipper look foolish.

There were, as I have written, no deft passes or pretty glides, but every bowler, every fieldsman, every spectator in Bradman's heyday sensed that he was using not a bat so much as an axe dripping with the bowler's blood and agony. He knew not pity; he was remoresless; a century rarely satisfied him. It has to be two or three, or even four against Queensland, when he made 452 and still did not yield. His dynamic and convulsive appeal to the spectator has never been equalled in my time. The roar that circled a ground when his magic name appeared in the vacant slot on the scoring-board was one of sheer anticipatory delight, and Bradman rarely failed his huge 'army'. I was often at the other end to him. Perhaps, with W. A. Brown, we had given our side a good start against keen bowling and fielding. If Brown had gone, I might have been 40 or so. In no time, Bradman would be past me, and in no time also the bowling and fielding would be ragged. Bradman had them where he wanted them — at his mercy.

He was, alike, aggravation to the bowler and despair to the batsman at the other end. He would take guard with a wide smile, survey the field, give his trousers a hitch, settle down and then with a piercing 'Right' he would be off to his first run from the first ball. Of this, he made a habit. In unnoticeable time he would be 10, 20, 40, 50 and so on to his inevitable century. He dominated the strike and the batsman at the other end felt an ineffectual goon. Bradman made it all look so easy and he always regarded the clock as another enemy to be trounced. I heard batsmen of his era, cast deep into the shadows, complain that Bradman got more full-tosses and long-hope that anybody else. They were trying to suggest he was lucky. Of course he wasn't. Bowlers bowled to him as Bradman made them. He dictated everything. His footwork, his abounding confidence, pulverised bowlers, mesmerised them, and they didn't know where to bowl to keep him quiet.

W. H. Ponsford, who was the magical record-breaker until Bradman ejected him from the throne, once told me that Bradman saw the ball

quicker than anybody else. He meant that Bradman judged the ball's
intent a whit quicker than others. And this was true. His judgment was
impeccable and the co-ordination between mind and feet was like
automation at work. His batting, his style, had many facets, but it was
built, principally, upon footwork. He believed, implicitly, in the drive,
and, often on the run, he drove in an arc from in front of point to wide
of square-leg. He regarded the crease purely as a place in which to mark
his guard. The keeper he ignored — he was stumped twenty-two times
in his 669 innings and most of those were sacrificial in minor games —
and he left 'home' like an arrant night-clubber. When the bowler, tired
of being drive, dropped short, Bradman was back in a flash to slash him
with pulls he learned on the concrete pitches of his country youth.

Some said he was unorthodox. I do not think he was to any great
degree because his batting was built on solid foundations. He stood with
the bat between his feet, an unusual stance, and his left hand was further
to the right of the handle than was orthodox. This was doubly effective
in enabling him to bring his devastating pull quickly to earth, the bat
face closing quickly over the ball. If he was unorthodox, it was in his
outlook. Where others suspected a long-length ball of being explosive
in content, Bradman sniffed contempt at it. I don't think there *was* a
good length to him. His confidence was incredible, his judgment
superb, his run-appetite insatiable, his temperament and self-discipline
unsurpassed. He was a study when not out during lunch of a big innings.
He had, in Sydney, the inevitable light batting lunch in the
dressing-room of rice custard, stewed fruit and milk. Each slow
mouthful was an essay in method, in digestion, in cold planning and
contemplation of the feast soon to follow in the middle. To suggest —
and he missed nothing of such suggestions — that a particular bowler
had his measure, was to invite that bowler's annihilation.

Frank Tyson once suggested in Australia on television that Bradman
would not have thrived against astute modern captaincy. I sensed that
Tyson was somewhat derogatory of Bradman's genius, and as I was
appearing at the same time I told him he would have changed his mind
had he bowled against Bradman. Tyson obviously thought that the
modern circle-field, nugatory in its purpose and much used these days,
would have limited Bradman. It would have made Bradman grin at its
challenge. He knew the circle-field and he played against some astute
captains. It was a matter of honour with Bradman to make
field-placements and skippers look ridiculous. A captain might take a
fieldsman from here and put him there to cut off a Bradman flow of
boundaries. Bradman invariably put the next ball where the fieldsman

had been and then grinned hugely. The crowd loved this. His footwork in getting to the ball was too brilliant. He could not be confined. He would have twisted the spokes of the circle-field in a twinkling, but perhaps Tyson was thinking the slow-over approach by his skipper, Hutton, would have eased Bradman down. I agree with that. There is no batting answer to that one.

Body-line did, comparatively (he still averaged over 50 in the series), subjugate him, but that was based on physical attack — in itself a tribute to Bradman's greatness — and was quickly outlawed. I think his pristine days were in England in 1930 when he made 131, 245, 334 and 232 — 974 in the series — with a century before lunch in his 334 at Leeds. Understandably, he was well past his murderous best when he came for the last time to England in 1948 at forty years of age yet he contrived to make eleven centuries! Jim Laker, who once bowled the 1956 Australian team out at the Oval for Surrey and got 19 of their wickets in the 1956 Old Trafford Test, never once got Bradman's wicket in 1948 while Bradman tallied almost 1,000 runs in games in which Laker played. Bradman's footwork, even at 40, killed every spinner.

Bradman was not a half-fellow with comrades of his own immediate generation. Jealousy often made his position a difficult one, yet there were times when he might have assessed his standing in the game and made more of a gesture himself. His genius tended to make him a man apart, his soul immersed in batting and (it seemed) in records. He was often a lonely man in his peak years and obviously the fault was not always his. Even as a very young man, he was an adroit businessman. Offers chased him and he capitalised on his unparalleled standing in the game and with the public. He seemed to most who played under him in pre-war years to be dictatorial in his captaincy and it was obvious the post-war Australians got on better with him.

Pre-war he did not indulge himself in gestures to his players or opponents. He did not bother to welcome or bid farewell to his opponents in their dressing-room on his home Adelaide ground, and once he had his innings against his former NSW side (of which I was captain) declared by an official over the loudspeaker. His vice-captain (McCabe), his greatest bowler (O'Reilly), Fleetwood-Smith and O'Brien were once summoned by the Australian Board to appear on a charge of not giving Bradman full support in his captaincy. Some Australian officials are odd birds, not deeply immersed in a knowledge of the game, and his team thought Bradman should have gone to the Board with his men. Bradman didn't. We had a surprise win over Allen's side in the interim — and the charge crumpled. Now, in a happy family life with a charming and helpful wife, Jessie, I think Bradman has mellowed. So, too, have some of his comrades of his early days. Cricket, I think, was more intense, more individualistic and held the public stage more then than it does today.

Bradman was a clever and astute captain, knowing all the moves, and he played the game up to the hilt. He was one of the most brilliant fieldsmen ever, fast as a deer, unerring in his low, screaming throw to the wicket keeper, often holding the ball in the deep and challenging the batsman to run. He is a capital speaker with a rich sense of humour. Spectators crowded the Lord's field in 1948 to bid farewell to the greatest batsman of his type the game has known. For all the thrashings he gave their bowlers — some of the greatest in the game — the English adored him. One analyses Bradman's art again and declares, uninhibitedly, that he would have been Bradman in any era of the game. He was, and is, a remarkable man. Today, from Adelaide, he holds about as many business directorates as he still holds cricket records.

CRICKET FICTION

THE MATCH AT CROW FLAT

By Frederick J. Mills, 'The Twinkler'
(FROM HIS SQUARE DINKUM, MELBOURNE, 1917)

'[AN] historic match occurred out at Crow Flat, up north, when the Crow Flats were at home to the Wattle Wonders from a neighbouring shire. When the Wattle Wonders arrived on the ground they were a man short. The Crow Flats couldn't lend them a player because their emergency man was away burying his grandmother. However, a frowsy-looking little man, a stranger, who had wandered across from the local hotel, offered to make up the team. He didn't look much of a cricketer, but he certainly did appear a dangerous man to leave in the vicinity of a barrel of ale. His offer was reluctantly accepted. The match was started. The Wattle Wonders batted first, and went down like chaff before a drayhorse to the wiles of the Cow Flats' googly bowler. Nine wickets were down for 71, and the Wattle Wonders' stonewaller had increased his score in half an hour from 0 to 1.

Then the frowsy-looking little man went in to bat . . . The first ball shaved his off stump, the second sniffed the varnish on his leg stump, the third breathed on the bails, the fourth hit the bat, the fifth went for a fourer, and the sixth for a fiver. After that the frowsy man never looked back. He batted for an hour, and ran up 85 before he got out. The stone-waller had increased his total to 4. The excitement was terrific. The spectator (a stout lady, the publican's wife) fainted. The frowsy-looking little man was a hero. The Wattle Wonders were jubilant. The Crow Flats were savage.

Then the Crow Flats batted. They got going, and put together 130 for 3 wickets, and every stock bowler was tried. "Ken yer bowl?" asked the captain desperately of the frowsy-looking little man. "Some" was the reply. "Then 'ave a oozle," said the captain. The first ball from the stranger was a wide, the second a grubber, the third a full toss, the fourth a yorker, the fifth a decent length, and the sixth took the wicket. Then the little man found his length. He went through the Crow Flats like a fire-reel through a poultry farm. He took 7 for 10, and the Wattle Wonders were victorious. There was a sensation. The spectator fainted again. The Crow Flats raised the question whether it could be counted a win, as the stranger wasn't a Wattle Wonder anyway. They accused the Wattle Wonders of importing the stranger from Adelaide, and he might be Clem Hill or Crawford in disguise. A free fight ensued, and three bats were broken through coming into violent contact with heads which no bats were made to withstand. In the confusion the frowsy little man entered the dressing shed, and after taking on a heavy cargo of watches and small change sailed for port unknown without troubling about a bill of lading. It was a historic day at Crow Flat.'

FATTY FINN'S PRAYER
By Bob Ellis
(FROM HIS *THE ADVENTURES OF FATTY FINN*, SYDNEY, 1981)

FATTY WAS in his little upstairs bedroom saying his prayers. On the end of the bed was Pal, already asleep. On the wall was a big magazine photo of Don Bradman awaiting the next ball.

'And please let me find a way I can fix Bruiser Murphy good,' prayed Fatty, 'and also get my crystal set before Don Bradman spifflicates the Poms at Old Trafford. In return I promise to do my homework all next term. Oh, and could I have a fine day tomorrow for our last cricket match, preferably with a light southerly wind so's I can deceive Lolly Legs with my off-spinner. That's all for tonight I think, Lord.

'I remain yours faithfully, Hubert Finn.'

THAT BARAMBAH MOB
By David Forrest
(FIRST PUBLISHED IN *OVERLAND*, NO. 15, JULY, 1959)

'EDDIE Gilbert?' said the publican at Murgon. He polished a glass for a moment and eyed us very carefully.

'Henry Stulpnagel's your man,' he said.

We went and found Henry Stulpnagel.

We had followed a long trail to find out about Gilbert, and we eyed our new source of information very carefully before we sat down. Mr. Stulpnagel somehow reminded us of dairy farms; and where most people would perspire we thought the Mr. Stulpnagel would sweat. He was a big, dopey-looking bloke with a couple of front teeth missing, and not very much hair left on top of his head. When we found him he was sitting on the post-office steps and staring down the Cherbourg Road across the Barambah flats. We said it was a good day, sat down on the steps, and stared across the Barambah flats.

He eyed us very carefully, said that the train was in but that the mail hadn't come over yet. He didn't say what he thought of the day. When he saw our note-book, we knew he was a dairy-farmer, because his eyes classified us with drought, fire, the pear, flood and Noogoora burr.

It appeared he thought we were from the Taxation Department.

'You got the lot last time,' said Mr. Stulpnagel gloomily.

We said we had come to find out about Eddie Gilbert, and for a moment Mr Stulpnagel transferred his gaze from the distant line of trees on the Barambah and looked us up and down. Amongst other things, his gaze noted that we would not sweat, but perspire.

'What would you know about Gilbert?'

We said that was the point. We didn't know anything about Gilbert, but we understood that Mr. Stulpnagel was an authority on the black and white streak from Barambah.

Mr. Stulpnagel said, 'Come from Queensland, eh?'

He went to collect his mail, leaving us to stare down the Cherbourg Road. When he came back, we asked whether it was really true that Mr. Stulpnagel had once hit a six into the Barambah from the Murgon Showground. His gaze followed ours, down the Cherbourg Road, out of the town, across the Barambah flats, over several farms and stopped at the line of trees. It was pleasant standing in the sun.

Mr. Stulpnagel said, 'The beer come up on the train, too.'

We went back to visit the publican. Mr. Stulpnagel had a glass of Four X and switched over to Green Death.

We asked whether it was true that he was the first white man ever to take strike to the bowling of Gilbert.

He surveyed our city clothes and said he believed so.

We wrote that down.

We wanted to know whether Eddie Gilbert was as fast as they said, and Mr. Stulpnagel's lip curled as though his beer might have been flat.

'He got Bradman for a duck, didn't he?'

We agreed very hastily that that was so. We made a new approach.

'Speaking of Bradman, Mr. Stulpnagel, they say you were no mean slouch with a bat yourself.'

He took the top off his beer.

'I was openin' bat for the district for seven years. Take the shine off the new ball. That was my job.'

Mr. Stulpnagel had flogged new-ball bowlers from Kilkivan to Nanango. We wondered whether this was the reason the touring M.C.C. omitted the South Burnett from its itinerary.

'Ah, there'd be more to it than that,' said Mr. Stulpnagel. He rolled a cigarette.

'Mind you,' he said, 'I was pretty fit in them days. Milkin' fifty cows single-handed twice a day.'

He licked the cigarette and spared us a glance.

'And no machines,' he added.

From his mental eminence, he surveyed our capacity for milking cows, and was reassured of his perspectives.

We drank our beer and pursed our lips. This sixer of Mr. Stulpnagel's . . . it really did go into the Barambah, did it?

'Well,' said Mr. Stulpnagel. 'That was what the bloke said who had t' go an' fox it.'

We ordered beer all round.

'While he was away,' said Mr. Stulpnagel, 'we took lunch. Some of the Goomeri blokes belly-ached about the way I was slowin' up the game, but I made up for it when the ball came back. I carried me bat right through, and after the shine was off the ball I gave their spinners somethin' to belly-ache about.'

We wrote that down.

'I didn't have a polish of a bloke like Bradman,' said Mr. Stulpnagel and sipped at his beer. 'But I was quick on me feet. What you call agile.'

Mr. Stulpnagel was very agile for a dairy-farmer. He got that way keeping out of the way of bumpers on concrete wickets. Later on when he had begun to slow up, he took to discarding his cap and parting his hair in the middle so that he didn't have to duck so far.

'But it don't make for polish,' said Mr. Stulpnagel.

We wrote that down.

We said Rex Rogers was a bit of a slogger, but he had been lucky enough to make the Shield.

That was so, but it wasn't luck that did the trick. It was circumstances.

'It was Gilbert,' said Mr. Stulpnagel gloomily. 'Concrete wickets an' Gilbert. Rogers never had t' handle that combination.'

Mr. Stulpnagel had never got to play Shield.

'Later on,' he said, 'we used t' go down t' Brisbane t' see Gilbert slippin' into Bradman.'

We straightened up with a bit of a jerk and poised our pencil.

We wondered, with bated breath, whether Mr. Stulpnagel had actually seen Gilbert bowl the ball that turned Shield cricket upside down.

He had, indeed!

'Bowled him for a duck!' boomed Mr. Stulpnagel. 'They say it wasn't one of Bradman's days, but don't let them kid y'. He got him fair and square and that's in the book for everybody to see.'

We scribbled furiously.

What sort of a ball was it that got him?

'It was a full toss. Bradman played all over it like a schoolkid. Fair on his off-stump. The 'keeper took it inside the fence. Just as well they had a fence.'

We finished writing.

We said, 'A bloke in Brisbane said it swerved as it came in.'

'Some blokes'll tell you anything,' said Mr. Stulpnagel curtly. 'Did he see that ball bowled?'

'He said he did.'

'Yeh,' said Mr. Stulpnagel.

We didn't tell him about the man in Ipswich who said it was an outswinger; nor about the bloke in Toogoolawah who said it was a yorker, right up in the block-hole.

'Look,' said Mr. Stulpnagel, 'Gilbert never swung the ball. Straight up and down.'

We scribbled very fast.

'He didn't have t' swing the ball,' said Mr. Stupnagel. 'He was the fastest bowler the world's ever seen. And when you're that fast, why muck about with the fancy stuff?'

We said that was a good question.

We said that a Mr. Meisenhelter had claimed to have batted against swing bowling from Gilbert.

'Meisenhelter?' said Mr. Stulpnagel slowly, and took another beer. 'You mean old Norm?' he said and shook his head. 'Gilbert was over the hill then. Probably down t' Larwood's standards.'

We said cautiously that some people reckoned Larwood was fast, faster maybe than Miller and Lindwall and the Demon.

Mr. Stulpnagel said that these things were relative.

We wrote that down.

Mr. Stulpnagel rolled up his sleeve over his biceps, and we examined the corrugated and dotted scare imprinted there by the seam of a cricket-ball.

Mr. Stulpnagel said, 'It wasn't Larwood done that.'

He inclined his bead and we studied the scar on the top of his head. The mark was old and brown and still recognisably a diamond in shape. Enclosed in the diamond, in reverse, the words '. . . nufactured in Austra . . .'

Mr Stulpnagel straighted up and said gloomily, 'Larwood never done that, neither.'

'Gilbert?' we whispered.

'Thirty years ago this summer,' said Mr. Stulpnagel.

We reached for our beer and changed direction, and wrote down what we had been told.

We wanted to know whether all that damage was done in one innings.

Mr. Stulpnagel grimaced at our intellect.

'You should try gettin' hold of the idea that Gilbert only bowled one ball t' you in an innings.'

There was a little silence.

We said, 'Just how fast was Gilbert?'

Mr. Stulpnagel reckoned it was a hundred mile an hour.

We said that was faster than Larwood and Demon Spofforth and Lindwall and Miller.

Mr. Stulpnagel said, 'We've been into that already.'

We stopped writing and asked him how he knew it was a hundred mile an hour.

'You could tell,' said Mr. Stulpnagel. 'Mind you, I don't know about them turf wickets, but on the concrete you could tell.'

'How?'

Mr. Stulpnagel said, 'You seen tyres smoke on the bitumen when they stand on the brakes?'

We had.

'When that ball hit the concrete,' said Mr Stulpnagel, 'she'd smoke.'

He measured with his finger and thumb. 'You'd see this little wisp of smoke when she come at y', comin' like the hammers o' hell. Hundred mile an hour.'

We wrote that down, and supposed that some blokes tried to get out of the way.

'Oh they tried,' said Mr. Stulpnagel.

We wrote that down.

'Mind you,' said Mr. Stulpnagel, 'blokes like that shouldn't take the game up.'

We wanted to know whether Gilbert scared him at all.

'Not the first time,' said Mr. Stulpnagel. 'That come afterwards. When you'd see the draw for the season, and see you was down for the first match against Barambah. Bill Ritter, who used t' live out on the Windera Road, he was my openin' partner, he sold up and bought a farm over in Barambah.'

'Just to get away from the black and white streak?'

'Mind you, he didn't put it that way,' said Mr. Stulpnagel, 'but he played for Barambah that year.'

If Mr. Stulpnagel wasn't scared the first time he met Gilbert, just how did he feel.

'Queer,' said Mr. Stulpnagel, and ordered a glass.

'They batted first that day,' he said. 'They was always bottom in the points table; and then Bill Ritter an' me, we went out t' belt a few sixes off them.'

He drank some of his beer.

'We didn't take much notice of the black bloke, because that Barambah always was a queer mob.'

He drank the rest of his beer.

'They gave Charlie Schultz the new ball, and we run a couple o' twos and a single. And so I come about t' face the other opener. Everybody started t' walk off, and I thought it must be drinks, so I started t' walk off, too.'

He rolled a cigarette.

'The black bloke was standin' there in his whites, and he said to me, he said, "No not you. You stay here." I said, "What's goin' on here?" And he said t' me, he said, "I am going to bowl to you, Mr. Stulpnagel."'

We ordered Mr. Stulpnagel a pot of Green Death.★

'I stood there an' I looked around, and by golly it made you feel queer. There was only the black bloke and the umpire in front of me. Ernie Vogel, he was their 'keeper, he was hunched up in front of the grandstand . . . and the rest o' them were scattered about on the fence. Everybody in the stand was as quiet as anything. They were feelin' queer, too. Wonderin' what it was all about. Except a couple of the Barambah womenfolk who were shiftin' along the stand out of the line o'wicket.

'It was so quiet you could hear the footsteps of the deep third walkin' up Taylor Street towards the power-house.'

We felt a bit queer ourselves. We ordered Green Death.

'Then,' said Mr. Stulpnagel, 'you couldn't hear them footsteps any more.'

He sank some of his beer.

'Then he give it to me,' said Mr. Stulpnagel. 'He only run about five yards, and I suppose that put me off a bit. But in that last yard or two he went all streaky an' I knew I had real trouble on me hands.'

★*Carlton draught beer*

96

We wanted to know whether he sighted it well. Mr. Stulpnagel looked at us doubtfully.

He heard it.

'It whistled,' said Mr. Stulpnagel. 'You could hear it comin'.'

He measured with his finger and thumb. 'And there was tis little wisp o' smoke when she come off the mat. That's when he gave me this.'

He inclined his head, and we examined the tip of his ear. There was a scar there but the letters were indecipherable.

'I'm a bit deaf in that ear,' said Mr. Stulpnagel.

We thought he was lucky he wasn't clean-bowled first ball.

'It depend on what y' call luck,' said Mr. Stulpnagel gloomily. 'He went back his five yards and give me the next one.'

'Did it whistle?'

'Maybe,' said Mr. Stulpnagel, 'I dunno, I didn't hear nothin'. I didn't see too much, neither. I was still waitin' to play it when something cracked behind me . . . and all that Barambah mob started yellin' Howsat.'

We wrote that down.

'They took one bail at deep fine leg, and there was me middle stump flat on the ground. In two bits and some splinters.'

He was silent for a while and we wondered what happened to the other bail.

'You hear yarns,' said Mr. Stulpnagel slowly . . . he shook his head, 'I dunno what happened to it. Fred Kleinschmidt always reckoned the deep third took it in front of the powerhouse.'

Was that possible?

'Oh, it was possible,' said Mr. Stulpnagel, 'but you don't want t' take too much notice of anything old Fred ever tells you.'

We supposed that his averages went to pot after that.

At the end of that season, Mr. Stulpnagel didn't have an average.

We said sympathetically that this must have made him feel crook.

'It did and it didn't,' said Mr. Stulpnagel. 'I was a bit hard t' take for a while. But then he made that trip to Brisbane t' clean up Bradman, and then Bradman's average didn't look so hot itself. So when you felt miserable you was in good company t' be miserable with.'

'It was all right when he made his trips to Brisbane. But then you'd come into town one day and a bloke'd say t' you, "Gilbert come home on the train this morning." And you wouldn't sleep so well as the fixture come up.'

Mr. Stulpnagel toyed with his glass.

'That was when it got bad. There you'd be standin' out there. All by y'rself an' only the umpire an' the black bloke in front of y'. And the other umpires a bit toey out there at square leg. And your partner down the other end prayin' t' God you wouldn't hit a single.'

We ordered Mr. Stulpnagel another beer.

'And Ernie Vogel, he was their 'keeper; he'd pat you on the shoulder and say good luck, Henry, and then you were on your own.'

There was a little silence.

We wanted to know whether it was Gilbert who had removed Mr. Stulpnagel's front teeth.

'That was the tractor,' said Mr. Stulpnagel. 'Startin' handle come back at me.'

We wrote that down.

He leaned forward and tapped the bar with his glass. 'The truth about Gilbert is that in his openin' overs there wasn't a batsman he met ever saw one of his deliveries. It was Gilbert or the game . . . somethin' had t'give. Write that down.'

We wrote that down.

'They had plenty to go on,' said Mr. Stulpnagel. 'He made an ape of Bradman, and he was black, and he was born in Queensland, and they didn't like the look o' that whippy wrist of his. They reckoned he wasn't bowlin'.'

We wrote that down.

'They'd have fixed him for keeps, only someone took a slow-motion film and that was that.'

'Yes?' we said.

'He was bowling all right,' said Mr. Stulpnagel. 'It's all right about them blokes who were makin' the fuss. The knew the day was comin' when they'd have t' stand out there, an' Ernie Vogel pattin' them on the shoulder before he buried himself under the fence.'

We fetched another beer.

'Not that I blame Ernie, mind you,' said Mr. Stulpnagel. 'He had a wife an' six kids t' think about and none of them was old enough t' help with the milkin'.'

We wondered what else Mr. Stulpnagel could tell us about Edward Gilbert.

He thought about it while he drank his pot.

He shook his head slowly. 'No, I don't think so. There's a bloke out on the Redgate Road might be able t' help y'. Old Augie Schulte. Although I supppose most o' what he knows he got from that Barmabah mob, and they always was a queer lot.'

We had one for the road with Mr. Stulpnagel, and he drove off to

Boat Mountain to get stuck into the milkin'.

We got ourselves lost in the main street while looking for the Brisbane Road, and enquired of a policmen.

As an afterthought, we wanted to know whether he knew anything about Gilbert.

The policeman put his foot on our mudguard and said that as a matter of fact he had seen Gilbert bowl Bradman for a duck.

'He snicked it,' said the policeman. 'It was a shooter.'

We didn't tell him about the bloke in Brisbane who said it swung in, nor about the man in Ipswich who said it swung out. We didn't mention the bloke in Toogoolawah who said it was a yorker, right up in the block-hole; nor Mr. Stulpnagel who said it was a full toss.

Policemen are reliable witnesses. We wrote it down that it was a shooter.

A black bloke walking down the street said, 'G'day.'

The policeman said, 'G'day, Mr. Gilbert.'

We scribbled at a tremendous rate of knots.

The policeman took his foot off our mudguard and said, 'Hey, Eddie, Just a minute.'

We met Mr. Gilbert. We don't really remember what he looked like.

We wondered whether he would be kind enough to describe the ball that got Bradman for a duck.

Mr. Gilbert looked at us very carefully for a while.

'I don't really know,' he said apologetically. 'When I let it go, I didn't see it again till the 'keeper threw it up in the air.'

He looked rather embarrassed.

He said, 'You'd have t' ask someone who was watchin'.'

We looked at Mr. Gilbert very carefully for a while.

Then we said good-afternoon to Mr. Gilbert, we said good-afternoon to the policeman, and we drove wildly back to Brisbane, anywhere, to get away from that Barambah mob. We ran out of petrol coming through Toogoolawah, but we had the pace, and we'd have got home all right it it hadn't been for that sharp turn out of Ipswich Road at the 'Gabba'.

That stopped us.

A CRICKET MATCH AT HOGAN'S
By *Edward S. Sorenson*
(FROM HIS *QUINTON'S ROUSEABOUT*, MELBOURNE, 1908)

A great test match between the Bolong Station hands and the experts of Warri Bore and township had been the talk of the district for months. So, when the eventful day at last came round, the scattered population of the district turned out to do it honour, and gathered in a wildly excited heap in front of Hogan's — a wayside pub, three miles from the station. Warri township was a long ride from Hogan's and the 'Borers' came out the day before, so as to be fresh for the contest. The Boundary-riders had some scouts at the pub to meet them, and these carried out their part of the programme so well that the visiting captain had considerable trouble in getting his hilarious team to bed at midnight. They were all Trumpers and Nobles by that time.

The captain had not long retired himself when he heard Tom Connors, the crack bowler, betting somebody £10,000 that he would bowl five Boundary-riders with the first six balls in the morning. Rushing out, he found the doughty Tom nodding over a pannikin, while 'Long' Macpherson, a scrub cutter, poured some vile decoction into it from a black bottle. A fight was prevented by the timely appearance of Hogan; and then the irate captain went round and carefully locked the doors to prevent his precious team being further tampered with. The eleven was considered the cream of the district, and was made up of bore workers, storekeepers, two squatters, a publican and a constable.

The Boundary-riders were a hardier lot, but with less experience of the manly game. Still they could all bowl, having practised in spare time with gibbers, using the hut for a wicket; and they all had a sharp eye for anything coming at them. Two of them were known to carry a ball and a tomahawk about on the run with them; and they would get off for half-an-hour on any level piece of ground, and chop out a rough bat from a sapling. They bowled at trees, and when one made a successful drive with the bat the other would mount his horse and canter after the ball. So it was naturally expected they would give a good account of themselves.

The pitch was on a strip of level ground in front of the hotel. The tussocks and lumps had been carefully chipped off, the sticks and cowdung had been gathered up for a short radius, and a heavy log rolled up and down between the wickets. Still, the ground had a very bushy aspect. At the back was a thick cluster of trees, and close at one end was a sandy mound, honeycombed with rabbit burrows. These things, Hogan said, would help to make the game more interesting.

The Borers felt a bit seedy next morning when the Boundary-riders arrived, and they were not sorry when the latter won the toss and elected to bat. An hour or two's running about, leather chasing, would shake the scorpions out of their eyes. Connors sent down the first ball, somewhere behind the batsman, and the manager of Bolong smacked it hard as it passed him. It was the only hit he made; yet with that single stroke he topped the score. The ball flew to the sandhill, and presently the fieldsman yelled out that it had gone down a rabbit burrow. The batsmen continued to run to and fro, while the outfield rushed to the pub, swallowed a 'longsleever', and hunted up a pick and shovel. Twenty-eight runs were scored before the ball was grubbed out. But Connors had his revenge, two wickets falling before another run was added.

In the meantime bunny's fancy work had been debated by the two captains, with the result that Hogan's groom was engaged to do pick and shovel work for both sides, and each time his services were needed the hit was to count 5 runs.

The fourth man to face the demon bowler, after snicking a couple of singles, drove one hard into the middle of Hogan's dam. The outfield streaked to the brink, and commenced to peel off his veneer of civilization for a swim. But Hogan rushed out, and strenuously objected.

'Kape yer fut out of that, now, or I'll murdher ye!' he cried.

'But I must get the ball,' panted the fielder.

'I tell ye I'll not have me dam polluted by any of ye. It's the water we drink!'

The fieldsman stood on his naked feet, nonplussed, desperate. 'It's a conspiracy!' he cried. 'Look at them running!'

Hogan looked. 'Bedad, thin, an' they're foine runners,' he said admiringly. 'But — niver moind, they'll knock up boy'n'bye.'

The fieldsman commenced to swear. Then young Hogan, aged eight, came on the scene. 'Sure Johnny will get it for ye,' said his father. 'There's not so much of him to pollute the water wid.'

The chagrined fieldsman was only too willing; but here the Bolong captain protested. Johnny wasn't a player. The Warri skipper joined them, and a hurried consultation took place. Then it was agreed that Johnny should act as swimmer for both sides, and the water mark should henceforth count as another five hit.

The dam was an easy boundary, and every bat now aimed for it; but as it was close by the end of the pub, their erratic shots more often hit the latter. Ball after ball clattered on the iron roof, one lodging in the spout, seven runs resulting while the ladder was being hunted up. The bowler claimed a catch, as it had not touched the ground, but the umpire disallowed it, holding that the spout had ground connections. Mrs. Hogan discreetly closed the doors and shutters, and hoped the awful match would soon be over. Hogan was caught napping. A ball crashed through the bar window and hit him in the eye. He staggered against the shelves, and three of four bottles were knocked down and smashed. A trifle disturbing this to a quiet business man. Still, Hogan said nothing — to the cricketers. He was making a big score himself.

The last wicket fell for 92, and the players adjourned in a body to inquire after Hogan's health. The inquiries refreshed them considerably, and then the Warri cracks went in to bat. The sun was a scorcher; but the spectators, counting flies, had swelled to five hundred millions. Play was slow, desultory; the people lounged in groups under trees, with bottles and waterbags distributed about, or yawned on the pub verandah. A few families, who had come out for a picnic, made fires and boiled their billies and quartpots, while the cart horses stood by, some with nosebags on, some nibbling at little heaps of bush hay.

Interest revived occasionally, as when the ball struck a wandering dog, and the resultant howls were greeted by a multitudinous yabbering from the Aboriginal stand. When the constable finally skied one, and it dropped into the hollow spout of a box tree, forty feet from the ground, the excitement was tremendous. The fielders gathered round the tree, and took bearings of the offending limb from various angles. One suggested chopping it down; another thought it would be easier to burn it. Meanwhile the cosherman and his partner were making runs. The skippers hastily formed themselves into a committee of ways and means, and it was agreed that the black trackers be put on to climb trees for both sides, and that the treed balls should also count 5.

The Borers had made 116 when the last man knocked his stumps down with the bat. Immediately afterwards Hogan rang the cowbell for lunch. There was more drinking. Anybody who would accept it was presented with a bottle. Hogan's liberality was unlimited. He handed in lager and ale by the dozen; the losing team had to foot the bill. There were toasts and speeches, each ending with 'fill 'em up again'. At 3 o'clock the game was resumed under somewhat altered conditions. The bowling was erratic, the batting more so. Everybody slogging — mostly at the air. Connors, making a vigorous swipe at a ball, missed, and, losing his grip, flung the bat into a cockspur bush. Connors was destined to become famous. Though a 'demon' bowler, he was a poor batsman; but, being a big man, with the strength of a bullock, when he did get fair on to one, in his own phraseology, it was bound to go somewhere.

The crowd liked to see Tom's mighty swings; they suggested magnificent drives if the bat and ball happened to come into collision. They did eventually, and the stroke brought the house down — at least it brought Macpherson down. Mac was sitting on his horse, leisurely filling his pipe, preparatory to going home. The ball whanged hard against the horse's flank, and with a sudden electrified spring the astonished animal dropped Mac on the grass, who, grasping an empty bottle in each hand, made a beeline for Connors.

'A cricketer yer call yerself!' he snorted. 'By the jumpin' wallaby, I'll bowl you out!' Whizz! 'I'll make a cricketer of yer!' Whoosh!

The constable left the bowling crease in a hurry to arrest Macpherson, and, slipping the bracelets on his wrists, handed him over to the black tracker, who chained him to a tree.

Tom's bat didn't have the good fortune to collide with the ball again, and duck eggs became plentiful. The Borers wanted only 52 runs to win, when they commenced their second innings; they still wanted 25 when the ninth wicket went down. Victory looked certain for the Boundary-riders. But here the natural resources of the field supplied a sensational turn in the proceedings. The last man in was a good wicket-keeper and a fair bowler, but a rank duffer with the bat. Like Connors, he hit wildly, but blindly, at everything. He fluked one, and it flew hard and high over the bowler's head, hit the ground, and bounded into an old fenced-in well. It was 50 feet to the water, the windlass was broken, and the rope missing. It looked hopeless from the outset. There was no emergency man engaged to go down wells, and, it being the last innings, the Borer captain would listen to no compromises — the Boundary-riders must get it themselves.

When half the required runs had been nicked off, Hogan strolled out to 'see how the play was goin'.' He saw — and grinned.

'Sit down and have shmoke, boys,' he said to the batsmen. 'Ye'll have plenty o' toime to make a schore in the cool of the even'. It's a bit hot now.'

But the panting Borers kept on till victory was theirs. After that Hogan did all the scoring, the disgusted Boundary-riders having acquired a thirst that was unquenchable. Some of them left next morning, some a fortnight later. They all got home eventually.

Poems
and Songs

GRACE BEFORE DINNER
Anon.
(*PUNCH*)

The Australians came down like a wolf on the fold,
The Marylebone cracks for a trifle were bowled,
Our Grace before dinner was very soon done,
And Grace after dinner did not get a run.

EIGHTY-FIVE TO WIN
By John Masefield, on England's second innings against the
Australian eleven at Kennington Oval on Tuesday, 29 August 1882
(FIRST APPEARED IN THE *TIMES*, AUGUST 29, 1956)

THE AUSTRALIAN ELEVEN	THE ENGLISH ELEVEN
A. C. Bannerman	R. G. Barlow
H. H. Massie	Dr. W. G. Grace
W. L. Murdoch (*Captain*)	G. Ulyett
G. J. Bonnor	A. P. Lucas
T. Horan	Hon. A. Lyttleton
G. Giffen	C. T. Studd
M. McC. Blackham	J. M. Read
T. W. Garrett	W. Barnes
H. F. Boyle	A. G. Steel
S. P. Jones	A. N. Hornby (*Captain*)
F. R. Spofforth	E. Peate

Though wayward Time be changeful as Man's will,
We have the game, we have the Oval still,
And still the Gas-Works mark the Gas-Works End
And still our sun shines and the rains descend.

Speak to me, Muse, and tell me of the game
When Murdoch's great Eleven overcame.
Laurels were tensely lost and hardly won
In that wild afternoon at Kennington,
When more than twenty thousand watchers stared
And cheered, and hoped, and anguished, and despaired.

Tell of the Day, how heavy rain had cleared
To sunshine and mad wind as noon-time neared,

Then showers (sometimes hail) on strong blasts cold,
Making a wicket good for men who bowled.
Such as the Day, when England's side went in
Just before four, with eighty-five to win.

Grace, and the Captain (Hornby), led the way,
(Grace to face Spofforth) in beginning play.
Spofforth was blowing from the Gas-Works End,
Garrett across.
                    The opposites contend.

What was this Spofforth, called The Demon yet,
For men forget, but cannot all forget?
A tall, lean, wiry athlete inly lit
With mind, and saturnine control of it.
Is it not said, that he, with either hand,
Could fling a hen's egg, onto grass or sand,
Clearly seventy yards, yet never crack the shell?

Then, when he bowled, he seemed a thing of Hell,
Writhing; grimacing; batsmen, catching every breath,
Thought him no mortal man but very Death;
For no man ever knew what ball would come
From that wild whirl, save one from devildom.

Now the sharp fears came tugging at the heart,
As Cunning strove with Care and Skill with Art.

Hornby and Grace, with eight-five to win,
Watched for some balls, then made the runs begin.

Ten had gone up, when Hornby's wicket went
(His off-stump), from a ball that Spofforth sent.
One, for fifteen; and Barlow took his place.
Barlow, our safest bat, came in with Grace:
Barlow, the wonder, famed in song and story,
The Red Rose County's well-remembered glory.
The first ball Spofforth sent him bowled him clean.
Two gone, of England's surest, for fifteen.

But Grace alone was power manifest,
(Of all men there, he is remembered best)
The great, black-bearded Doctor, watchful-eyed,
Next to our Queen, that vanished England's pride;
Grace was still in; and Ulyett joined him there.

Slowly the scoring mounted from the pair.

To Twenty, Thirty, Forty, and anon
Garrett was taken off and Boyle put on
And Spofforth changed to the Pavilion End.

Thirty odd runs and seven bats to spend,
Surely a task so simple could be done?
Ulyett and Grace seemed settled and at one.

Fifty went up, and then a marvel came,
Still something told by lovers of the game.
And Spofforth sent down a ball that Ulyett hit,
No barest chance (it seemed) to mortal wit.
Snicked, high and wide it went, yet with one hand,
Blackham just caught it and dissolved the stand.
Three gone, for fifty-one.

    Lucas joined Grace,
Two partners famed in many a happy case,
But not, alas for them, for two runs more,
Grace was caught out, as fifty-three for four,
Caught from a ball by Boyle, for Boyle had found
All he could wish in that uncertain ground

Still thirty-two to win, with six to fall,
Lyttlelton joined, and brought delight to all,
Enchanting promise came, for runs were scored,
Lucas and he put sixty on the board.
And then the conflict quieted to grim.

For master-spirits shine when hopes are dim;
Australia's best, all their best, were there.
Light, wicket, and themselves, all bade beware.
The field were all lithe leopards on the pounce:
Each ball had a new break upon its bounce.

Twelve deadly overs followed without score.
Then came a run, then deadly maidens more.
then Spofforth shattered Destiny's arrest.
And Lyttleton's mid-stump was scattered west.

Five gone, for sixty-six, but Hope, still green,
Felt, the last five would make the last nineteen.
Had we not Steel, and Studd, and Maurice Read,
Three superb bats? how could we fail to speed?
Here, Hornby, saving a reserve to win,
Re-made the order of the going-in,

Putting in Steel, not Studd, at fifth man gone,
Thinking that Studd might save us later on,
If any later on might need a stay.

A strain and anguish settled on the day,
As Steel came in; but Lucas cut a four;
Not nineteen now but only fifteen more.

Steel hit his first ball back to Spofforth's hand.

Then Maurice Read gave centre and took stand . . .

Read, Surrey's pride, who ever made hope thrill
In doubtful games when things were going ill.
If Read could stay . . .
        But Spofforth's second ball
Made the mid-stump of Surrey's pride fall.
Seven men out, and fifteen still to get.
But William Barnes was never careless yet;
A watchful batsman he, though skilled to smite,
Barnes joined with Lucas in the doubtful fight.

Wild was the cheerless weather, wild the light,
Wild the contesting souls whom Hope had fired.
All the Australian team were men inspired,
Spofforth had said the matter 'could be done',
And all the live eleven were as one
The Hope was theirs, the Hope that ever wins,
The Hope that sways the tossed coin as it spins,
The starry Hope that ever makes man learn
That to the man who Hopes the luck will turn.
The twenty-two at bay were face to face.

The watchers' hearts stood still about the place.

In risk so hateful, hoping so intense,
One English watcher died there, of suspense.

Barnes hit a two; three lucky byes were run;
Ten more to win, what joy to everyone.
All cheered for every run and faces shone,
Then Lucas played a ball of Spoffoth's on.
Eight, of ten, out, and seventy-five the score.
'Over' was called: the fieldsmen loitered o'er.

They paused in little groups to mutter low
The secret hints the bats were not to know.
Then, watching Studd, they tautened, each in place.
Studd, our reserve, acclaimed a second Grace.

Studd stood at watch by Boyle, the Gas-Works End;
On Boyle and Barnes the minute's issues pend.

The ball had come to Boyle, who paused awhile,
To give it hand-hold in the sawdust-pile,
Then walked, intent, as he turned to run,
Saw twenty thousands faces blurred to one,
And saw, ahead, a great bat tensely wait
The ball he held, the undelivered Fate.

He ran, he bowled, his length ball took its flight
Down the drear wicket in uncertain light,
It lifted, struck on Barnes glove, and leapt
To Murdoch, watching point, who caught, and kept.
Nine gone, for seventy-five, and last man in.
Just nine more runs to tie, and ten to win.

Peate, Yorkshire's bowler, came in Barnes's place.
The last man in, with three more balls to face.
Could he but stand until Boyle's over ended,
Stand, keeping in, then all might be amended.
The other end would bat, and Studd was there;
Studd, Cambridge Studd, the bright bat debonair.
A prayer to Peate went up from England's sons:
'Keep stead, Yorkshire, Studd will get the runs.
You, who throughout the game have done so much . . .
Now, stand . . . keep in . . . put nothing to the touch.'

Peate took his stand: Boyle bowled his second ball.

A tumult of glad shouting broke from all,
Peate smote it lustily to leg, for two.

The ball returned and Boyle began anew.

Seven to tie, and eight to win the game.

Boyle launched another, subtly not the same;
And half the white-faced watchers, staring tense,
Bit their umbrella handles in suspense.

The third ball came, but like a deedless day
It passed unhit, and ceased to be in play.

An instant's respite: only one more ball
And Studd will play, unless Peate's wicket fall.

Boyle took the ball; he turned; he ran; he bowled,
All England's watching heart was stricken cold.

Peate's whirling bat met nothing in its sweep.
The ball put all his wickets in a heap;
All out, with Studd untried; our star had set,
All England out, with seven runs to get.

The crowd sat stunned an instant at the blow,
Then cheered (and none had heard men cheering so),
Cheered the great cricket that had won the game.

In flood onto the pitch the watchers came,
Spofforth and Boyle were lifted shoulder high.

Brief, brief, the glow, even of Victory.
Man's memory is but a moment green.
Chronicle now the actors in the scene,
Unmentioned yet, as Massie, who had made
Life-giving runs, with Bannerman to aid;
Jones, Giffen, Bonnor, Horan, all who shared
Those deadly hours when disaster stared.

Quickly the crowd dispersed to life's routine
Of Life and Death and wonder what they mean.
A thunder muttered and a shower fell
As twilight came with star and Vesper-bell.
Over the Oval, stamped where Spofforth bowled,
Reviving the grass-blades lifted from the mould.

THE GREAT CRICKET MATCH – BREWERS V. PUBLICANS

Anon., c. 1878
(FROM 'IRONBARK'S' *SOUTHERLY BUSTERS*, SYDNEY, 1878)

THE day was wet, down poured the rain
    In torrents from the sky;
Great coats, umbrellas, were in vain.
    But every lip was dry.

The clouds seemed disinclined to part,
    The wind was from the *West*,
Yet worked each brewer's manly heart
    Like (y)*east* within his breast.

Along the road each brewer spent
   His coin in frequent drains,
For mere external moisture went
   Against those brewers' *grains*.

And with a bright triumphant flush,
   Their Captain, Mr Staves,
Swore they should crush those suns of lush
   Who dealt in 'tidal-waves'*

For, speaking of the L. V. A.,*
   The brewers said, and laughed,
'A most efficient team were they
   For purposes of *draught*.'

'Twas thus they talked upon the way
   Until they reached the ground;
But in their friends the L. V. A.,
   Rum customers they found.

I haven't space to speak of all
   The glories of the match —
Of every well-delivered ball
   And every well-caught catch.

I fain would tell of Mr Keggs
   (they *spiled* and *bunged* his eye)
Of *Barley*-corn, and how his legs
   Got twisted all a *rye*;

How Stoups, the umpire, stood too near,
   And came to grief and harm;
How, when he fell they gave him beer,
   Which acted like a *barm*;

Of Hope, who keeps the Anchor bar
   And vendeth flowing bowls
(My feet have often been that far
   And anchored fast their *soles*)

Mark how he bustles, snorts and spits —
   His brow he mops and wipes,
And though I couldn't praise his hits,
   I'll gladly praise his '*swipes*';

*Tidal-wave — a large glass of colonial beer.

*Licensed Victuallers' Association

Of Corks, who funked the second ball,
   And by a sudden turn
Received the straightest one of all
   Upon his ample stern.

He raised a loud and fearful roar —
   With fury he was blind,
And, though they called it *'leg-before'*,
   He felt it most *behind!*

Of Marks, the scorer — best of men!
   Sure everybody talks;
He chalked the runs correctly when
   He couldn't *walk* his *chalks.*

Despite the flasks of monstrous size
   He'd emptied to the dregs,
He scored 'wides', 'overthrows', 'leg-byes',
   And runs attained *by legs.*

For all the ceaseless rain which flows,
   The rival teams care naught;
Though *runs* were made by many a nose,
   And many a cold was *caught.*

Inside and out they all got wet —
   Each drank what could hold;
I'm sure a bowl was overset
   For every *over bowled.*

The daylight fails; at length 'tis gone:
   There's little left to tell;
For as the shades of eve drew on
   The stumps were drawn as well.

Then to the tent each man resorts;
   On food intent were they.
Who won the sport? the pints and quarts —
   The gallant L. V. A.

Beneath the canvas let us pass —
   Old Bottle-brush was there,
And well he filled his empty glass,
   And well he filled the 'chair'.

At length the Maltsters cleared the tent,
    And several hops ensued;
But stay! Both time and space are spent —
    In truth, I must conclude.

A vict'ler rose amid the host —
    A burly man was he —
'My lads', he said, 'I'll give a toast,
    And here's my toast d'ye see:

'John Barley-corn, the king of seeds!'
    And round the glasses go,
'For that's a *corn* that ne'er impedes
    The light fantastic toe!'

THE GAME OF CRICKET
By Daniel Healey, 1894

WELL, what is cricket after all,
    That so delights the masses?
Six bits of stick, a bat and ball,
    And two and twenty asses.

Yes, two and twenty donkey-men —
    I wish I could impound them;
Yes, asses I repeat again,
    With thousands more around them.

And then the asses bowl and bat,
    Knock down, or keep a wicket;
And run, and cheer, and shout, and that —
    Why, that's the game of cricket.

BUMP
Anon., 1898

BUMP 'em down and keep 'em short,
It's the essence of the Sport;
Bowl 'em very fast and short,
Make 'em bump, and that's the sort;
Hit him — body, head, or wicket —
'Tis the soul of Modern Cricket,
And if tries to score from you, he's certain to be caught.

SOLDIERS OF THE WILLOW
By George Essex Evans, 1894

PLAY the grand old game once more,
Soldiers of the willow,
While two nations keep the score,
Watching o'er the billows,
Play it true and play it strong
While we crown it with a song
That shall ring the world along
Soldiers of the Willow.

NEW SOUTH WALES V VICTORIA, 1898
By 'Woomera'
(*CRICKET*, FEBRUARY, 1898)

HE started from his pleasant sleep
    And gazed in wonder round,
Roused by the wild exultant shout
    That echoed o'er the ground.

'And wherefore all the row?' he cried.
    'Has Trumble missed a catch?
Is Worrall in or Giller out?
    Has Sydney lost the match?

'Oh, say why do the people rave?
  What great deed has been done?'
They broke it gently, as they might,
  'Victoria's made a run.'

'Ah, woe is me,' the old man said,
  And bitterly he wept;
'I've waited long to see that run;
  They got it while I slept.'

Ah! vain indeed are simple words
  To solve so great a sorrow;
They only said 'You'll come again;
  They might make two to-morrow.'

HUGHIE'S THE BOY
Anon.
(THE *AUSTRALASIAN*, FEBRUARY, 1899)

WHEN the running batsmen stumble,
  Or at one another mumble,
Perhaps the fieldsmen make a fumble,
  And the crowd begin to grumble.
But when the batsmen sad and humble
  See their wickets quickly tumble,
As the ball comes with a rumble
  Till the stumps are in a jumble,
Then the bowler's Hughie Trumble.

SPIRIT OF AUSTRALIA
Anon., 1899

SPIRIT of Australia (to Australian Cricketer) — Shall I speak for
    you?
Cricketer   If you kindly will.
Spirit — Down under we're not talkers, for our skill
      Lies all in action. Take us as we stand
    Leal sons and lovers of the mother land.
        Song — 'Advance Australia.'

Though a trav'ller's eyes with longing turn to lands where he may
   roam,
To the England and the loves ones he has left across the foam;
Still other lands exist which much resemble home, sweet home,
And a very grand dominion is Australia,
Her people loving England, and by England well beloved,
Two hearts that beat in unison by but one impulse moved,
Australians are welcome here, and oft it has been proved
That an Englishman is welcome in Australia.
   Chorus —
   In the land they call Australia, which, though far across the
      foam,
   Is the daughter of Old England and a chip of home, sweet
      home;
   Where the mother tongue is spoken, and their hearts are loyal and
      true —
   Advance, Australia! England number two.

THE COWED AND DODGING BRITISH LION

Anon.

(*ADELAIDE OBSERVER*, 1899)

AT the British Lion not a foe might jeer,
   While breath of life he drew;
But now 'tis queer how he yields to fear
   At sight of the kangaroo.
On cricket field he will tamely yield,
   And a roller skulk behind;
With lowered tail, lest his Ranji's bail
   A ball from E. Jones might find.

Like beaten hound — oh! he will not bound
   At his foe in open fight;
But crouch below his slave 'Barlow,'
   And pray for the fall of night.
His mean cubs yelp round the greensward's bound,
   As a jackal's pack might do,
To save the game, and their dad too tame,
   From the lusty kangaroo.

If the poor old beast cannot fight, why then
    Let him carpet-bag his roar,
And slink by night in his palsied fright,
    From the sight of a foeman's score.
Let him vaunt, if he will, of his pluck and skill,
    As the halt and the blind may do;
But never agen, to his sea-girt den,
    Let him challenge the kangaroo.

THE BOWLER'S TEAR

By 'W. A. B.', inspired by Ernie Jones's loss of form, 1900
(*CRICKET*, FEBRUARY, 1900)

Upon the pitch he turned,
    To take a last fond look
Of the hole he made within the crease,
    And the length of run he took:
He listened for applause,
    So familiar to his ear;
And the bowler looked upon the ball
    And wip'd away a tear.

Inside that scoring box
    They added fours and threes:
And held aloft their hands in awe
    For runs were thick as bees.
They breathed a word or two,
    'Twas well he could not hear,
But he paused to bless them as they worked,
    And wip'd away a tear.

He turned and left the ground,
    Oh! do not deem him weak,
For dauntless was the bowler's heart,
    Tho' he'd slightly lost his cheek.
Go watch the av'rage lists
    In 'Wisden' year by year,
Be sure the hand that's foremost there
    Has wip'd away a tear.

CLEMENT

By 'W. A. B.', on reports that Clem Hill was considering retirement
(*CRICKET*, c. 1900)

O Clement, Clement, this is hard
    To bear. We cannot bear it.
Your name must be upon the card
    In future 'tests.' We swear it.

What will your colleague, Victor, say
    (You two were boys together)
If you with him no longer play
    At punishing the leather?

Must the Australians take the field
    While you sit in pavilions?
Must they to every foeman yield,
    And sadden waiting millions,

Because they can no more rely
    On you to paste a swerver?
O Clement, Clement, go and buy
    An *Adelaide Observer*,

And see what pretty things it says
    About your plucky cricket;
Then think about the bygone days
    Before you leave the wicket.

RHYMES FOR TRUMPER

By 'Oriel'
(FROM THE *ARGUS* (MELBOURNE), JANUARY 9, 1904)

SOME talk of Alexander,
    And some of Hercules,
Of Hector and Lysander,
    And such great names as these;
Yea, all those heroes breezy
    Will live beyond all time,
Because their names were easy
    To jingle in a rhyme.

But there is one Australian
  Whose praise few poets sing,
Because his name is alien
  To almost everything.
Unjust it is, I know it,
  But he must yield his claim —
The most perspiring poet
  Can hardly rhyme his name.

Long life to Victor Trumper,
  That record-breaker fine;
I drink it in a bumper
  Of clear Australian wine.
And verses would come thronging
  Ev'n as I drink it down,
If only (foolish longing!)
  His name were Jones or Brown.

Long life to Victor Trumper!
  That brave, hard-hitting soul,
That pounder, smasher, thumper
  Of all that Rhodes can bowl!
Ground, press-box and pavilion
  Have seen what he can do;
His worshippers are million,
  Although his rhymes are few.

Ask no more rhymes for Trumper;
  There is no English name,
From king to counter-jumper,
  That knows a wider fame.
And in my verse I'd gather
  His records till the morn.
If only Victor's father
  Some other name had borne.

VICTOR TRUMPER

Anon.

(THE *CORNSTALK*)

V ictor he in name and deed, pride of Austral seas,
I n a blaze of glory such as few recall.
C linking strokes that blind us, dazzle and remind us,
T rumper, Victor Trumper, is the peer of all;
O nward still where'er he be, England or Australia,
R eeling out his hundreds while the crowds acclaim.

T iming driving, glancing, hooking that's entrancing,
R ushing up the pathway to the Hall of Fame;
U nder all this triumph what do we discern —
M odesty, refreshing as a desert rain,
P ride, well-curbed and glowing,
E arnest and straight-going
R ound his brow the victor's wreath will long remain.

TOO MUCH 'OBBS

Anon., during the 1911–12 season

(*EVERYBODY'S*)

THERE's sumfin up with our nash'nal game —
an' its cost me a good bob;
Orstralian Cricket is not the same —
It suffers from too much 'OBBS!
They've got this feller — I've watched 'im bat —
'e's good as any you've seen!
'E goes in first, an' strike me fat!
'e bats like a fair machine!
Our fellers give him lightnin' ones,
An 'googlies, an' swerves, an 'lobs,
But 'e makes 'is 'undred-an'-fifty runs,
where our caps is makin 'blobs!

C. V. GRIMMETT
By J. A. Gibney, March 1925

BATS off to C. V. Grimmett,
  The wizard of the ball,
Who routed England's champions.
  Hobbs, Sandham, Hearne, and all.
Who in his opening test match
  Displayed such magic skill.
Australia sought a bowler
  And Grimmett filled the bill.

Hats off to C. V. Grimmett,
  We're justly proud to-day
Of South Australia's champion,
  Who quickly forced his way
Through England's grim endeavours
  To guard her polished sticks.
Success attend his efforts
  In nineteen twenty six.

CRICKET IS IN ON THE FLAT
By Baker James
(BALLARAT SPORTING WORLD, 1932)

CRICKET is in,
I can tell by the din
Of a kerosene tin,
  On the flat.

A broken old ball,
And no pads at all,
A lath from a wall
  For a bat.

First on the field
Gets the "willow" to wield,
His wicket to shield
  Takes his stand.

His field placed with care,
The second "man" there,
With arms shining bare,
  Ball in hand.

His coat is the crease,
He steps out his "piece"
Away fly the geese
  To the shore.

Now striker takes block,
Feels firm as a rock,
He's going to knock
  Up a score.

But "Bag full of tricks"
Clean bowls him for nix,
And down go the "sticks"
  To "How's that."

Yes, cricket is in,
I can tell by the din
Of a kerosene tin
  On the flat.

DAD ON THE TEST
By C. J. Dennis

I reckon (said Dad) that the country's pests
Is this here wireless an' these here Tests.
Up to the house and around the door,
Stretchin' their ears for to catch the score,
Leavin' the horses down in the crop.
Can you wonder a farmer goes off pop?

I'm yellin' at Jim or I'm cursin' at Joe
All hours of the day; but it ain't no go —
Leavin' their work and hangin' around
When they think I'm down by the fallow ground;
Sneaking away when I start to rouse,
An', as soon as me back's turned, back at the house.

"Who got Wyatt? Is Sutcliffe out?"
Wot do they care if I rave an' shout?
Bribin' young Bill for to leave his job
To twiddle the switches an' twist the knob.
"Has he made his century? Who's in now?" ...
And I bought that machine for the price of a cow!

There's a standin' crop, an' the rain's not far,
An' the price is rotten, but there you are:
As soon as these cricketin' games begin
The farm goes dilly on listenin' in;
Not only boys an' the harvester crew,
But Mum an' the girls gits dotty too.
An' I reckon (said Dad) that a man's worst pests
Is this here wireless an' these here Tests.

ADVANCE AUSTRALIANS
By Alan Herbert, 1948

ADVANCE Australians, best ambassadors of all,
And test once more the love this island bears for you.
The world may laugh at us—our games of bat and ball,
But what a pity certain folk don't play it too.

RAINING IN ENGLAND
By C. J. Dennis
(QUOTED IN BARRY WATTS' *THE WORLD OF THE SENTIMENTAL BLOKE*, SYDNEY, 1946)

OH, to be in England
    Now that summer's there!
For who plays the Game in England
    Is each morning well aware
That the cricket-pitch is water-logged,
And the in-field's wet and the out-field's bogged:
    For it's surely raining, anyhow,
    In England — now!

A BOY'S CRICKET DREAM
By John Henderson
(THE *BULLETIN*)

BILL drove the cricket ball
And all the crowd lay flat,
For Bill was hitting right and left
—Explosion in his bat—
And hitting for a boundary
Where all the future lay
An oval in the field of time
Ringed by a golden day;
And still that Bowler at the end,
Elated, huge and dim,
Came looking through the hot still air
And bowled the world at him.

A CHRISTMAS CARD
By F. E. Weatherly

WITH Christmas Greetings
See here a token small I send
   For life's a game of Cricket,
But with a Bat called "Pluck" my friend,
   You can defend your Wicket

So when the Ball comes rolling in,
   The Ball that men call "Brother",
Take up your Bat and make it spin,
   You'll never have another.

LILLEE
By Jeff Clores
(*THE CRICKETER INTERNATIONAL*, FEBRUARY, 1983)

O Lillee of the valley of the shadow
O shade of the vale of tears and fears
Wizard of Oz — O raging prima donna
accept this bunch of humble belladonna
from the ranks of stricken batsmen — and
with this testimonial and valediction
mark the venomed blackness of the berry
scent the sullen purple flower
clasp them to your lilied bosom — my
how they complement your glower.

LILIAN THOMSON
By Richard Stilgoe
(FROM DAVID RAYVERN ALLEN, *A SONG FOR CRICKET*, LONDON, 1981)

Ev'ry morning on the radio, the news comes to Australia
The English batsmen once again have had a ghastly failure
It was Lilian Thomson's bowling once again caused the collapse
I always thought Test Cricket was intended just for chaps
But Lilian Thomson is Australia's finest flower
A maiden bowling overs at a hundred miles an hour.

She's the fastest lady bowler that the world has ever seen
Her bumper's awe-inspiring and her language far from clean
Just imagine the reaction of Greig or Knott or Amiss
As this six foot six of Sheila runs up, do you wonder they miss?

She hit Randall on the ankle, then she hit him on the forehead
She finds the happy medium she could hurt him something horrid.

She's Lilian Thomson, the first of cricket's dames
A mixture of Joan Sutherland, Rolf Harris, or Clive James
She'll hit you on the temple, in the groin or knee and kidney,
To prove that liberated Adelaide's as good as Sydney.

G.S.C., IN TRIBUTE
By Irving Rosenwater, 1982

Of those who unleash bat on ball,
Who is most graceful of them all?
With surest eye and nimblest feet,
And bat as broad as King William Street?
Extolled by gamin and Q.C.,
With the sweetness of touch of Debussy.
A caress through point or through the covers
Is pabulum for cricket lovers,
Who, in Perth or on the Hill,
Understand a rare-sent skill.
So, be upstanding, raise a cheer
To the lordliest player in the hemisphere.

A GAME THAT WE PLAY
An old song revived in England during the 1921 Australians' Tour
(*AUSTRALIAN CRICKETER*, OCTOBER, 1924)

There's a game that we play on
a bright summer's day,
With a bat, and a ball, and a wicket!
And we always have thought,
When we joined in the sport,
That we really were playing at Cricket.

But the Australians came just to give
us a game —
It's a fact, though it's painful
to say it —
They are teaching us fast that
we're things of the past,
And we really don't know how
to play it.

TWO HUNDRED YEARS OF CRICKET
By Richard Stilgoe
(FROM DAVID RAYVERN ALLEN, *A SONG FOR CRICKET*, LONDON, 1981)

IN Melbourne on the Ides of March in 1877
The English team encountered an Australian eleven,
They couldn't see how possibly an English team could fail
Although that chap behind the stumps could not get out on bail,
'We'll show the convicts how,' they cried,
'We'll play these chaps alive.'
But as you know it wasn't so
They lost by forty-five.
In nineteen seventy-seven to proclaim the century,
Another team of Englishmen went to the colony,
'Your Chappells and your Lillees don't scare me,' cried Tony
   Greig,
And Lillee chewed his gum, and bowled, and hit him on the leg.
And Randall scored a century, but still t'was all in vain
T'was just the same, we lost the game by forty-five again.

In twenty seventy seven, when the bi-centenary's played
What bumpers will be bowled, how many centuries made?
As in the Cornhill, Texaco, John Player, Dunhill Test,
The Aussies in their Brearley patent caps take on the rest
As Arlott, Johnson, Frindall in the commentary box in heaven
Compare them to the English team of ninteen seventy seven
One thing is sure, the final score, however hard they strive
Our national pride, the England side will lose by Forty-five!

CRICKET
MISCELLANY

TIBBY COTTER'S LAST BOWL
By 'Blue'
(FROM THE NSW CRICKET ASSOCIATION ARCHIVES)

I was "Tibby" Cotter's cobber in the 12th Light Horse and on the night of October 30, 1917, we were at Khallassa, in Southern Palestine, the most remote portion of the southern position. We watered our horses there, and prepared to move off in the attack on Beersheba.

"Tibby" was one of the best foragers in the A.I.F. He would come to light with a bottle of champagne in the middle of the desert, and the lads in the section all looked at him to turn up with something unusual.

About 1.30 on the morning of the attack, "Tibby", who had received instructions to report to Echelon on a guard, turned up at the unit. He said to me: "Bluey, I've skittled a Turk in one hit; and what do you think he had on him? Here it is — a yard of ling".

He wasn't going to Echelon, he insisted, but said he would treat the boys to a Stammell fish supper in Beersheba, and be damned to the consequences.

We moved off at 4.30 a.m. from Khallassa, and attacked Beersheba that afternoon. "Tibby" was next to me on one side in the charge, and Trooper Jack Beasley on the other. Rex Cowley was there also. The other three were skittled by a machine-gun, and after we had cleared the Turks out, the troops went back half-an-hour later to bury the dead.

"Tibby" was still alive when I got to him, and he recognised me. "Blue", he said, "You can have the fish supper on your own". He died shortly afterwards.

He should never have been in the charge. Had be obeyed orders, he would probably have been alive today.

Just before we left Khallassa, "Tibby" — who, in a bowling competition at Tel-el-Fara, bowled over 18 single stumps at full pace out of 24 — took up a ball of mud, and throwing it into the air, said: "That's my last bowl, Blue; something is going to happen".

THE DEATH OF CHARLES BANNERMAN
(THE SYDNEY MORNING HERALD, AUGUST 21, 1930)

MR Charles Bannerman, the famous international cricketer, collapsed and died suddenly yesterday afternoon. Mr Bannerman was 79 years old.

He had been extremely ill for several weeks at his home in Chapman Street, Surry Hills, but on Tuesday felt better, and went for a walk. Yesterday he watched the events at the Kensington Racecourse, and later in the afternoon, while at a tram stopping-place at the corner of Flinders Street and Moore Park Road, Moore Park, he suddenly collapsed.

Ambulance men from the Central District Station quickly conveyed Mr Bannerman to Sydney Hospital, but on arrival there life was extinct. The body was taken to the city morgue, pending funeral arrangements.

He had been widely regarded as the father of Test cricket.

THE NIGHT THE SELECTORS CAME TO BLOWS

The official report by the secretary of the Board of Control, Syd Smith, of the fight between two Australian selectors, Clem Hill and Peter McAlister, at a selectors' meeting in Sydney in 1912. The third selector was Frank Iredale

I beg to state that I convened a meeting of selectors for Saturday evening, February 3, for the purpose of selecting the Australian eleven to play in the fourth test match, and also to select as many players as could be agreed upon for the Australian eleven leaving for England in March next.

I was the first to arrive at the rooms of the N.S.W. Cricket Association, getting there about 8 o'clock. Mr Iredale arrived about ten minutes later, and I informed him that the other selectors had not arrived; so he stated he would wait for them at the front door. In the meantime Mr Joe Davis, of the *Sydney Morning Herald,* came into the small room, and was chatting with me on various matters connected with cricket. Mr Sinclair rang up on the telephone about 20 minutes past 8 to say that Mr Hill had left Manly, and to ask the other selectors to wait for him. Mr Hill arrived about 10 minutes to 9, and the other selectors came upstairs immediately afterwards.

The three selectors and myself were seated at the table, Mr Hill on one side, Mr McAlister and Mr Iredale on the other, and myself at the end, whilst Mr Davis was standing up near the door.

The conversation was started with regard to the match being played in Melbourne on that day, Mr Hill remarking that it was strange that one of the best bowlers in Australia — Mr Laver — should have been omitted from the State team, and one who should be playing in the test matches. Mr McAlister then remarked that in his opinion Mr Hill had not sufficiently used Messrs. Kelleway and Minnett in the bowling department, so as to rest Messrs. Cotter and Hordern. Hill stated that he considered that neither the bowlers in question were any good on the Melbourne and Adelaide wickets. Mr Davis in answer to a question from Mr Hill, also participated in the conversation and remarked that whatever Frank Laver may have been on English wickets, he did not consider he was a good bowler on Australian wickets, and quoted that gentleman's averages for the last 19 years, and at the same time informed the selectors that he would be only too pleased to go down to the office and bring his assistance to them in their work. He also remarked that he considered Minnett was a splendid bowler in so much as he had seen of him on New South Wales wickets. In view of his remarks, Hill informed Mr Davis that he did not consider that he was any judge of cricket.

The discussion again got round on the captaincy question, when McAlister reiterated his statement with regard to the using of Kelleway and Minnett. Hill remarked that McAlister had better take over the captaincy, and that he was quite prepared to hand his resignation to the Hon. Secretary at once. McAlister stated that he was not giving his view as a captain, but as a judge of cricket.

At this stage, Mr Davis, at my request, left the room. I had some telegrams ready to show the selectors with regard to Mr McLaren being available for the fourth test match, and was only waiting on opportunity to give them this information before leaving the meeting myself.

Hill then asked McAlister where he got his experience as a captain, and he (McAlister) stated that he had captained teams in Australia, and also captained several matches as vice-captain of the Australian Eleven in England, and he considered that he had done all that was necessary. Hill remarked, was it not a fact that Warwick Armstrong had refused to play under him as a captain in the Old Country. This McAlister denied, and Hill asked him to name any match in which Armstrong took part, and in which he (McAlister) acted as captain. McAlister replied that he played under him as captain at Lords on one occasion, when Mr Noble had to leave the field, but that he did not play under his captaincy in other matches because he always stood down when Mr Noble was not playing. Hill then asked McAlister what matches he had ever won as captain and asked him to write them down on a sheet of paper. McAlister numerated several, and Hill remarked that they were very second-rate matches. McAlister said, "At all events, I did quite as well as Victor Trumper had done in captaining the Australian Eleven against

Gloucestershire, when he almost made a hash of things." Hill then stated, "Fancy you comparing yourself to men like Trumper and Armstrong." McAlister replied, "At all events, I consider I am as good a skipper, if not better, than the two players you have mentioned." Hill then informed McAlister that he had no idea of captaincy, and McAlister replied, "At all events, I reckon I am a better skipper than either Trumper, Armstrong, or yourself."

Hill got up from his chair and informed McAlister that he had better take the position of captain and pick the team himself. Hill then sat down again, and informed McAlister that he knew absolutely nothing about skippering a side which brought forth a retort from McAlister that he (Hill) was the worst skipper he had ever seen. When this remark was passed, McAlister was leaning with his two hands in front of him, and Hill immediately jumped up and said, "You have been looking for a punch in the jaw all night and I will give you one," immediately leaning across the table and dealing McAlister a violent blow on the side of the face. McAlister was somewhat dazed, but jumped up and rushed round the table to where Hill was standing, and a fight ensued, both selectors grappling and trying to punch each other in the small space between the table and wall. McAlister sat down between the telephone-box and the table and Hill leant over him but did not strike him whilst on the floor. I eventually managed to separate the two combatants, and I might state here that when the scuffle first took place the table slewed round and Mr Iredale was jammed into the corner, and thus powerless to act. I urged Hill to get out of the room, but he went to the other end of the table near the door. As soon as McAlister got on to his feet I tried to stop him from rushing at Hill, but they again got to holts. The furniture was knocked all over the room, the pictures were broken, and Hill grappled with McAlister and forced him onto the table and window-sill — another couple of feet and both selectors would have been out the window into the street, three floors below, but this was prevented by Mr Iredale leaning across and catching McAlister by the arm, whilst I pulled Hill off by the coat-tails. As soon as I got Hill away, I at once shoved him out of the door, and told him he "had better stay outside." Mr Iredale and myself holding McAlister he shouted to Hill: "You coward! you coward!" Blood flowed from McAlister's face copiously, and it presented a sorry spectacle. My clothes, collar, hat, etc. were covered in blood. After getting McAlister to sit down, I went outside and interviewed Hill and told him that he had better go home. He said, "Syd, I will not remain a member of the selection committee any longer, as I refuse to sit with McAlister as co-selector." I replied that I could not take that as official, but if he would put the matter in writing, I would place same before the board. He said he would write it out at the hotel, and I would call for it. I then gave Hill his hat, papers, etc., and he said that he had had enough the day before at the board meeting, when Colonel Foxton practically branded him a liar in connection with the publication of the telegram he received from McAlister on the eve of the third Test match.

I might also state that during the disturbance, Hill accused McAlister of being drunk, but in my opinion neither Hill nor McAlister were intoxicated.

The two selectors were very heated in their arguments before the climax was reached, and the language was anything but gentlemanly. . .

Mr Iredale and myself took no part whatever in the arguments, but endeavoured in a joking way to try and get the two selectors into a better humour, but without avail. I regret exceedingly that this report has been necessary, but can positively state that this is a true account of the proceedings.

WHEN IN ROME

Victor Richardson's account of a match an Australian touring side played against a local team at Yorketon, Canada, in 1932

I FOUND it advisable to greet umpires everywhere in the most friendly and cordial manner, and as usual, when taking the field, I approached the two gentlemen with long white coats. One was a veteran of some seventy summers. I congratulated them on their interest in the game, and thanked them for offering their services.

The old gentleman informed me that the association had done him the honor of inviting him to umpire, but he had not umpired for forty years. He called me aside out of hearing of the other umpire and asked me if there had been any alterations to the rules in that time.

Following the usual principle of "doing as Rome does," and that rules wouldn't matter very much, I replied, "Oh, no, sir, just the same now!" He said, "There is only one thing I don't like. It is the right-arm bowler who bowls over the wicket." I replied, "Why don't you like him?" Swinging his arm over, he said, "He might hit me with his arm as he comes over." I reassured him that in that case it would be all right if he took up his position two or three yards wide of the wicket on the on side, which he did. The batsman at the bowler's end was then hiding his view, so he had to be moved still a yard or two further out.

Don Bradman, then a great stickler for the rules and quite ignorant of my conversation with the old gentleman, stood this for an over or two, but at last went up to him and said, "You can't give a man out l.b.w. from where you're standing, umpire." Armed with my authority for his position, the umpire dismissed Don with the curt reply, "Can't I, my boy!"

Don found that he was right, for when he went in to bat later I think he gave him out about second ball for a "duck."

UNLUCKY 87
By Keith Miller, 1984

So MUCH guesswork by the Media over this so-called "Hoodoo" among the batsmen has prompted this despatch. Among a lot of guesses it is now the popular belief that it is 13 less than 100. The true story is a simple one.

When Don Bradman was hitting centuries, double and triple centuries, I saw Victorian fastbowler Harry Alexander bowl Bradman for 87 in the Vic.-N.S.W. match when I was a kid sitting in the outer. It stuck in my mind — what a great delivery to bowl the great man with when he was scurrying to get another century-plus.

Looking through various scores in all grades of cricket, somehow the dismissal at 87 often appeared. Later, when playing for South Melbourne Cricket Club, Ian Johnson, now Secretary of the M.C.C., was dismissed at 87. I remarked that I expected it. I then told him the story.

Johnson and I later played together for Australia usually fielding together in slips. A few more dismissals at 87 and we were laughing at this odd dismissal number. Soon it caught on among the other players, with no explanation for this strange dismissal number.

The T.V., radio and press in recent years have put more emphasis on this hoodoo number, with wild guesses as to its origin.

To check my facts, I recently looked up the record books. Thumbing through, there it was — the year 1931. Vic. versus N.S.W. at the M.C.G. Bradman bowled Alexander 89. What — not 87!!

Obviously, as a kid, the last time I looked at the scoreboard, Bradman was 87. Obviously a couple of runs went unnoticed before his dismissal. So 87 should in effect be 89. Let it stay 87.

THE COMING OF THE AUSSIES
By Michael Parkinson
(FROM HIS *SPORTING FEVER*, LONDON, 1974)

THE hibernation of the cricket lover is just about over. Soon we'll be waking and stretching and sniffing the air. There might not be many of us left but those that are dwell in the delicious anticipation that only comes when the Aussies arrive.

My first view of an Australian was Ray Lindwall at Sheffield sending the first ball of the game past the 'keeper and into the crowd sitting on the grass. When he got it back every bit of shine had been rubbed off it, and what moments before had been a glittering example of the ball-maker's art now resembled a piece of volcanic rock. It made no difference to Lindwall. Nor did it matter that second time at Bradford when Hutton walked out to meet Miller and Lindwall, the two men he had played on his own, and the crowd rose to him just to let the Australians know that anyone getting cute with their hero had better know a secret exit from the ground. Lindwall went through his ritual set of exercises and, with the ground still and silent as the moon, bowled Yorkshire's hero for a duck.

'It was a good ball,' said Uncle Jim grudgingly. 'It had to be,' said my old man, looking sadly at Hutton's back as he walked from the wicket.

For all he was so obviously the master of his craft, it was not Lindwall but Miller who captured my young imagination. He was the most glamorous figure I had ever seen. He was all my heroes mixed together into an unlikely but irresistible compound of Biggles, Rockfist Rogan, Jelly Roll Morton, James Cagney and the Great Wilson. I pictured him arriving at Lord's in his Spitfire, making a ton before lunch, spending the break lunching Lana Turner in her sumptuous caravan on the set of her latest film, returning to Lord's to bowl England to defeat and celebrating victory knee deep in champagne and showgirls at a London nightclub.

It was an extraordinary fantasy for anyone to live up to, but Miller never let me down. Nor did he disappoint me so many years later when we were colleagues on the same newspaper and played together in the office team. It is fair to say in these games the wine flowed freely before, during and after play, and more often than not the result was decided by whichever team could muster a player capable of finding his way to the wicket without the help of a guide dog. Miller added his own individualistic touch to these often bizarre proceedings by having his own tic-tac man who stood by the sight screen and signalled to his master the results of all the day's races.

In common with most Australians Miller was not averse to putting money on the ponies, and it was a little disconcerting to stand in the slips with him, crouched low, tense and coiled in a spring only to have one's concentration totally destroyed by a long and colourful dissertation on the crookedness of racing as Miller learned that the 2.30 at Wincanton had not been won by his fancy.

It was during one of these moments when I was watching the edge of the bat and Miller was gazing at his tic-tac man that an extraordinary thing happened. He was first slip, standing up, hands in pockets looking at the far horizon. I was second slip, crouched low, hands cupped, hoping to God that the batsman didn't nick it, when he did. He nicked it hard and low and it came like a missile towards my ankles. I was contemplating taking evasive action when Miller dived across in front of me, took the ball off my boot tops, turned a somersault, gave me the ball and looked towards the tic-tac man. 'What the hell won the 2.30?' he said, as if vexed that the bowler and batsman had conspired to interrupt the real business of the afternoon.

A rare bird, Keith Miller. People say they don't make 'em like him any more. The fact is they never did. Like all great athletes he was unique. To bemoan the fact that he has no double in the modern game is to wish there was a replica for the Parthenon. But with or without a Miller the prospect of an Australian team touring this land — any Australian team — is sufficient to waken the connoisseur's taste buds. There will be no easy games for anyone while they are around. Our cricket fields will ring with the noise of bitter battle — and a good thing too. The Australians put everyone on their mettle, players and spectators alike.

I once went to Lord's with my old man to see them at the start of a tour when O'Neill was the great white hope. We sat in the free seats and leaned forward in anticipation as O'Neill came to the wicket. He was nervous and out of touch, but he was lucky and started accumulating runs with any number of streaking shots.

My old man observed the progress in silence. Not so the man behind who applauded every miscue as if it was textbook. The old man could stand it no longer. 'What's tha' doing?' he asked the man, who was applauding an off-drive that took fine leg by surprise.

'Clapping,' said the man. 'Tha' wants to be careful. O'Neill will die of embarrassment if tha' carries on like that,' said the old man. Ten minutes later O'Neill went on to the back foot and crashed a sumptuous boundary through extra cover. The old man applauded for the first time. He was interrupted by the man behind him. 'Do you mind if I clap that shot?' he said sarcastically. 'Clap? If tha' knew owt about this bloody game tha'd be on thy feet cheering,' said the old man.

It is good for cricket and good for cricketers and even better for lovers of the game to have the Australians with us. The moment is particularly ripe for their visit. The present crisis in the game is being countered by an increasing and fairly bewildering number of one-day competitions. I have no doubt they are needed for cricket to survive and I have no objection to one-day cricket in principle.

But the fact remains that to be seen in all its glorious complexity the game needs a larger canvas. There is nothing in the whole of cricket so satisfying and aesthetically complete as a five-day Test between England and Australia.

The next series will prove that fact and all other fixtures will be insignificant in comparison. The Aussies are welcome and I hope they lose. And if you think I'm being ungracious, I'm sure the tourists will know exactly what I mean and approve the sentiment.

A GLORIOUS UNCERTAINTY
By Terence Rattigan
(THE CRICKETER, 1964)

THE "dullest ever" series between England and Australia has "ended fittingly in a dreary, water-logged draw". So you will have read, no doubt, as also the fairly widely-held critical verdict that Test cricket, as a crowd-drawing spectacle, is as good as dead.

If you should also have read the theatrical critics — but why should you, when you don't have to? — you will also have learned that the present London Theatre Season has been the "worst in living memory" and that "panic reigns in Shaftesbury Avenue" because plays are so bad today that audiences "simply can't be drawn to see them".

Now I suppose if I were as young as some of your readers I would be seriously alarmed by these judgments. My two favourite pastimes, watching Test cricket and going to the Theatre, would both seem to have had it, and the future would be quite unlivable. I would take to drink and, happily, die of it.

But, also happily (anyway in this case) I am not young, and I can assure my fellow cricket and theatre lovers alike that the expert writers on both subjects have been regularly pronouncing their irrevocable death sentences for as long as I can remember, and that is for well over forty years.

In 1921 Test cricket was killed by Warwick Armstrong's "determination to win at all costs," and by England's "appalling mediocrity." A couple of years later the West-End theatre was killed by "2 L.O." and by "the dearth of good new plays." At very regular intervals since they have both died a number of times through some sad and irremediable concatenation of circumstances.

In 1930 Bradman killed Test cricket by making too many runs. In 1931 talking films killed the Theatre, by giving the people more entertainment for less money. Bodyline killed Test cricket again the following year. Somerset Maugham killed the Theatre again the year after that by writing two failures and retiring. In 1934 Bradman killed Test cricket by making too many runs once more. (And in 1938 too, come to think of it.) Meanwhile the Theatre had been completely and finally destroyed by the war-scare, and the war; and after the war, by Mr Baird's interesting invention, which later finally destroyed Test cricket too.

The obituaries in fact have been innumerable but the two "fabulous invalids" seem to have somehow tottered on. Until 1964, anyway, when, I admit, they have been both, for the first time that I can remember, clearly pronounced dead in the self-same year.

This coincidence induces an analogy between Cricket and the Theatre which, though patently inexact, has always, to me, had a kernel of truth.

At about the same time that Dexter was taking guard on Saturday evening at the Oval, while thirty thousand spectators watched in an electric hush of expectation (hadn't they read their morning papers, the idiots? Didn't they know that the game had been killed the day before by Lawry? And the day before that, by England's inept battling?) Laurence Olivier, in another arena, but in Dexter's county, was just about finishing his own innings in Othello; and with:

"I kissed thee ere I killed thee; no way but this,
Killing myself to die upon a kiss"

was about to score his anticipated but still breathlessly awaited hundred between lunch and tea. (In fact his Othello, when on form, I would rate as slightly better than three hundred and nine runs, in a Test, in a day. Forgive me, Sir Donald — but there it is.)

One wonders how many of those theatre critics who have firmly buried the British Theatre, 1964, have tried to get a seat for Othello at

Chichester, 1964. I did, and succeeded only by a calculated blend of toadyism, patience and corruption. The same methods got me into the Final Test 1964, but only just — the corruption and toadyism had to be rather more, the patience only little less. (And Test cricket was buried, remember, at Old Trafford.)

Now does this prove anything at all, except that the critics are almost always wrong? As I have said, only the very young and very gullible need reassurance there. Yes, I think it provides evidence for a belief I nurture about cricket — a belief unpopular with sports masters and possibly with your readers — that cricket is no more a team game than Othello is a team play. Test cricket, like great drama, needs a star.

True that I cajoled my way into the Oval in the *hope* of seeing a great drama. A Final Test, with the rubber still at stake, might well have produced one. But would I have cajoled quite as eagerly if Dexter and O'Neill hadn't been in the cast?

True, too, that I slimed my way into the Chichester Festival Theatre in the *certainty* of seeing a great drama. Othello is nearly my favourite play, and with McKenzie playing it opposite Trueman as Desdemona it would still give me pleasure. (Rather a lot, come to think of it.) But would I have slimed quite so eagerly if Olivier had been standing down that evening with a slipped disc? — and believe me, in that performance, he can easily slip almost anything.

The answer to both questions is surely a resounding "No". We queue to see great stars. For group acting we may wander to our local rep. For team cricket we may meander to our county ground (and in neither place do we always get what we have come to see). But for Test cricket, and for Shakespeare's drama we demand our dram of genius.

Unhappily neither Dexter nor O'Neill made his anticipated ton at the Oval and "Oh the pity of it, Iago! Oh, Iago, the pity of it!" (which, incidentally, is a line that no plodding club-cricketer of a playwright could ever dream up and shows Shakespeare's genius as clearly as a Wally Hammond off drive) but the "glorious uncertainty" of cricket has always included the strong possibility of seeing our idols ingloriously dismissed. Even Olivier is capable of an injudicious slash at a rising ball, notably, he tells me, when, in Othello, he tries to take the "Pontic Sea" speech in one breath, as Kean apparently did. Then he too can return to the pavilion to a muted and disappointed ripple of applause.

'YABBA'

By Ray Robinson
(FROM HIS *FROM THE BOUNDARY*, SYDNEY, 1951)

THE green slope of the Hill at the southern end of Sydney Cricket Ground is intersected by a diagonal streak. The streak is a footworn track, beginning at the asphalt path at the foot of the Hill and leading up the couch-grassed rise to the concrete scoreboard towering in the far corner. The pilgrims who trudge up this track are not the short-sighted, seeking a closer view of the names and figures on the scoreboard, but the thirsty, bound for the bar tucked away under the informative facade.

The bar, the track and the green stretch down to the ringside benches close to the white-lattice sightscreen lay in the domain of Yabba.

Australian barrackers are known as masses of people, silently intent, talkatively bored or noisily angry. Yabba was the only one who stepped forward from the ranks of the chorus, so to say, and established himself as an identity. This colloquial wit had a comedian's sense of timing. He had an old soldier's vocabulary, dating back to the South African War, for which he enlisted while on a visit to that country in his early twenties.

On a sleepy afternoon, watching J.W. Hearne break a long scoreless spell with a sudden single, he bellowed: "Whoa, he's bolted!"

Though nothing was known of his playing experience as schoolboy and youth, he had a knowing appreciation of the game. From his viewpoint almost in line with the wicket he could tell when the batsman was not to blame for slow play. Persistent off-theory or leg-theory bowling soon brought him to full cry as spokesman for the resentful crowd. Sarcastically he thundered at one Victorian medium-pace bowler: "Your length's lousy but you bowl a good width." Midway through an over in which a bowler consistently pitched the ball well outside the off stump Yabba yelled: "Wide."

Again, next ball (louder): "Wide."

Next ball (fortissimo): "DOUBLE wide" (in a tone implying that the bowler had committed an error like a double-fault at tennis).

He would not rhapsodize about fast scoring if batsmen were gathering runs by the armful on an easy wicket. "Can I go in with a walkin'-stick?" he would ask.

Yabba was credited with having originated many of the sayings from which tedious repetition has since drained all humour. When two batsmen in long partnership had the fielding side in despair everybody laughed when he suggested sending for the fire brigade to put them out,

141

or calling for a nurse of shady reputation. He became more widely known in Sydney than many members of Parliament. Cinesound made a newsreel about him. A 14-stone man, about 5.10 or 5.11 tall, he used to walk through the turnstiles carrying a hamper and a couple of bottles of beer. Lolling or standing on the Hill he would soon be surrounded by a cluster of admirers who made sure his throat never ran dry. His face was fleshy, with more than a hint of a double chin, and his expression was that of a man enjoying himself. He dressed for the part in an open-neck shirt and sometimes a white coat, like a barman who had temporarily deserted his post to steal a peep at the play. On hot days the coat was discarded, exposing his braces. He wore a cloth cap, or a felt hat pushed back.

His voice, coarse and penetrating, had a brassiness which rang through the nondescript yells and mutterings of the mob like Harry James' trumpet above the noises of the band. On Saturdays when there was no first-class match he watched the Glebe club, and was a loyal supporter of *The Cricketers' Arms,* of Warren Bardsley, the left-hand opening batsman, and of Albert Cotter, the fast bowler.

To add to the discomfort of a batsman facing the dreaded Cotter, Yabba would bawl: "Give him one on the big toe, Tibby!" One afternoon when Cotter was running through North Sydney's batsmen a tail-ender had his middle stump smashed first ball. The crowd laughed unfeelingly. As the shamefaced batsman retreated to the pavilion Yabba consoled him with: "Don't worry, son; it woulda bowled *me.*"

A harsher note was heard in his voice in an Annandale pub late one winter afternoon in 1940. As he raised a pint from the counter somebody bumped his elbow, spilling the beer on the floor. In righteous wrath, Yabba blasted the clumsy oaf with tavernacular invective, including words which, though some of them appear in *The Bible,* are forbidden out loud in a public place. For the language, Glebe Court fined him £1 in default 48 hours. Yabba served only one of the 48 hours. He described his liberation in these words: "It was the longest hour of me life. Also the quietest. When the juice went around that the One and Only was in the clink some of the boys in the village had a zak in the tit-for-tat to get me out."

By occupation he was a dealer who hawked rabbits. In every street and back lane between Long Nose Point and Iron Cove they knew his two-wheeled cart, with its row of disembowelled rabbits hanging by their tied hind-legs, white tails bobbing to the pony's gait. All the cats in Balmain trooped behind his cart; he threw them rabbits' heads. When a customer hailed him Yabba would hitch a rabbit's hindlegs around a hook, expertly peel its skin up to its neck with a flick of the wrist, behead it with a blow of his snickersnee and slap it on to the housewife's plate almost in one action, like a fieldsman picking up and returning a ball. He would drive on, standing up in his striped apron with his vest open to the breeze, calling his wares: "Rabbie — wild rabbie!" A corruption of his call gave him his nickname, Yabba. Watching one of his cobbers, Alan Bowen, playing football for Balmain, he combined comment and advertisement in one breath: "You ought to eat my rabbits!"

His voice was not always as bold as brass. One day a batsman was having a sightscreen moved, and umpire George Borwick was holding an arm aloft as a signal to the attendant to keep pushing. The operation took some time. Yabba stared at the umpire's upraised hand and piped up in a schoolboyish falsetto: "It's no use, umpire; you'll have to wait till playtime like the rest of us."

The Hill at Sydney has hardly been the same since Yabba died in 1942, at the age of 64, a grandfather. He was a first-generation Australian, born in the inner suburb of Redfern, son of an Englishman and a Sydney woman.

Yabba's name was Stephen Harold Gascoigne. His father was a storekeeper who migrated from that centre of learning, Oxford.

BAIL FEAT
(*CRICKET*, 1908)

AT Laidley, Queensland, on New Year's Day, a bowler named James Higgins, of the Milton C.C., bowled a bail 51 yards off the wicket. The distance was measured by four of the players.

A BOX OF MATCHES
(THE *REFEREE*, 1910)

A PECULIAR accident happened to a batsman in a match Sackville v. Windsor, on the former's wicket, a few days ago.

He failed to strike a ball, which struck one of his pockets wherein reposed a box of wax matches, igniting them; but, beyond consuming a portion of his clothing and singeing his side, no damage was done. The incident produced no little amusement.

THE GREAT GLORY OF CRICKET
By J. M. Barrie, from a luncheon address to the Australian cricketers,
Piccadilly, 1926

IN conclusion — for I was out long ago (caught Gregory) — in conclusion, as Mr Grimmett said when he went on to bowl in the last Test Match — let us pay our opponents this compliment, we are sure that if we had not thought of cricket first, they would have done it, and whether we win or lose, O friendly enemy, you cannot deprive us of our proudest sporting boast, that it was we who invented both cricket and the Australians. And let us not forget, especially at this time, that the great glory of cricket does not lie in Test Matches, nor county championships, nor Sheffield Shields, but rather on village greens, the cradle of cricket. The Tests are but the fevers of the game. As the years roll on they become of small account, something else soon takes their place, the very word may be forgotten; but long, long afterwards, I think, your far-off progeny will still of summer afternoons hear the crack of the bat, and the local champion calling for his ale on the same old bumpy wickets. It has been said of the unseen army of the dead, on their everlasting march, that when they are passing a rural cricket ground the Englishman falls out of the ranks for a moment to look over the gate and smile. The Englishman, yes, and the Australians. How terrible if those two had to rejoin their comrades feeling that we were no longer playing the game! I think that is about the last blunder we shall make.

S.P. JONES'S RUN OUT
By Charles F. Pardon, 1882

MURDOCH hit Steel to leg, a fluky half-hit that went up in the air, and might have been a catch had we been playing a short-leg sharp. As it was Lyttelton ran for the catch, but could not quite get to it. The batsmen ran, and after the first run had been completed Jones strayed out of his ground, Lyttelton returned the ball, and Grace put the wicket down and appealed for the run out. Thoms, the umpire, immediately gave Jones "out", as he was bound to do. It was reported to me that Thoms, on being appealed to, answered: "If you claim it, sir, out!" Now, I thought this unlikely, so I took the first opportunity, after the match was over, of asking Thoms what he really did say, telling him at the same time what I had heard. He, as I expected, denied having said anything more than the necessary word, "Out!" Thoms told me the point was a very simple

one, the ball was not dead, and the batsman was run out. If Grace, instead
of going up to the wicket and putting off the bails, had thrown at the
stumps and missed them, the batsman could, and probably would, have
run again, and then every one would have said what a smart thing the
Australians had done. Jones did a foolish, thoughtless thing in going out
of his ground, and he paid the penalty of his rashness. Grace did what he
was perfectly justified in doing, and there can be no doubt that the run
out was legal and fair. It was in my hearing called "Cricket, but dirty." I
can't agree in this opinion. It may not have been a particularly courteous
or generous action, and if England had won a close match we should
never have heard the last of the matter. The thick-and-thin supporters of
Australian cricket would have talked about sharp practice, and
ungentlemanly play, and there would probably have been some revival
of the old ill-feeling. I don't mean that the Australians themselves would
have been weak enough to make a serious complaint as to an action
which could not be attacked on any but sentimental grounds. But
Murdoch expressed his disapproval openly in the field, and was
evidently angry, and we all know how strong sentiment is, and how
easily a grievance grows and spreads. I personally cannot say I approve of
what Grace did. It was strict cricket, but it was taking full advantage of
the thoughtlessness of a young player, and I am sorry that anything
should have been done to give any one a chance of saying with any basis
of truth, however small, that a member of the picked eleven of England
played a discourteous game.

ALBERT TROTT'S SUCCESS IN THE THIRD TEST, 1894-95
(CRICKET)

IN THE Test match at Adelaide his all-round success was astonishing,
seeing that he scored 38 not out and 72 not out and took eight wickets in
the second innings of England for 43 runs. *Lika Joke* celebrated the
achievement as follows:—

> THE KANGAROO TO MR STODDART.
> You didn't expect it, my sonny?
> Yet, truly, complain you must not;
> For you wanted "a run" for your money,
> And, complying, we gave you A. Trott.

Fingleton's Run-Out
(THE *AUSTRALIAN CRICKETER*, FEBRUARY 10, 1934)

Several comments have come in on the Fingleton run-out in the last N.S.W.-Victoria match. The actions of all concerned, Fingleton, Woodfull and Barnett, seem to have been misunderstood. None were at fault really, although that seems to be a paradox. Fingleton was beaten by a ball and attempted to hold up his morale and damage that of the bowler in the orthodox way by patting down an imaginary patch on the wicket. In doing so, he carelessly dragged his foot over the crease. The ball was quickly returned to Barnett from the slips, and Barnett, resenting the liberty that had been taken with him, removed the bails and appealed. It was a very fine point, and Fingleton deserved to go out, as he obviously did not go cleanly out of his ground, in which case Barnett might have let him off, although he might have waited for the ball to become dead. Fingleton rather resented being given out for taking what he considered to be a batsman's privilege. Woodfull, not caring to have it thought that he was taking any kind of unfair advantage, decided to give Fingleton the benefit of the doubt, particularly as he was batting for a place in the touring team, and asked the umpire's permission to allow Fingleton to return. In a similar case in England quite a long time ago, W.G. Grace ran out S.P. Jones, the Australian, and many of the Englishmen thought that it was not sporting, although Jones' case concerned a bad wicket and was not nearly as glaring as Fingleton's. Cricket, after all, is really only a game, and a win or a run out is neither here nor there in a hundred years of cricket. It is the spirit of cricket that has made the game what it is today, and those who sacrifice advantages to do the sporting thing, particularly in big cricket, do the game a great service.

Cricket – A Definition
By *Keith Dunstan*
(FROM HIS *A CRICKET DICTIONARY*, MELBOURNE, 1983)

Cricket (crikk-itt in England, criggit in Australia). Like living in igloos, skateboarding and eating tripe, unless taught at birth it remains forever as unfathomable as nuclear physics.

A SNAKE IN THE OUTFIELD
By 'Felix', 1889

AN unusual incident occurred last Saturday on the Frankston cricket ground. The Richmond Ramblers had journeyed down to play the local team, and during the course of the match, whilst the Ramblers were fielding, the ball was hit into the out-field, and the fieldsman, on stopping the ball, discovered a large brown snake within a few feet of him. He at once called the attention of the players to the fact, and both players and spectators rushed *en masse* to the spot, armed with bats, wickets, tin cans, and other weapons of destruction. The fatal blow was struck by the evergreen Bob Greig, who rushed up to within 20ft. of the snake, and then handed his wicket to another of the team with instructions to "hit it with that." It was hit with that and succumbed. The snake was about 4ft.6in. long. The cricket match was then concluded, and resulted in the defeat of the visitors, despite the bowling of Greig and the batting and wicket-keeping of H. Brock, who scored 16 in excellent style. The visiting team, after braving the terrors of the deep and perilling their lives in a cranky fishing boat, returned to town on Sunday night, having spent a very pleasant trip.

BILLY'S GREAT THROW
By Arthur Haygarth
(FROM MCC CRICKET SCORES AND BIOGRAPHIES)

THE following appeared in an English sporting paper of April, 1889:—

"THROWING THE CRICKET BALL — THE WORLD'S RECORD

There is a great diversity of opinion as to the longest throw on record with a cricket ball. One of the American baseball team, when in Australia, threw 128 yards 10½in., but the *Peak Down Telegram and Copperfield Miner,* of February 16th, 1889, asserts that this is not a record, and upon referring to their files, publish the following:— "On December 19th, 1872, a cricket match was played on the old cricket ground, at the north side of the Lagoon, between teams representing the Town and Country. The *Telegram,* of December 21st, 1872, says:— 'The fielding generally was good, Billy, the aboriginal, who played for the Town, showing himself the best hand not only of the players on the ground, but we venture to think in Queensland.' The same issue contains the following paragraph:— 'A wonderful throw was witnessed by the spectators at the cricket match on Thursday. Between the innings some discussion arose amongst the players as to the distance some of them could throw, and it was decided to test the powers of those who professed to excel in this line by a match. Amongst other good throwers, Billy, the aboriginal, astonished everyone by sending the ball a distance of *one hundred and forty yards,* as measured with the tape, and allowances made. After making every allowance (a tape not being as accurate in practice as a chain), this throw surpasses anything we have ever heard of in the Colonies or England.' On March 22nd, 1873, another paragraph appeared with reference to the matter. It appears that the *Australasian* of February 16th, 1873, doubted the throw, to which the *Telegram* replied:— 'The throw was witnessed and measured by several gentlemen still in town. We have not the slightest doubt as to the accuracy of the report we gave on the previous occasion. The measured distance was 142yds. 1ft. 6in., and 2½ yards were allowed for deviation in measurement. Everyone who saw the throw allowed it surpassed anything they had deemed possible. The hero is known as Billy, the Black Boy. He is a native of Brisbane, 5ft. 11in. in height, 34in. round the chest, and about twenty-four years of age.' "

The Editor of a newspaper of 1889, writes as follows:—

A correspondent forwards me the enclosed cutting from the *Sydney Mail* on the subject of the record for throwing the cricket ball:— "Once more we are able to publish a very interesting communication on the subject of the record of the 140 yards throw at Clermont in 1872 by an aboriginal. The letter in question comes to us from Mr W. O'Shea, of Brisbane, formerly of Clermont, and in answer to out note for some particulars, he replies as follows — 'On December 19th, 1872, a cricket match was played in Clermont, Queensland, on the ground lying between the town and Sandy Creek. The match was between a team representing the town and a team representing the country. The town team was composed of the following, viz., J. Thorne, T. Thorne, G.W. Waddell, C.J. Graham, Row, Miller, Spencer, Dearing, Pegus, J.A. M'Garin, and Billy, the Aboriginal, who that day made the record for cricket ball throwing. The country team included the following:— D.S. Wallace, H. de Satge, F.C. Lyon, W.H. M'Kean, Langley, Baldwin, Reed, Harris, Elliott, and Edkins. During the interval in the match a number of the players indulged in cricket ball throwing, amongst whom was Billy. His then employer, Mr J. Thorne (who was playing) backed him for a wager of £5 to throw over 130 yards in the first attempt. Billy's throw for this wager, when measured, was 142½yards. The throw was measured more than once, and amongst the tapes used for this purpose was an entirely new one. The throw was measured once by Messrs. Wallace and Graham, and every measurement with different tapes gave the same result, but so unprecedented was the throw it was deemed that a cotton tape could hardly measure such a distance correctly, and it was agreed to call the throw only 140 yards. But when the *Australasian* of February 13th, 1873, doubted the throw, Mr Graham indignantly replied through the columns of his paper, and gave the full and correct measurement. This throw was witnessed, and also its measurement, by all the players and many other respectable residents of the town, some of whom reside in Brisbane now. Billy was an aboriginal native of the district surrounding Brisbane. He was then 5ft.11in. in height, and about twenty-four years of age. He was splendidly made, was a good sprinter, and very fair with his fists. Altogether he was a typical athlete. Mr J. Thorne, his then employer, kept the Clermont Hotel. There are many gentlemen still residing in Clermont, Brisbane, and Rockhampton who well remember to have seen and measured some of Billy's big throws at practice. In no case did he throw under 130 yards. He is stated to have been possessed of an abnormal reach. A few years later he joined the Queensland Native Police, from which time he is lost sight of. A Sydney paper mentioned that he was at an intercolonial cricket match there in 1879 or 1880, and remarked on the possibility of his being able to repeat his great throw. But it is a matter of great doubt whether he ever was there or not. His throw has often been quoted in sporting records, but very seldom have the correct particulars as to place and distance been given."

KIPLING AND CRICKET
By Peter McAlister
(*CRICKET*, FEBRUARY, 1913)

WHEN I was at Canterbury with the Australian Eleven in 1909, a well-known cricket writer came to me with a bat, and asked me if I would obtain the signatures of the team on the face of it. Printed on the other side were the words, 'John Kipling, his bat'. 'Mr Rudyard Kipling would be very much obliged if you could do this for his son', said the writer alluded to. I was glad to be able to do it, for it showed me that the one poet who had written against cricket had been converted to it.

A REST DAY IN 1977

By Adrian McGregor

(THE *NATIONAL TIMES*, JUNE 27, 1977)

IT is midday at the Waldorf and in the Palm Court lounge Doug Walters, David Hookes and Len Pascoe idle at a table, overlooking the sunken floor portion where guests read and write.

The Palm Court is a scene of anachronistic splendour. A massive expanse of white marble floors covered with runner carpets in deep wine red and gold floral design. Brass abounds.

The lounge maitre in tails, white bow tie and flyaway starched collar hovers near the players, and across the lounge a pianist at a Steinway is bending to a sotto rendition of the Moonlight Sonata.

The three players, in their tracksuit tops and casual clothing, are like actors on the wrong set, but they are oblivious. There is an important matter at hand.

Hookes is reading aloud Ted Dexter's Sunday newspaper story which accuses Len Pascoe of being a chucker. He reads with appropriate disbelief and humour.

"The funny thing is I can bowl faster than I can throw," says Pascoe. Kerry O'Keefe wanders up. "I'll put a splint on my arm," offers Pascoe, stiffening from the shoulder like a tin man.

"No, you'll be as slow as Skully (O'Keeffe)," says Hookes.

"That quick, eh," retorts O'Keeffe. Then, more seriously: "They said the same thing about Thommo when he cleaned them up in Brisbane, you know."

It's Sunday, rest day in the Jubilee Test between England and Australia but captain Greg Chappell early that morning has already given a brief conference with the touring press corps. "It's a load of garbage, not worth commenting on," he says.

Some of the players are off to play golf, some for a drive in the three low-slung Triumphs which British Leyland have made available.

Though they banter about the chucking accusation, captain Greg Chappell's sharp rejection is symptomatic of the team's edginess about controversy on this tour. The first Test has come as a relief to them; at last the purpose of the tour is being realised; to play cricket.

The Packer revelations in early May all but destroyed this cricket tour. It worked in two ways. It split the Australian team into those who were signed and those who were not, and it diminished the importance of the Test series for both players and public.

In truth the announcement on tour of the Packer series caused to surface feelings of doubt and discontent which have burdened some team members ever since the Melbourne Centenary Test in March, when most of the signings were completed.

For the young players just beginning, with none of the seasons of discontent with financial rewards justifiably felt by the senior players, it has been a crisis of conscience. The natural trajectory of their sporting careers has been knocked out of kilter.

It was confusing in the extreme for young players to discover that responsible players like Chappell, Walters and Marsh, who they held in high regard, had precipitated events which threatened to bring their beloved cricket into bad odour with the general public. Instead of heroes they were being labelled villains.

It led to schisms which even now have not healed. Ian Chappell was in England on his own business, but whenever he was seen drinking with Greg an interpretation circulated eventually that Ian was influencing Greg on team or tour decisions.

And Ian's at the root of it all right. Not here, but back a year when the whole of the South Australian cricket team went on strike for Ian Chappell over his demand for what amounted to higher player payments and more influence for players in Australian cricket decision making. "It has all come to pass" he told me, though not in the way he would have preferred.

The Packer crew, in their wisdom, ignored South Australian captain Gary Cosier, and in doing so crucified him. His form on field on tour has been wanting and his self confidence plummeted with his exclusion. His eventual omission from the Test side was a formality.

Ian Davis is another. Because he hasn't had good scores he was replaced in the Test team by Richie Robinson as an opener. Packer's squad has Rick McCosker and Ian Redpath as openers. Where will they place Ian Davis? From possessing a promising Test career, Davis now faces cricket oblivion.

It may be coincidence or it may be allied, but there is also on this tour a sense of laissez-faire which is a product of the tour management's attitude that players are adult enough not to have to be organised or disciplined.

The senior team members rarely wear their blazers. In fact there is strong peer pressure not to. One night Kim Hughes changed into his country's blazer and, sure enough, was roasted by team colleagues. That is not to say the team does not look respectable: indeed they are, to a man, Beau Brummels on their nights out, but it emphasises their singularity.

The players themselves recognised this element of disorder in their tour when, before the first Test, they called a team meeting with manager Len Maddocks to ask for more notice of team obligations so they could plan ahead.

Given all these factors it is remarkable Australia performed so well in the Lord's Test. In the end it served as a catalyst to concentrate the team's maelstrom of conflicting energies into one external foe: England.

WATCH YOUR WICKET
A sign on the wall at a solicitor's office in Tully, Queensland

"WATCH your Wicket when the Devil puts a woman on to bowl!'

HONOURABLE
MEMBERS

THE LORD'S WICKET
A remark made by John Curtin during World War II

'AUSTRALIANS will always fight for those twenty-two yards. Lord's and its traditions belong to Australia just as much as to England.'

BOB HAWKE IN FORM
Bob Hawke's account of an innings he played for the Australian Capital Territory in Newcastle
(QUOTED IN BLANCHE D'ALPUGET'S *ROBERT J. HAWKE*, SYDNEY, 1982)

SOMETHING happened — I felt as if I were out of my body. I was hitting the ball and I suddenly knew that I couldn't miss it — every ball was coming straight to the bat. They changed bowlers and went through contortions to try to get me out but I just hit them and hit them — fours and sixes — until I was 78 not out. There was a New South Wales spotter there and he rushed over and talked about selection trials for me, said I should try out for a non-metropolitan team. I told him that wasn't me out there, it was someone else playing. Next game I was out for a duck.

DR EVATT'S GIFT
(THE *SYDNEY MORNING HERALD*, DECEMBER, 1940)

ARTHUR Morris, who scored two centuries in the New South Wales v Queensland cricket match, at his first appearance in a first-class fixture, yesterday received a gift, which he will always treasure, in recognition of his record-making feat.

Dr H.V. Evatt, M.P., a vice-president of the New South Wales Cricket Association and a member of the Sydney Cricket Ground Trust, took Morris in S.J. McCabe's sports store. "Choose the best bat in the shop," invited Dr Evatt. Morris chose, and went away, more excited than when he had completed his second century on Saturday.

Dr Evatt is a keen supporter of the St George District Club, with which Morris plays in the first-grade competition.

CRICKET AND THE LAW
By Sir Robert Menzies

IN MY County Court days, I had been appearing a good deal before an elderly judge who was not a great lawyer but who had for a brief period been a better than average cricketer. He was somewhat pernickety and abhorred slang expressions, but he was always approachable through his three special hobbies; roses, poultry and cricket. I suppose that purists will say that no advocate should play upon the weaknesses or foibles of a judge. My reply is that any advocate who does not study and know his judge or judges is going to lose many cases, most needlessly.

Anyhow, my story is this. I was for the defendant in a civil action which arose out of events in the neighbourhood of Ballarat, the famous old gold-mining city. My client, as I discovered after a conference with him and his solicitor, was a very decent and honest, but dull, man, quite incapable of stating the facts in any consecutive fashion. Right through the first day of the hearing, the plaintiff and his witnesses were heard. I cross-examined with no particular success. Yet I had a feeling that my bucolic client was right, if he could only be coherent, and register himself with the judge. The plaintiff's case closed just on the adjournment. The judge looked at me, kindly enough (he approved of me because he thought I spoke good English!) and said: 'Mr Menzies, I think I should tell you that I find the plaintiff's case and witnesses most impressive.' With my usual air of confidence, I replied: 'I would ask Your Honour to suspend judgment until you have heard my client, who will, I am sure, impress you very much!'

After the adjournment, I led the solicitor and client (we had no other witness) down to my chambers. All efforts to extract coherence from the client failed. I then produced my cards.

M. 'Mr X, have you ever grown roses?'

X. 'I think my wife has some in the garden.'

M. 'But can you distinguish a La Belle France from a Frau Carl Drushki?'

X. 'Not a hope!'

M. 'Do you keep fowls?'

X. 'The wife has a few.'

M. 'Can you distinguish between a White Leghorn and an Orpington?'

X. 'Not for the life of me!'

M. 'Have you ever played cricket?'

X. 'Ah! Now you're talking. I played for Ballarat and District against Ivo Bligh's Eleven!'

M. 'Good. Conference ended!'

The next morning I opened my case and called the defendant. He was quite dreadful as a witness. At one stage it became necessary to ask him about a date. Before he could reply I said, in the most helpful manner: 'Take your time, witness. I know that dates are not always easy to remember. Now, if I were to ask you about the date when you played cricket for Ballarat and District against Ivo Bligh's Eleven, that would be much easier!'

The judge, beaming with excitement and delight, switched round in his chair and said, 'Is that so? Tell me about the match. Were you batsman or a bowler?' And at once they were into it. For half an hour we had cricket reminiscences galore. By the time my client, completely relaxed, had returned to and concluded his evidence, the judge turned to the plaintiff's astonished counsel and said: 'Of course, Mr Y., you may cross-examine if you like. You have a perfect right to do so. But I think I should tell you that in all my years on the bench I have never been more favourably impressed by any witness.'

It is hardly necessary to add that the defendant won and, I think, rightly, on the merits. But it was cricket that did it!

While I am in this mood, I crave leave to record another reminiscence of cricket and the law.

A case had occurred, well over thirty years ago, in the local court at Mildura, the famous irrigation settlement in the far north-west of Victoria, on the River Murray. The Mildura solicitor concerned on the losing side, an old friend of mine, wanted to obtain, in the Supreme Court, an Order Nisi to review the decision. But he overlooked the time factor — the Order had to be applied for within thirty days — and filed his papers and briefed me almost at the last moment. Alas! It was Christmas time, and the Supreme Court was not sitting! But there was a Test Match on at the Melbourne Cricket Ground, and Mr Justice Cussen was the President of the Club.

I hared off to the ground; it was my only hope. The judge was in the Committee Box. I found my way in, waited until the end of the over, and then caught the eye of the judge. Happily he was a patient and generous man. I told him the circumstances. He at once caught on. 'I quite see the position. Have I your assurance that the necessary papers are filed?' I assured him that they were. 'Very well,' he said, 'I think the rule is that if you formally apply within the time, and the papers are in order, I can note the fact that you have applied, and adjourn the actual argument to a future date!' I vigorously agreed. He noted the application, turned to the field, and said with a smile: 'That was a fine bit of bowling wasn't it?'

THE CHINESE AND CRICKET
By Douglas Darby, MLA, 1970

. . . IF the Chinese nation is to be made great, they must learn to play cricket too.

RUBBER CRICKET BATS
From a letter to Pat Mullins by Queensland Premier Joh Bjelke-Petersen in 1983

I AM writing in reference to your recent letter requesting details of my interest in cricket and how I conceived the idea of a rubber cricket bat.

At school I was always a keen sportsman and played cricket for a number of years. During this time you would appreciate that at a small country school we were constantly finding problems with sporting equipment, in particular the handles of the cricket bat, which would break off. It was because of this that later in life I decided to develop a rubber cricket bat.

Unfortunately the venture was doomed from the start because the rubber companies whom I approached to market such a bat informed me that no one would buy a cricket bat made of rubber, due to the fact that cricket was always traditionally played with a wooden bat.

WHY DON'TCHA PUT BILLY HUGHES ON?
By Keith Dunstan
(FROM HIS THE PADDOCK THAT GREW, MELBOURNE, 1962)

THROUGHOUT the Second and Fourth Tests [in 1920–21] a barracker called out monotonously, 'Why don'tcha put Billy Hughes on?' This was a reference to the remarkable bowling prowess of the Prime Minister. On 29 November last there had been a match at the Albert Ground between the Federal and State Parliaments. As a cricketer Mr

Hughes was somebody to see. The *Argus* reported that he wore 'a picturesque if scarcely orthodox cricket costume which consisted of a blue shirt, a striped collar, a flowing silk tie, white trousers well rolled up and tennis shoes'.

The State side batted and three wickets fell for 12 runs, but then the batsmen dug in, and when they passed 50 the Federal men became alarmed. "It's time somebody did something", said Mr Hughes. Whereupon he took the ball and a spectator in the pavilion had the courage to call out sardonically, 'Bowler's name?'

The *Argus* said, 'The Prime Minister has a peculiar action that is faintly — very faintly — reminiscent of Wilfred Rhodes. He takes three long strides and tosses the ball well up, and then apparently prays for something to happen. To everybody's amazement his first ball clean bowled Mr Hannah, the captain of the State side.' If the easy catches had been held off his next two balls he would have taken the hat-trick. The Federal Parliamentarians were incredibly inefficient at catching the balls which were hit at them, and this gravely affected the Prime Minister's analysis. He finished with 4 wickets for 45 with six dropped catches. It looked as if a new Australian bowler had arrived, but one of his wickets was open to question. Mr Hughes appealed for an l.b.w. with such prime ministerial ferocity that the startled umpire felt he had no choice but to give the man out.

Fortunately Australia did not have to call on Mr Hughes for any of the Tests, for Arthur Mailey was bowling as never before.

CRICKET FOR PEACE
A comment by Bob Hawke at a cricket match in Canberra, January, 1984

IF I had my way I'd certainly introduce cricket into China and the Soviet Union. I think that if we could make them play cricket we'd have a much more likely chance of a peaceful world.

A CRICKET PERSPECTIVE
By Rodney Cavalier, 1984

CRICKET is a landscape of the mind that is forever 1930.

From the Press Box

THE QUIET AUSTRALIAN
By John Arlott
(THE *CRICKETER*, 1982)

RAY Robinson died without an enemy in the world. He was 76 years old, and surely the most underestimated of all cricket writers.

Perhaps he lacked — and certainly never aspired to — the racy, trenchant, critical self-certainty of a Jack Fingleton; he was rather the quiet Australian. He never adopted the romantic attitude of Neville Cardus; and in common with all other cricket writers, he could not command the sparkling humour of Raymond Robertson-Glasgow.

Ray Robinson, though, had his own particular field, in which no one else has matched him. He was the great mosaic-artist of cricket writing; a builder of infinite taste, talent and perception. He had not always the luxury of time to create work of his highest standard.

He was generally earning his living as a highly competent match-reporter: often — far too often — writing three or four different match accounts for three or four different papers or agencies. Each would be dispatched, to length and to time; sound and accurate; no facts would be missed; the prose would be unprententious but completely workmanlike and without clumsiness; amiable but not fulsome; essentially clear and professional.

That was Ray Robinson, the match-reporter.

Not for him the opportunity to lean back in the press box rolling a phrase round the tongue, an image across the mental palate, or an idea through the critical filter.

His output was high; his work-rate fast; his reliability monumental; his patience inexhaustible; his good humour unfailing.

If a merit table were compiled for running story and instant summary cricket reporting, Ray Robinson would win it. That was his rock, but not his ambition. He did his agency and hour-by-hour accounts in order to be at the cricket; watching the game for which he had such a deep feeling and in which lay so much of his happiness.

Even as a sick man — and tour by tour in recent years he looked yet more ravaged — he found his enjoyment at the match. He did not need to be in the company of famous cricketers though, of course, he relished that. He was happy in the company of his fellow enthusiasts; and he was unendingly appreciative of the work of his colleagues (he did not see them as rivals).

He was happiest of all, though, when, with the intuitive skill of a lapidarist, he built up his studies, especially those of great players. They were created from his own observation and reading — he was a profound student of cricket and had an eye for the apt quotation — the shrewd questioning of a fine journalist, his sense of form, and his basic knowledge of the game.

So he built such profiles as those of M.A. Noble, Bill Johnston, Bertie Oldfield, his potted history of fast bowling, and the concise and balanced survey of the 'Bodyline' Tests (he reported that series). He was a master not only in the arrangement, but the discovery and confirmation of minutiae.

At one juncture he writes: "About the same height (5ft 11in) Kippax modelled his stance at the wicket on Trumper's, an ideal pattern for young players. Cover the heads on photographs of each awaiting the bowler and there are few clues to tell one from the other. The similarity extends even to the shirtsleeve folded half-way up the forearm instead of the elbow. The feet are some 12 inches apart, weight evenly balanced on both, the left leg hiding the right shin from bowler's view. The body is inclined no more than necessary for comfortable grip of the bat with the hands together, high on the handle, between the pad tops."

When he wrote like that you could be sure that every fact had been checked. The picture was completely accurate.

In bulk, though, such details would cloy. So they are balanced with anecdote and animadversions.

He first wrote the story: "After all that had been said about Ponsford's wonderful sight, the doctor who examined him when he volunteered for the Air Force was astonished to find that he was colour-blind; he could not distinguish between red and green. A dialogue like this followed:

Doctor: "What colour did the new ball look to you?"

Ponsford: "Red".

"What colour did it look after it became worn?"

"I never noticed its colour then, only its size."

. . . He wrote only five books — he did not count "Cricket's Fun", a twenty-page humorous pamphlet — and each was written with pains, care and pride. It is true that Ray Robinson wrote for money, but he never wrote without the pride of the true craftsman. His books will last; and, so long as any of his friends live, so will his memory.

THE FIRST BALL
By Denzil Batchelor
(*PLAYFAIR CRICKET MONTHLY*, JULY 1965)

THE first Test match I ever reported between England and Australia was begun at Brisbane on December 4th, 1936. No one who played in that match was half as nervous as I was. The incomparable Neville Cardus was in Australia for the first time, and I was engaged by the *Sydney Morning Herald* to meet this challenge to their circulation by writing a signed column on the cable page — the first of its kind in over a century — giving my views in my own airy-fairy style of what happened in each day's play of the series. (I had got the job through writing a trial draft; the subject I had chosen being that of a day on which rain washed out play, and one was left arguing with a pavilion bore that the nucleus of the ideal team was: Jean Batten, John Boles, the film star, and Gracie Fields.)

Well, I got the job. I spent the evening before the match dining with Arthur Mailey and Arthur Gilligan, protagonists of that fantastic finish at Adelaide in January 1925, when England were left at the weekend with 26 to get and two wickets in hand. Australia won by 11 runs. Gilligan made 31, and told me he never slept a wink on the Sunday night. Mailey may be said to have won the match for Australia by taking the last wicket. He spent the weekend with Herbie Collins, his captain. A bookmaker called on them with an offer, if they would throw the match. Instead they threw him — down a flight of stairs. On the eve of Waterloo, so to say, Mailey spent the whole night dancing. There you are. One protagonist sat awake all night: the other enjoyed himself — dancing. And, of course, in this unfair world the dancer won.

Those were the stories the two Arthurs told me the night before my own debut: and is it to be wondered that I found myself that night belonging to the school of Gilligan rather than Mailey? Next morning I walked from my hotel to the ground obsessed by one devouring terror. Nervous indigestion tore at my stomach muscles with crab-like claws. Suppose *nothing* — nothing dramatic — happened during the day? Suppose nobody hit a six, or dropped a catch, or spreadeagled a wicket? Suppose Bradman batted all day for a hundred and fifty — this happened almost every day of the year at that time and was hardly worth commenting on. What was I to write? In the name of heaven, how was I to fill the first signed column on the cable page of the *Sydney Morning Herald* for more than a century?

I remember turning some graceful phrases at the spectacle of the purple bougainvillea spilling over the fence on the side of the ground opposite the press box and how this sight would have amazed the Hambledon men: but even I knew in my heart of hearts that this could not be expanded to a full column to the complete satisfaction either of the reader or the editor.

And then — it happened. G.O. Allen beat Bradman in the toss. Australia took the field. And Stan Worthington faced E.L. McCormick for the first ball of the match. There was a puff and — I swear — a spark, and almost before the long hop came to earth a couple of short legs were closing in, their necks protruding like vultures. Worthington played a strange stroke: half hook, half a defensive shot to preserve his face. The ball went from his bat in a gentle parabola. For a moment time stood still. Then Oldfield, never straightening up from his couch, sprang forward and clapped his great gloves about the catch.

Such was the first ball of the first Test match I ever reported. In a matter of minutes there wasn't a crab in my stomach, and my column was half completed. (For the record, the next man in, Fagg, was to score 4, to be followed by Hammond who was out for a duck; and — such is cricket — England was to win by 322 runs.)

But whenever I remember Brisbane in 1936, it is that first ball of the match that comes to mind. Poor Worthington, poor luckless Worthington! There he was; there he wasn't. He had looked forward all the 31 years of his life to that day — his first appearance against Australia. And then — first ball.

And this has set me wondering about those whose whole careers have been blighted by these fatal first balls. And do I mean, by the way (I never know), the first ball of an innings, or the first ball of a day? If the latter, then Bobby Simpson's failure to survive the first ball of the day, when set and apparently leading his side to victory in this year's Jamaica Test against the West Indies, may well have had immeasurably serious results not for himself, but for his team. He certainly accused himself in no uncertain terms at the time.

It is pleasanter to remember a merely personal failure. Dr R.L. Park of Victoria was the bright particular star of Australian batsmanship in the 1920/1 season. He scored 152 against South Australia; 111 in the first match against New South Wales; 100 in the second. Everyone in Australia clamoured for his inclusion in the Test side against England; and at Melbourne, in the second antediluvian era, Australians had as yet no conception of the Superbatsmen. Ponsford was to be the first of the tribe: Bradman its greatest member. But R.L. Park was near enough to having originated the species.

It was Arthur Mailey (who was playing) who told me what happened in the first Melbourne Test of 1920/1: I only hope he was right in detail and that I have remembered him correctly. There was a vast crowd to greet the hero, who came in to bat — he had taken Macartney's place — after the first wicket had added over a hundred runs. The crowd stood up to cheer him all the way from the pavilion steps to the pitch. He took guard against Howell — was immediately bowled — and retired in dead silence to be swallowed up by the pavilion and oblivion. He never had a second innings, nor played in a Test match again.

Now it is at this point that memory and reminiscence cease and theory and prophecy take over. It is only in cricket, and then only if you are a batsman, that such total failure can claim you for its own *in one ball*. If you are playing in a golf championship you may make an air shot on the first tee, and still win the title. If you are playing in a Wimbledon Final you may miss the simplest smash in the first rally, and still be champion. You may be put on to bowl the first over in a Test and begin with a wide — three wides — six wides — and still win the match for your team. But one ball can settle your destiny if you are a batsman: for having made your duck, life being what it is you will surely never have a second knock — either it will rain, or (as in Park's case) your side will win by an innings.

Now, though we are all conservatives when it comes to cricket and bitterly deplored the revolutionary spirit of change when the tea interval was prolonged to twenty minutes, the plain fact is that cricket is not and never was a static game. If it were, we should still be bowling under-arm to two stumps. The sempiternal pageantry of county cricket itself is dying on its feet — the spirit of the knock-out competition for the Gillette Cup has given it the *coup de grace*: it is only because the county championship gives us something to read about in the papers other than the decline and fall of the British Empire or fresh examples of diminished responsibility in crimes of violence that this form of the game survives.

And, having proved that cricket must for ever change if it is to live, I am here to suggest that no batsman need forfeit his status as the result of a first ball: every batsman should have the right to two chances in a match — and, if he is out first ball in the first innings (I can't help him in the second), he should be allowed to opt whether he would prefer to go on until dismissed a second time — thereby forfeiting his right to a second innings; unless, of course, he is not out at the end of his side's stay at the wicket.

You think it would detract from the high drama of the occasion? Not at all — just imagine if in the first innings that Melbourne scoreboard had read *Dr R.L. Park b. Howell 0; b. Howell 0.*

But perhaps you think the idea too revolutionary, and opposed to the very spirit of the game. . .? I submit that you are wrong. Is it not said that at the height of his career W.G., having been bowled first ball, calmly put the bails back and went on with his innings, pausing only to remark: 'Trial ball.' He had, you see, my own view of the need for reform, and an idea of how to cope with the situation. And in my opinion it was just what the Doctor ordered.

FINGLETON, THE CRICKET WRITER
By *Michael Parkinson*
(FOREWORD TO FINGLETON'S *BATTING FROM MEMORY*, 1981)

THE joy of being a true lover of cricket is that the season never ends. When winter comes we have its literature to sustain us, to carry us through the dreary days by reviving memories of seasons long burned out. We are lucky in that the game attracts and stirs the imagination of creative writers; no sport has a more varied and rich treasury of poetry and prose.

The men who write about the game remind me irresistibly of the men who play it. A Cardus essay is an innings by Graveney, all elegance and silken flow. John Arlott is Len Hutton, superb technique and classic style. To read Robertson-Glasgow and Ian Peebles is to watch an over by Johnny Wardle at his most humorous and imaginative; while Jack Fingleton, the man who has set down his life story in this book, writes about the game in a way which Keith Miller played it, which is to say in his own inimitable fashion.

John Lovesey, the Sports Editor of the *Sunday Times,* and a friend and mentor to both Jack and myself, once told me that when he came new to the job and looked for the first time at an article by Jack Fingleton he wondered how he might edit it. To his trained eye the writing lacked form and structure, it did not conform to accepted patterns of journalism. He brooded a long time about the problem and then made a startling discovery; namely, the secret of editing an article by Jack Fingleton is to leave it alone.

Quite simply his journalistic style is unique. It's a combination of gossipy information, blunt judgment and telling anecdotes, all seasoned with a dash of humour. What Jack Fingleton illuminates (and has always done so) is what a lot of us tend to forget: that cricket is not only the loveliest and most difficult of games but also the most humorous. And, in doing so, he puts into proper perspective the fundamental truth that any sporting pursuit, whether it be as complicated and cerebral as cricket or as simple as soccer, is, when all is said and done, only a game.

Jack Fingleton knows better than most the certain truth of cricket's proper place in the order of things because, for most of his journalistic career, he has reported the doings of politicians in the Australian Parliament. And no matter how beguiling the sound of willow on leather, no matter how seductive the smell of new mown grass or the sight of flannelled fools flitting o'er the greensward, he knows, more certainly than most, that these sensations are insignificant compared to the decisions that men make on behalf of mankind.

His years as a parliamentary reporter have also given him a sharp insight into both the foolishness and the grandeur of man. Of all my friends, many gifted with great perception, I am acquainted with no-one who can make a sharper and sounder assessment of his fellow man than Jack Fingleton. It was he who befriended Harold Larwood at a time when the majority of Australians believed him to be the Devil incarnate, discovering beneath the fearsome aspect, the simplicity, courage and essential niceness of the man.

It was he, in one of his best essays, who sensed that the traditional enmity between an Australian cricket team playing Yorkshire was not, as commonly supposed, caused by two conflicting and thereby varying philosophies. Rather, the conflict was due to two tribes of blood brothers competing for a reputation which, both truly believed, belonged to them. Moreover, each was agreed (but would never admit it) that if it didn't belong to one it belonged to the other, and the rest weren't worth bothering about.

I knew Jack Fingleton before I met him and, in truth, was a little hesitant in making proper contact with someone I admired so much as a writer and broadcaster. I needn't have bothered. The writer is the man. The image on the screen is not the disguise but the real person.

When, in 1979, I went to Australia to do a series of television shows, I was saddened how little his reputation mattered in his own country. Therefore it delighted me beyond measure when he came on my show and, simply by being himself, reminded his countrymen that he was a very remarkable and singular man. His television style, like his writing, is unique. And, as with editing his copy, the way to interview Jack Fingleton is not to try.

During the course of that interview, another one when I returned to Australia in 1980 and again in England later the same year, he told jokes with the timing of a comedian, rattled through 'On Ilkley Moor B'aht at', flirted with actresses, gave advice to trades union leaders and enraptured the audience with anecdotes about everyone from Bradman to Jack Kennedy, Trevor Howard to Douglas Jardine. But through it all shone his own distinctive humour. When I asked him to do the second interview in Australia he agreed, but worried about the wisdom of it. After all, his first interview had been little short of sensational, and he felt he couldn't top it. He said he'd go away for a while and think about what he might do on the show to make it different. For my own part I was perfectly happy for Jack to come on and do exactly what he had done before, namely be himself. The night before the show I had a call from Jack.

'I've been thinking about tomorrow,' he said.

'Come up with any ideas?' I asked.

'Think so. Tell me, have you ever had anyone croak on your show?' he said.

Just a couple more things I know about Jack Fingleton which I'll mention because I know he won't. Sir Robert Menzies, a fair all-rounder himself, described him as the best of cricket writers. Harold Larwood, not much given to excessive praise of anyone, particularly batsmen wearing baggy green caps whom he bowled at, told me that Fingo was simply *the* bravest of cricketers he bowled against.

I never saw him play, but I have come to know the man. He is a beguiling mixture: a humorist who is never flippant, a serious man but not po-faced. He is someone of deeply-held beliefs, but never censorious of others. He has walked with kings and commoners, fools and wise men, and never been anything but his own man. My only regret is that I might have met him sooner, and known him the better and the longer.

———————

VICTOR TRUMPER

A LAW UNTO HIMSELF
By M. A. Noble
(FROM HIS THE GAME'S THE THING, SYDNEY, 1926)

MY first recollection of Trumper was at school. He came just as I was leaving. A short, spare, narrow-shouldered boy, he did not inspire one with the idea of athleticism in any direction, yet it was not long before some of the old brigade were asking: "Have you seen Trumper playing for Crown Street School? He is going to be a champion." His admirers little knew how true their prophecy would be. But his triumph was not instantaneous.

When he was old enough (seventeen years) he joined the South Sydney first grade club and played with it for two seasons (1894–1896). In the club games he did not perform any great feats, but was considered good enough to be included in the team of Colts to play for New South Wales against England (Stoddart's XI). When the day of the match arrived he was very unwell and his mother pleaded with him to withdraw from the team. But, for fear that people should think he had funked, he resolved to battle it out, and that was the day on which he started to climb the ladder of fame, not rung by rung, but by bounds that carried him to the top in a remarkably short space of time. In making 67 against the bowling of such men as Lockwood, Peel and Humphreys, the lob expert, he completely astonished everyone by his versatility and his utter contempt for regulation stokes.

But, much as his batting was admired, there were many who shook their heads and said: "He is too flash; he cannot last. His methods are not those of a great batsman." How Victor dumb-founded those wiseheads of the older school is now a matter of history. But I must not forget to mention that on his return home from the match he went to bed and remained there for several days.

Soon afterwards he was sent for by the manager of the New South Wales team, then on its annual visit to Melbourne and Adelaide, and played against South Australia, but met with no success. Later the same season he was given a place in the New South Wales team against Queensland, but made only 6 and 5 (not out). It looked as if his critics were right, and so he was left out of representative cricket for the next two years. In 1896 he transferred to the Paddington Club, of which I was a member, and the following year (1897–98) achieved a run of success that has never been equalled in Australian cricket. In eight innings he scored 1021 runs and was three times not out, making his average 204.20.

Curiously enough, when selected against Stoddart's second team that season he made only 5 and 0. If he had little success with the bat, however, he made amends on the field by bringing about Hayward's dismissal with, perhaps, the most sensational and spectacular catch ever seen in the out-field. Hayward hit a ball which I bowled, long and low over mid-off's head. Calculating where it would lodge, Victor dashed in at top speed, made a baseball dive at the ball, caught it, turned a somersault, and finished on his back with the ball in one hand held high in the air. It was a catch such as one sees but few of in a lifetime. From that match onward Trumper became permanently associated with New South Wales cricket.

Before dealing in further detail with Victor's cricket career — which is the main purpose of this chapter — I should like, just briefly, to mention a few facts connected with the man himself. On leaving school he became a teacher for a short time, then accepted a position in the New South Wales Government Stores Department, and, later still, transferral to the Probate Office, where, under the wing of Mr T.W. Garrett, the old international cricketer, he received much advice and encouragement. About this time several of his friends urged him to open a sports depot in Sydney, but he resolutely refused to do so on the ground that it might injure Syd Gregory (also of international cricket fame) who was running a similar business. When the latter gave up his depot, however, Victor opened a shop in conjunction with Hanson Carter, the great international wicket-keeper. Subsequently he joined J.J. Giltinan (the international umpire) in a cricket depot and mercery business. It is worthy of note, in passing, that these two were primarily responsible for the establishment of the Northern Union Rugby League in opposition to the New South Wales Rugby Union — a football force that has grown in strength and popularity ever since.

When Giltinan left the business, Victor took Mr Dodge into partnership, and, later still, joined Mr King in a wholesale tie business. But none of these ventures were financially successful. Victor was not the sort of man to succeed in commercial pursuits. He was too soft-hearted, too generous. As an instance of this, I remember how, at the beginning of one season, a team of newsboys came to his shop to buy some cricket material. Victor helped them to select it, then, looking at the few shillings they had collected, handed them the lot for nothing. But the newsboys did not forget it, and at Christmas time they bought a pair of vases with the money and presented them to their hero. Till the end of his days I believe these were among the most cherished of Victor's possessions. They meant more to him than all the gold and silver ware that later came his way.

His generous nature, however, was often imposed upon, especially by "cadgers" and seekers after free tickets to the cricket matches. Both at his shop and in the streets he used to be pestered by them, and many a time have I seen him, outside the Cricket Ground, if he could not give a ticket, give the necessary amount in cash to pay the entrance fee. I could relate scores of incidents to illustrate this side of Victor's nature, but one more will do. Coming out of the London Coliseum one cold wet night he saw a boy shivering in a doorway selling music. Victor broke away from the rest of us, spoke to the lad, bought the whole of his stock-in-trade and sent the youngster home happy.

Victor's modesty was one of his most charming qualities, yet it was often taken for stand-offishness, even among those who should have known him better. On one occasion, just prior to the departure of the Australian team for England, Jim Kelly, Trumper, and I were being entertained at a farewell banquet by the Paddington Cricket Club. Nothing we could do would induce Victor to sit anywhere but at the back of the hall, and even when his health was being drunk he resolutely refused to join us at the front. That was typical of the man. The only thing he hated about his cricket success was the notoriety it brought him. He was innately shy and was more nervous walking off the field amidst the deafening cheers of the crowd than he was when facing the best bowling in the world.

He hated display of every description and took very little pride in his own appearance either on or off the field (the privilege of genius). His cricket-bag was a byword among his team mates. Held together by a strap at each end, the lock being broken, it was invariably full to bursting with clothes pushed in and jumped on. It was as funny as a circus to watch his futile efforts to close the bag. It did not worry him in the slightest that his cricketing uniform was disgracefully creased, neither did the jocular epithets hurled at him ruffle his composure.

He had only one interesting mannerism on the field that I can recollect. When he was bowled early in his innings, he would, before leaving the crease for the pavilion, stoop, pick up the bail and put it back in position on the stumps, as though he were sorry for and trying to make amends for his failure.

But to return to cricket: In the season 1898–99 a very handsome shield was offered for the highest aggregate in international cricket. Towards the end of the season Victor was well behind, requiring about 200 runs in order to have a chance. When he left his home on the morning of the last match he said to his mother: "I'm going to get you that shield today," and, to the surprise of everyone, he did. He won it with an aggregate of 674 runs, 253 of which he made in the final match.

It was a great delight to me when, after strongly advocating Trumper's inclusion in the 1899 team for England, and having given up hope — for the team had been finally selected — Major Wardill, the manager, came to me towards the end of the third trial match, in Adelaide, and said: "Do you want Victor Trumper to go to England?" "Rather," I replied. "Well," he said, "you can go and tell him that he is selected." I could hardly believe my ears, for I had been greatly disappointed at his non-inclusion and, as we were then on the eve of our departure, had quite given up any idea of having him in the team.

Most of the opposition to his inclusion came from Victoria and Adelaide, for, they said, and with plenty of justification: "We have good young cricketers with records to prove their ability. And, in any case, we haven't seen Trumper." That was just what we had been telling them. They had not seen him; "but once you do," we declared, "there will be no doubt in your minds." That prediction was fully borne out in the trial matches played in Melbourne and Adelaide.

Strange to say, though I was so keen on his inclusion, to my great disgust I was the very unwilling instrument in his dismissal on two occasions during these trials. The Sydney one in particular was exceedingly trying. I was bowling. He had made 26 when he hit a catch back. As it came along the thought ran through my mind, "Miss it, miss it." It was not an easy catch and could very easily have been dropped without creating suspicion; but I did not miss it. My disappointment at his dismissal was, I believe, greater than his.

It was not long afterwards, however, that he thoroughly earned his selection — and I had no regrets. One incident which, I believe, helped very largely in securing his selection was a visit of the late Mr J. McLaughlin, a vice-president of the Melbourne Cricket Club, to Sydney to see a trial match. He journeyed to Waverley where the local club was playing Paddington and saw Victor play one of his masterpieces for 260 not out. Mr McLaughlin at once recognised his genius and was not long in expressing his opinions to the cricketers of Melbourne.

The innings which opened England's eyes to his outstanding ability was his 135 (not out) in the Test Match at Lord's in 1899. He was then twenty-one years of age and looked younger. Australia had opened badly and no one could foretell what would happen till Trumper joined Clem Hill (who got 135) and the pair gave a glorious exhibition. The partnership put Australia in an unbeatable position, and, in conjunction with some fine bowling by Jones and Laver, eventually won for us the only finished game of that series.

Later in the same tour (in the fourth Test, at Manchester) Victor played a masterly innings for 63 when runs were very badly needed. It was the last day of the match. Australia had followed on 176 in arrears. Some of this deficit had been wiped off at the end of the second day's play, but heavy rain came that night, and the next morning the wicket was pretty bad. Victor came in and, while I stone-walled, he knocked the bowlers off their length, making it much easier for his partner than it would otherwise have been. Eventually we were able to make a creditable draw after being in an apparently hopeless position.

The summer of 1902 was a very wet one, and bad wickets prevailed during the whole English tour, yet Trumper made 2570 runs, including 11 centuries, and was, of course, the mainstay of the team. We invariably drove to the cricket grounds in a charabanc, Joe Darling, the captain, being always first aboard. He was very severe on the laggards and a heavy fine was imposed on those arriving on the field late. Sometimes, I fancy, he had the impression that, provided Vic and a few others were there, nothing else mattered, for, when the time arrived to leave, he would look around and ask "Is Vic here?" If the reply was "Yes" he would tell the driver to go on, without even troubling to inquire if any were missing.

Victor was a law unto himself. You could talk to him and coach him; he would listen carefully, respect your advice and opinions, and, leaving you, would forget all you had told him, play as he wanted to play, and thereby prove that, although you might be right, he knew a better method. He would hit the first ball in a Test Match for four if it suited him. Sometimes, but not often, this would lead to his early downfall. It is necessary for most batsmen to play the game for a few overs before unfolding their strokes. Not so with Victor. He was off at the jump, making an amazing stroke off a ball which would probably have clean bowled most of his comrades. His defence was his offence. If, on a bad wicket, a left-hander was troubling anyone, he would immediately set about knocking him off, and generally succeed in doing so.

Perhaps his finest innings on a bad wicket was in a Test Match at Melbourne in 1904, when he made 74 out of 122 runs. He was so severe on a famous left-hand bowler that the latter gave up bowling at the wicket and plied him with off-theory — a complete triumph of the bat over the ball on such a "glue-pot." On another occasion, when New South Wales was playing Victoria, J.V. Saunders, bowling on a bad wicket (at Sydney) beat him twice in the first over. After that he gave them the long handle and made 100 before lunch, that is, from noon to 1.30 p.m.

One well-known bowler worked out a scheme to defeat him in a club match. It was to bowl a ball a yard behind the wicket instead of from the usual crease. This ball came as a surprise and beat the wicket. The next one Victor tipped and it was missed by the wicket-keeper. The third he jumped into and hit with terrific force just over the bowler's head. It went at great pace, straight and low, hit the fence on the full and came back to the bowler who picked it up and went on bowling as though nothing unusual had happened. On that occasion Victor and his partner registered the century in thirty-three minutes.

Victor had a particularly keen dislike for the boaster. He was not resentful, never harboured ill-feeling, and seldom retaliated. If the fate of the match had been decided he would occasionally allow a young bowler to get him out so that he might derive some encouragement thereby; but, if he deemed it necessary, not to show his own superiority, but to administer a corrective to an over-confident opponent, he would drive home the lesson with all the force of his wonderful ability. The following incident is an illustration of this side of his character. On one occasion a young, slow bowler who was about to meet him in a club match, informed his friends that he had developed a ball which would get Trumper any time he like to bowl it. He may have been quite conscientious, but made the mistake of talking about it. It became public property, and eventually reached Victor's ears, without losing anything by constant repetition.

Quite a number of people journeyed to the ground primarily to see the young man make good his boast. Every one was agog with excitement as the captain put him on to bowl. Then the thing happened. As he bowled the first ball Victor went down the wicket after it, and hit it long and low. It bounced over the fence for four. The next hit the fence on the full and bounced back into the playing area. The following four balls were hit out of the ground for six, 32 runs coming from the over thus: 4, 4, 6, 6, 6, 6. The first and second balls of this bowler's next over were played by Victor's partner, who scored one off the second ball. Trumper played the third without scoring, then hit the next three for six each. Thus he received ten balls and scored 50 runs off nine in five and a quarter minutes. Needless to say the young bowler was taken off, a sadder and wiser man.

In another premiership match, playing for Paddington against Redfern, Trumper made 335 in two hours forty minutes, being associated with D.A. Gee (172) in a first wicket partnership of 423. It is worth noting that only 5 were allowed for over the fence in those days, not 6 as at present. This meant that the batsmen had to change ends each time the ball went over the pickets. The bombardment of these two batsmen was so great outside the playing area that a game of bowls which was in progress just outside the cricket ground, and in which the late Hon. James McGowen, afterwards premier of New South Wales, was engaged, had to be discontinued owing to the danger from balls landing on the green from the lusty strokes of the batsmen next door.

Perhaps the greatest tribute ever paid Trumper was the statement of the English bowlers in 1902. "As batsmen you can have Jackson, Fry,. MacLaren and Ranjitsinhji," they said; "there is only one Trumper." When he played his great innings of 185 (not out) against Warner's team in 1903-4, Braund was bowling leg-theory, with most of the fieldsmen on the on-side. Victor stepped to leg and continually back-cut him to the fence. Braund afterwards said: "It didn't matter where I pitched the ball, Trumper could hit it into three different places in the field."

Bowlers frequently appealed for l.b.w. against him, only to find that the bat had connected at the last moment. Fast bowlers particularly appealed when they sent down a yorker on the leg-stump before the foot was removed and a beautiful on-side shot resulted. He made great players at the other end look like schoolboys by comparison; often have I seen them stand staring with astonishment at the audacity of his strokes. When he made 300 (not out) against Sussex in 1899, I asked Joe Darling, who was 70 (not out), when the innings was closed: "What do you think of the boy?" "What do I think of him?" he replied; "I thought I could bat!"

Every stroke he made seemed to be absolutely correct and he was always in the best position to make it. Even when he changed his mind, which he often did, he was invariably in position and the stroke seemed the only possible one to make. In many ways he reminded me of a great orator. You follow the discourse, even anticipate correctly the words he is going to use — it all seems so natural and easy — yet, if you try to do it yourself you fail miserably. He would pick up a bat everyone else had scorned, go in and make a century with it, come out and say: "What is wrong with the bat; it is a very good one." He never used a cover for the best handle. Both he and Reggie Duff, Australia's brilliant opening pair, used to roughen the handle string with a piece of glass and apply powdered resin. He disliked chamois leather and rubber covers because, he said, they interfered with the instinctive movement of the hands. He like the weight of the bat to be more in the centre back than is customary, and for that reason would shave off some of the lower and thicker portion of the hump in order to secure a more even distribution of weight.

It was not generally known that Victor was an excellent bowler in his earlier days. He bowled a very fast ball and introduced variety by occasionally sending up a slow one with exactly the same action. He was also a wonderful long-distance thrower of the cricket ball. In a competition held on the Sydney Cricket Ground he threw 115 yards while standing still and 125 yards with a run.

Although very strong physically, Victor had not a robust constitution, and when, at the age of thirty, he contracted scarlet fever, it seemed to undermine his health. Yet he never complained. He continued to play, and occasionally we got a glimpse of his real genius. Two seasons later (in 1909) he left the Paddington and joined up with the Gordon Cricket Club and played with the latter for six seasons. His last cricket tour was to New Zealand with Arthur Sims's team in 1914, in the course of which he made one brilliant stand (258), against Canterbury at Christchurch, he and Sims putting on 433 for the eighth wicket. It was a remarkable innings, the score being compiled at the rate of over 100 runs per hour. He did just as he liked with the bowling and provided a batting feast for the New Zealanders such as they had never seen before.

That was his last great effort. Soon afterwards he became ill, Bright's disease developed, and he lingered on till June, 1915, when he died in great pain at his home at Chatswood. The irony of it. He was a teetotaller, a non-smoker; he never gambled, and he never kept late hours. Indeed, he was such a clean liver and had such a wholesome mental outlook that one would have expected him to live his full measure of the allotted span. But it was not to be. The last person he would have thought of taking care of was himself. No matter how much his friends remonstrated with him, he would only reply, "Oh, I'm all right," and look around for an opportunity to do someone else a good turn. He was considerate, kind, and unselfish to a degree.

He was lovable, genial, modest and humble, absolutely without conceit. He was as clean in mind as he was generous in spirit. He always had a kindly thought for others, particularly for the down-and-outs. He never stopped to ask if a case was a deserving one. To him all under-dogs were "poor chaps" and if he could help them by word or deed so much the better. That was the spirit that endeared him to us all. The funeral was a great public one, attended by many international and inter-state cricketers, and as it passed through the streets of Sydney on its way to the cemetery, tens of thousands paid their last tribute of respect to the greatest, yet most modest, batsman the world has known.

THE GREAT TRUMPER
By Victor Daley

Ho statesman, patriot, bards make way!
Your fame has sunk to zero:
For Victor Trumper is today our one Australian hero.
High purpose glitters in his eye,
He scorns the filthy dollar;
His splendid neck, says Mrs Fry,
Is innocent of collar. . .
Is there not, happily, in the land some native borne Murillo to
    paint,
In colours rich and grand,
This wielder of the willow?
Nay, rather let a statue be erected his renown to,
That future citizens might see the Gods their sires bow down to.
Evo, evo, Trumper!
As for me it all ends with the moral that fame grows on the willow
    tree
And no more on the laurel.

VICTOR'S SLEEVES
By Tom Horan

I remember the first time ever Victor put 'em on. I mean the pads, and I am referring to the first time I saw him shape at the practice nets on the Melbourne Cricket Ground. That was at Christmas time, 1897. He did not play in that match against Victoria, but going on to South Australia he was included a week later in the New South Wales eleven, and performed well. While on the Melbourne ground the veteran Harry Hilliard introduced me to him, and I was struck by the frank, engaging facial expression of the young Sydneyite. After a few words he went away, and old Harry said to me, "That lad will have to be reckoned with later on." My word! But do you know what particularly attracted my attention when first I saw Victor fielding. You wouldn't guess it in three. It was the remarkably neat way in which his shirt sleeves were folded. No loose, dangling down, and folding back again after a run for the ball, but always trim and artistic. It is a small thing, perhaps, to some, but to me it counts and suggests a good deal.

CLEM HILL'S DEBT TO TRUMPER
By Clem Hill

THE second Test in 1899 was the game Australia won by 10 wickets, and it was the match when I reached the height of my ambition — a century in a Test match at Lord's. It was also the contest in which Vic Trumper got his first century in a Test. What a lot other batsmen have owed to Trumper! In that particular game Mead was worrying me, although I was feeling quite at home to all the other bowlers. I casually mentioned the matter to Trumper, who promptly replied: "You stop up the other end and I will have a go and will try to knock him off." He did so, for during the next two overs he treated Mead in such a manner that the English captain could not get him off quickly enough.

TRUMPER
By A. H. Garnsey
(THE CRICKETER, 1930)

HE handles his bat like a whip, does he,
As if 'twere a rod such as anciently
   Was wielded by Roman Lictor.
He cuts and he pulls 'em for fours and for fives,
He glances and hooks, he pushes and drives,
   And piles up the centuries — Victor!

He runs like a hare, he is brilliant at slip,
Or long-off for a change, and his throw comes clip,
   Right into a grip of the stumper;
Has the safest of hands for all species of catch,
Can bowl a good ball — oh, where is the match
   Of the trump of Australia — Trumper!

The pluck of a hero, a veteran's head,
And modest withal, though his fame it has spread
   To the limits of Empire. A bumper!
We'll call it, and take the goodwill for the deed.
(He drinks not, nor smokes, let us follow his lead),
   Here's health to you, Vic. — Victor Trumper.

TRUMPER'S SUPERSTITIONS
By Clem Hill

WITH ALL his greatness the crack right-hander was superstitious. Bowlers had no terrors for him, sticky or fiery wickets did not unnerve him in the slightest, but he had a decided objection to members of the cloth. At Manchester on one occasion after he had missed the bus, he came back into the dressing-room and said, "I knew I wouldn't score with all those parsons hanging round our pavilion; why don't they keep to the collection plate, or marry people, instead of coming worrying us Australians?"

Trumper always wore an old Australian Eleven cap. It was bottle green, but nevertheless he stuck to it to the end, and there was always no end of bother if Duff or some of the other humourists of the side got hold of the cap and hid it. He could make runs with any old bat. Just as we were beginning a county contest on one occasion an amateur bat-maker came along with a most unwieldy looking piece of willow, which weighed well over 3lb., and asked Vic. whether he would try it. Trumper said, "Yes, so long as it's got a spring in it." He made 100 with it straight away. He had wonderful wrist power, and could almost bend the spring of a bat in two. He played some wonderful knocks in England, but one stands out above all others, his 135 not out at Lord's — his first Test century and also his first century in Great Britain.

A BATSMAN OF THE THOROUGHBRED ORDER
By 'Long Leg'
(SPORTING LIFE, 1915)

NO OTHER batsman has played cricket with greater grace or attractiveness. There was charm in all he did. His every shot had distinction, and at his best his innings, even his shorter innings, could be described as masterpieces of artistic cricket. His was essentially the thoroughbred order of batsmanship.

The gods had been wonderfully good to him from the physical point of view. If ever a man was built to play cricket well and delightfully, it was Victor Trumper. A wonderful eye (wonderful is the only word), a wonderful pair of wrists, and a wonderful looseness of limb — all these were his, and the wonderful combination of it all enabled him to play wonderful cricket. "All eye and whipcord," he was once described as, and the description was very apt. His eye was his greatest asset. Next came his wrists. All his strokes, even his defensive stroke, were colored by wrist-work.

But, of course, his exceptional physical advantages would have profited him little had he not had an exceedingly practical method. C.B. Fry said of him that "he has no style and yet he is all style," and the truth of the seeming paradox will be appreciated by all who saw Trumper play. He was orthodox in so much as he kept his bat very straight when he chose, used his feet correctly, and unless the situation was such as to make "hoisting" good policy — say on a heavy ground — he kept the ball well down. But so great was his quickness of eye and wrist and foot that he could cut balls that would to ordinary men have been good length off the middle stump for four; he could step back and hit decent length straight balls to square leg; and such was the perfection of his timing, such was the perfect harmony of wrist and eye, that he has been known to turn to the on-side boundary a fast yorker dead on the leg stump! In brief, he was a genius. With the exception of "Ranji", no one within the memory of living man has been so quick with his bat. How vividly he comes back. The slight lithe figure, easily posed, with the straight blue eyes square on the bowler, with the bat nursed close to the legs, that were eased at the knees to facilitate a quick dash up the pitch, or a movement right back on the stumps. And then came the judgment of the ball, earlier in its flight than would be possible to most men, and the stroke flowing out as effortlessly as a swan swims. There was about all he did an air of consummate naturalness. No flurry or hurry or jerk. That is why the most daring things he did appeared perfectly easy and orthodox. For him to hit a good length breaking ball to the boundary seemed the only possible thing to do with it — as proper a stroke as the ordinary first class batsman's back-stroke applied to a similar type of ball. He always seemed as if himself and the bat were of a piece. To put the case in another way, the bat worked in such unison with the rest of his movements as to suggest that it was an extra limb.

But for all his lithe movements, his rapidity of action, he was never what could be called a strong man. Long ago it was rumoured that he was threatened with consumption.

His face was tanned, his eye was clear, but even in 1905 there was a strained look about him. He was too fine drawn for health. And yet, something like a contradiction to his appearance — and a very real contradiction, so it seemed, to the "rumors" — was given by his lithe movement, his obvious joy of life. Quite unassuming, he was a man who found delight in the touch of the sun, the green of the turf, the scents and sounds of the open-air life. Had you asked him to decline Mensa, or to explain the first proposition of the first book of Euclid, you would probably have stumped him first ball, as it were. But he knew all about birds and the way to grow things.

TRUMPER'S BURIAL
By W. Walsh, an old Goulburn cricketer

VICTOR Trumper was buried in the Waverley Cemetery, a charming site, overlooking a vast expanse of the Pacific Ocean. The waters were calm, glorious sunshine overhead, and the blue sky flecked by fleecy clouds. The coffin was borne from the hearse to the grave on the shoulders of M.A. Noble, A. Cotter, H. Carter, S. Gregory, Warren Bardsley, and another. I was subsequently informed he was Warwick Armstrong, but I failed to recognise him. They were his worthy allies in the contests on the various cricket fields of the world, and it was fitting that the final post of honour should be allotted to them. Clem Hill was absent, but we all felt that he was there in spirit, for he had a great regard for Victor. As the coffin was being lowered M.A. Noble showed much emotion, and so did Warren Bardsley. The scene was pathetic, and I think appealed to most of us as a practical sermon of life. All the mourners have gone home, and I am alone looking out over the ocean. Victor died of Bright's disease. His kidneys wasted away.

> "There is no death!
> What seems so is transition;
> This life of mortal breath
> Is but a suburb of the life Elysian,
> Whose portal we call death."

BETWEEN
THE WARS

HALFORD HOOKER'S HAPPY CHRISTMAS
By Arthur Mailey
(FROM *SUNDAY TELEGRAPH*, SYDNEY)

DEBONAIR Halford Hooker, 11th man, joined Alan Kippax. New South Wales were 263 behind on the first innings, and the result was a foregone conclusion.

'I'll try to hang around for a couple of overs, "Kippy," while you have a little practice for the next Test match,' said Hooker.

We though tail-ender Hooker would do well if he kept his wicket intact even for one over.

'Dainty' Ironmonger, 'Rock' Blackie, 'Stork' Hendry, and other Victorian bowlers, scenting a cheap wicket, were almost fighting over the ball.

The early New South Wales wickets had crashed. In fact, when Hooker joined Kippax the score was nine for 113.

'Come on, "Hook",' said Jack Ellis, the Victorian wicket-keeper, impatiently, 'let's get it over.'

Hooker and Kippax began, and when stumps were drawn on Christmas Eve they had carried the score to 117. New South Wales were still more than 250 runs behind on the first innings.

The Victorian bowlers said that Hooker had a Chinaman's luck, otherwise he would have been out before 6 o'clock.

Next day, in front of about 200 spectators, Kippax and Hooker again faced the strong Victorian attack.

Kippax played for the strike, and the pair were still together at lunch time.

'Gosh! This is funny. They'll get a shock up in Sydney when they hear that we're in at lunch time,' said Hooker.

The Victorian dressing-room was about as congenial as a creditors' meeting.

'Stone the crows!' roared Jack Ellis. 'I'll eat my gloves if I couldn't bowl better than you fellows.'

Considering Ellis's gloves had been padded with obsolete beef steak for a couple of hours, his was no mean boast.

'We'll get him after lunch,' chorused the Victorian bowlers.

It was Christmas Day, but the Victorians only toyed with their roast chicken and plum pudding.

The score board at lunch showed nine for 150.

Kippax continued to play for the strike, and his score mounted towards the century.

Hooker seldom scored. He was content to play out unfinished overs.

The news of the amazing stand filtered through Melbourne, and at tea time on Christmas Day the crowd had increased from 200 to about 10,000.

And for the first time in the history of cricket, or any other game, Victorian barrackers were barracking for New South Wales.

Halford Hooker sat sipping his tea as he looked across at the scoring board.

'Am I dreaming? Or is this real? Are we still batting? Our names are still up on the board, "Kip." '

After tea the Victorian bowlers were done to a frazzle, but still Hooker kept on the even tenor of his way, and made no attempt to force the scoring. Fieldsmen came in to within a few feet of his bat.

'I don't mind your standing there,' said Hooker to one daring suicide fieldsman, 'but must you breathe on the back of my neck?'

One over to go before stumps. Ryder threw the ball to Baring.

'What'll I bowl, Jack?'

'Anything you like, Fred. Full tosses, long hops, shooters, wides, anything at all.'

Then he called Baring aside.

'Keep Hooker away from the bowling, so that we can open out on him with fresh bowlers in the morning,' he said.

One ball to go.

Kippax strolled down to Hooker, 'Run for your life, "Hook," as soon as the ball is bowled,' he whispered.

Barling bowled a double wide on the off.

Hooker almost raced the ball through the air.

Kippax rushed out, blocked the ball, and scrambled for the other end.

Jack Ellis, with a face as red as an embarrassed turkey, sensed the move, and pounced on the ball like lightning.

He looked back at the wicket, but Hooker was well in. Then he prepared to throw at "Kippy's" wicket, but was too late.

He spat in the dust disgustedly, and gasped an uncomplimentary remark about tail-enders.

At the end of the day, Kippax had taken his score to 220, while his steadfast and faithful companion had scored 7!

The most pleased man on the ground was the caterer.

When play began on Christmas Day and the crowd was 200, he spent the morning looking for a revolver and a quiet place.

The hundreds of pounds' worth of food which looked like being wasted was sold out by 6 p.m.

Hooker, showing definite signs of wear, meandered back to the dressing-room.

'What are your impressions of the day's play, Mr. Hooker?' asked a bright young newspaper man.

'Well,' he said, 'the accuracy of the Victorian bowlers was amazing. How they bowled through that lane of fieldsmen all day without hitting one was remarkable.'

On the third day of the partnership, Hooker's hip pocket bulged.

He was carrying a pair of shrunken woollen socks that had brought him luck in previous contests.

They were too small to wear, but, to use 'Hook's' own words, he 'always liked to have them around the house.'

Again the two New South Wales batsmen defied the Victorian bowlers, and shortly before lunch the long-looked-for run which gave them victory was posted on the board.

Then Hooker went mad. In half an hour he scored 50 runs, and was batting like a champion.

This, I feel, was the greatest partnership ever made in cricket.

The pair added 307 runs for the last wicket — a world's record.

Kippax made 260 not out, and Hooker 62. New South Wales totalled 420 in reply to Victoria's 376.

The feat would have been extraordinary, even if two class batsmen had performed it but it must not be forgotten that Hooker was an absolute rabbit, and the Victorians were fielding their best bowling side.

BILL O'REILLY
By Neville Cardus
(PLAYFAIR CRICKET MONTHLY, JUNE, 1964)

WILLIAM Joseph O'Reilly ('Bill' for short) was one of the most skilful of bowlers, and very hostile on his day — which occurred too frequently for the liking of most batsmen. Off the field he would beam on the most prolific of run-makers. On the field he disliked all opposing batsmen at sight. His Australian colleagues called him 'The Tiger'. Whenever he was driven in front of the wicket for four, his Irish 'Paddy' would be seen almost visibly to rise. He would glower down the pitch, his attitude a whole vocabulary of invective in itself. His next ball would most likely be delivered with a view to rendering stumps, batsman and all, momentarily recumbent. He was, in fact, a bowler mainly of medium to slow pace, commanding extraordinary changes of flight. But without palpable alteration of action he could send down a really formidably fast ball — a catapult of a ball. He brought his right arm over quicker than the keenest eye or anticipation would infer from the rhythm of his action in general. You would not truthfully say his action was rhythmical at all. He ran lumberingly to the wicket, like a man going uphill in the face of a strong wind. He bent his right knee very much, and awkwardly, as the arm came over in a windmill swoop. Yet it was a strongly concentrated action at the moment of the ball's propulsion. The bent right knee allowed him to get a lot of flight, a lot of 'air', at his end. His slow (and disguisedly slow) 'googly' had a surprising bounce from the earth. This was the bait for a catch to the 'short-leg' trap, rapaciously led by Jack Fingleton. In his repertory was contained nearly every device known to the bowler's art. Bradman argued that the probability was that O'Reilly was a greater bowler even than S. F. Barnes, maintaining that O'Reilly was master of all the tricks known to Barnes — spin, flight, length and so on — and also he could bowl the 'googly', which Barnes didn't.

When I put this argument to Barnes himself he meditated a while, then said, 'It's quite true that I didn't bowl a "googly". I never needed it.'

In Test matches O'Reilly took 144 wickets, average 22.59, 102 against England at 25.36 each. Barnes's wickets against Australia amounted to 106, at 24 runs each. We need to bear in mind, as we compare these two bowling geniuses — not to belittle but to glorify each — that O'Reilly had to get his wickets and his work done on pitches which were, over a long period, much more favourable to batsmen than those of Barnes's period, especially those in England. O'Reilly took 52 of his 102 Test wickets against England in Australia, at a time when pitches there were hard and without flaw for days. O'Reilly, in fact, was the product of cricket as it was played on heavily-rolled wickets and grassless. Also he was brought up in a period which, in Australia, insisted that all Test matches should be played to a finish. In short, O'Reilly learned his comprehensive arts against heavy odds to bowlers, against some of England's most thoroughbred batsmen enjoying heavenly conditions in which to make their strokes. In Test matches O'Reilly's opposition (and victims) usually consisted of such as Hammond, Sutcliffe, Leyland, Paynter, Jardine, Hendren, Walters and, at the close of his playing career, Hutton and Compton. He had the stamina to support the heat and burden of the most scorching days. At

Old Trafford in 1934, England batted first under a blazing sun, temperature 90° in the shade. In sixty-five minutes England scored 68, C. F. Walters magnificently cutting and driving 52 of these runs. Then O'Reilly actually dismissed Walters, Wyatt and Hammond in one over. Nonetheless, England's total reached 627 — 9 declared; O'Reilly bowled 59 overs for 189 runs and 7 wickets. At Kennington Oval in August 1938, as every schoolboy knows or should know, England scored 903 — 7 wickets declared, Hutton 364. In this gigantic longitudinal innings of England's O'Reilly bowled 85 overs for 178 runs and 3 wickets. When Hutton passed the existing record of an individual total in a Test match the crowd rose to acclaim the hero. The Australians gathered round him shaking his hand — all except O'Reilly who, the first to see drinks being carried onto the field, made a bee-line for them. Years afterwards, when he was sitting in the Press Box at Sydney reporting on an Australia v. England Test match on a hot day, I asked him, 'Don't you ever wish, Bill, that you were out there in the middle again?' 'No,' he promptly replied, 'it's easier work here.'

For a great bowler he certainly gave the impression that he was often labouring and sweating. Sometimes he became curiously negative, pegging away on the leg stump, particularly on Hammond's leg stump, supported by the legtrap. At such moments I would ask myself, 'Is he truly a great, as distinguished from an extremely good, bowler?' Batsmen also seemed to lull themselves with some similar quietist view of O'Reilly's attack. And, like dwellers on the slopes of Mount Vesuvius in a calm season, they would become easily complacent. Then the O'Reilly eruption would break out. No warning. A rush of blood to O'Reilly's head, plenty of it Irish. He would galvanise his run, his arms flailed the air, the swing over of the arm was convulsive, the ball delivered was an expletive. The batsmen, comfortable only a moment ago in the sunshine, were overwhelmed, uprooted, 'assaulted and — possibly — foxed out'.

O'Reilly's balding head shone in the burning light of day. In Australia I have seen him shaking off drops of honest sweat. He stood six feet two inches high, and was broad-shouldered. As I say, he didn't as a bowler make the most of all this height — at least, the casual observer of him said that he didn't. But many of his victims were lured to their ends because of the slower ball tossed up from the bent right knee. He had in him enough original Irish to know the uses of blarney. At bottom, though, he was a bowler of classic precision of length. He is wrongly put into the category of leg-spinners and 'googly' experimentalists. O'Reilly seldom served up loose or untidy bowling. His 'googly' was never overdone; he used it as bait. He is not properly to be described as a 'back of the hand' spinner. His leg-break was spun by the fingers mainly, with the wrist turned at the last point in the process of motivation — there wasn't a pronounced elbow turn. He liked a dry dusty pitch, as at Nottingham in 1934, when in his first Test match in England he took 11 wickets for 129. Other times, other manners — thirty years ago England batsmen of the calibre of Cyril Walters, Sutcliffe, Hammond, and Hendren regarded as good policy quick strokes while the Australian fast bowlers were getting the shine off the new ball; for they knew that soon O'Reilly and Grimmett would come on with spin, and also with flight asking twenty questions in the air. In the five Test matches of 1934 O'Reilly and Grimmett accounted for 53 of England's wickets between them.

Australia's fast bowler 'Tim' Wall — and he was a very good and really fast bowler — had to be satisfied with 172 overs and 6 wickets. It was a joy to watch the skill, the allurements of flight, the varieties of spin and of length, sent along over and over by these two highly gifted bowlers — Grimmett, silent, stealthy and quizzical, a tiny man of sly humour, his arm as low as his grandfather's, a feline, 'pussy-foot' spinner — and giant O'Reilly, lumbering heavily into action, windmill and bulldozer, yet a wonderful combination of physical effort and well-thought-out strategy. At Sydney in 1936, England lost Arthur Fagg's wicket for 27, in England's first innings on a batsman's firm pitch. In came Hammond in all his majesty. The battle between Hammond and O'Reilly for an hour was as thrilling and as cleverly pointed and counter-pointed as any I have seen on the cricket field between two great players. O'Reilly onslaughted Hammond's bat. He attached his leg-stump, he held back his 'googly', he hurled down his fast one, he exploited his dipper — he gave Wally no rest. At the end, Hammond conquered, 231 not out, his lion's share of England's aggregate of 424 for 6 (declared). But O'Reilly had the last laugh; he had found out during this nobly sustained and endured 231 of Hammond, that England's premier batsman could be tamed by a gnawing length on his leg-stump, or thereabouts. Hammond once again, in 1938, asserted himself in all his claim grandeur against O'Reilly; but, all in all, O'Reilly clipped Hammond's wings incisively enough from 1937 onwards.

Most of England's master batsmen of O'Reilly's heyday agreed that he was the greatest and most versatile bowler of their actual acquaintance. One day, though, at Brisbane, Maurice Leyland, in conversation with O'Reilly before the 1936-7 rubber began, said, 'Well,

Bill, result of this rubber is in lap of gods. But there's one thing Ah can tell you, Bill, and knows it — Ah've got *thee* taped all right': O rare Maurice Leyland! O rare Bill O'Reilly, full of the milk of human kindness, a good son to his mother, friendly and considerate, a nature's gentleman, with Irish in him, wouldn't hurt a mouse — in domestic and private life, well away from a cricket field, a cricket ball, and from sight of an incoming batsman. The 'Tiger' and the lamb. Sometimes they lay down together, the lamb inside the tiger.

THE BIG MAN
By Jack Gregory

WHICHEVER way you like to take it, Warwick Armstrong was the BIG man in Cricket. He knew the game of cricket and was au fait with the ability and temperament of every man in his team, also with those in opposing sides, and he knew when and where to apply the knowledge. His deeds with bat and ball were greater than his bulk, and that's saying something.

Armstrong was one of the wonders of cricket and he played until he was 43, an age at which most cricketers are well and truly in the smoker's stand, criticising.

A writer once said, 'Armstrong's strategy was uncanny. He furnished a revival to cricket that was a salvation, and the greatest batsmen in the world were uneasy when facing him, knowing that some new ruse would be perpetrated by the bulky Victorian.'

I'll not forget my first appearance in a Test Match. It was at Sydney in December, 1920. Strudwick caught me behind off Frank Woolley when I had scored eight. I felt that I had made a poor start, and Armstrong evidently felt that he had to put me at ease. He said, 'Don't worry about the runs; you are in for your bowling.'

It was just the kick I wanted, and, although I knew my skipper was trying to buck me up, the words of encouragement were not wasted. When I got Jack Hobbs clean bowled, Armstrong just grinned and said, 'Any complaints?' No player could complain at this treatment from Armstrong.

Other incidents in that Test will remain in my memory forever. And my performance in getting run-out for a duck is not the only one. I was in with my bulky captain, who was well over the century when I came in ninth. I hit the ball to third man and started to run, when Abe Waddington threw the ball to Strudwick.

I stopped in the middle of the pitch, feeling disgusted at my foolishness, when I saw that Strudwick had fumbled the ball. I made another dash to regain my crease, but was too late.

Armstrong didn't scold me, but he taught me a lesson by asking whose call it was. It was my fault entirely, as I should have waited for a call from Warwick. He went on to make 158.

In England's second innings, Hobbs reached 50 when he was out l.b.w. to Armstrong. I can't recall ever seeing such a battle of wits between two veterans. Armstrong sent up a couple of his leg theory balls, which Hobbs ignored. Anticipating a break in the next Hobbs was surprised to find it was not there, and his pads were in the road. An appeal sent him back to the pavilion, and he was heard to say that Armstrong would never get him like that again.

In the Fourth Test at Melbourne, Armstrong put Mailey wise to the same stunt and Hobbs was out l.b.w. for 13. He fell to the Armstrong ruse, effected by an apt pupil. Mailey put up a few wrong 'uns and then let go a straight one.

Another day on which Warwick showed his greatness was in the Third Test at Adelaide in 1921 and were I not to mention the left-handed catch taken by him in dismissing Douglas, it would be to pass over one of the finest pieces of fielding I have seen.

I was particularly pleased, as I was the bowler. My congratulatory words to my captain were wasted. He only grunted and asked, 'What am I fielding here for?'

Armstrong's consideration for his bowlers was appreciated. He impressed on E. A. McDonald and me that we were to give him the wink when we were feeling the slightest bit tired. He always told us that we could recover from tiredness quicker than from strain.

He opened with McDonald against the wind and me at the other end and Mac was the first to spell. Before the batsmen got used to the fast ones, Warwick and Arthur Mailey would swing into action, and it certainly was a varied attack.

To those who do not know, McDonald and I were totally different bowlers. Mac was faster and he came back from the off, whereas I swung away to the off.

No bowler put more guile into his bowling than Armstrong, and just quietly, but firmly, no batsman ever drove a ball with so much power as he did. I never envied the fieldsman who had to stop his straight drives. Possibly he was the hardest driver the game has known, and that can be easily understood when one recalls the width of his massive shoulders.

Friendships made in cricket are lasting, and I left the game with the happiest memories of the Tours I had with that great leader and cricketer — the greatest of my time — Warwick Armstrong.

GREGORY AND MCDONALD – A COMPARISON
By Bert Oldfield
(FROM HIS *BEHIND THE WICKET*, 1938)

FOR the first time in Test cricket, Gregory and McDonald came together as a fast-bowling combination at Adelaide's picturesque oval. This was in the third match of the 1920–21 series which our side won by 119 runs, giving us the first 'rubber' of post-war Test cricket. Inevitably from my position behind the stumps I found myself studying these two bowlers and noted the contrast they presented. It is notable that throughout their association in Test cricket, Gregory always had the advantage of bowling with the wind. I found McDonald's approach to the wicket rhythmical and graceful by comparison to the bounding and somewhat ungainly run and delivery of Gregory.

Gregory, to my mind, always swung the new ball much more effectively than his team-mate and he was, if anything, slightly faster whilst the sheen remained on the ball. Once the newness was worn off he relied entirely on pace, whereas McDonald was able to turn the ball back from the off even at his fastest speed, and with this ball he could be most destructive. The spin which McDonald imparted added speed to his delivery in a most deceptive manner, after the ball made contact with the pitch. On the other hand, Gregory's delivery did not gain pace from the pitch, rather did it lose impetus, particularly on a lifeless wicket.

Jack Gregory flashed like a meteor across the cricket firmament. Wherever he played he was a centre of interest. Unknown before the war he became famous as a product of the A.I.F. team with his high bound and speedy deliveries, his marvellous slip-fielding and his capable and aggressive left-hand batting. Strangely enough he was a right-hand bowler and provided an interesting contrast to Macartney and Collins, who both bowled left, but batted right-hand.

Not of the fastest of bowlers, nevertheless his high deliveries, bounding run and controlled accuracy made him a dangerous and effective bowler. Using the new ball he swung it more disconcertingly than any other fast bowlers to whom I have ever kept wicket. His good-length deliveries lifted awkwardly, as though they were short pitched, and so proved extremely troublesome to all types of batsmen.

Nothing in cricket was prettier than the action of the late E. A. McDonald. He bowled with such rhythm that his action seemed to flow as smoothly as a river. All his energy went into flinging the ball down and none into superfluous pounding of the earth or waving of the arms. At an age when most fast bowlers have long since burned themselves out, McDonald still could achieve tremendous pace. When McDonald decided to return to England after our 1921 tour, Australia lost for all time one of the greatest fast bowlers it has ever produced. I shall never forget how in 1930, when playing for Lancashire against Australia on the Aigburth Ground at Liverpool, McDonald amazed me by his speed, which was particularly disconcerting. In the first innings he dismissed Jackson, Bradman, and Richardson for 51 runs. Even when past his prime he could make established batsmen nervous when his blood was up.

Having kept wicket to both these great bowlers under all types of conditions in England, South Africa, and Australia, I unhesitatingly hand the palm to McDonald as the greater because of his versatility and remarkable stamina. Proof of his great stamina was manifest during the fourth Test at Manchester in 1921 when McDonald, operating against the wind at the opposite end to Gregory, bowled unchanged until the luncheon adjournment. And well had he earned his lunch, as he had overslept that morning and was too late to get breakfast at the hotel. He reached the ground just in time to change, swallow a glass of water, and snatch two or three puffs of his indispensable cigarette before taking the field.

A BRIGHT PROSPECT
(THE *DAILY TELEGRAPH*, SYDNEY, JANUARY, 1902)

THE Chatswood Superior Public School possesses a player whom Noble — who, as sole selector for New South Wales and a member of the Australian selection committee, ought to be a judge — describes as the best boy cricketer he has ever seen. His name is Macartney, and he is an all-round performer. Playing the other day for his school against North St Leonards, he made 121 not out, out of 219, and took seven wickets for one run. This is only one in a series of notable achievements. Macartney is a left-hand bowler, and probably it would be worth the while of the authorities of the North Sydney District Club to give him some 'attention.' Macartney is the grandson of the veteran cricketer, Mr George Moore, senior, of West Maitland, and it is pleasing to note that he is likely to uphold the great cricketing reputation of his family.

MACARTNEY
By Neville Cardus
(*PLAYFAIR CRICKET MONTHLY*)

IF cricketers were long-playing records, and I were asked to select eight to keep me company on a desert island ('that is, assuming you possess a gramophone'), I should unhesitatingly choose Victor Trumper, G. C. Macartney, Denis Compton, George Gunn, Frank Woolley, Cecil Parkin, Keith Miller and R. H. Spooner (I could, of course, name at least eight others). Macartney would be included almost first choice. His batting was a constant thrill and delight. Even the most attractive players occasionally disappoint and bore us on days when they are 'out of touch'. Macartney was never uninteresting; when he had to suffer one of those dull fallible moods which come inexplicably over the greatest, he got out. On one occasion, as he told me, he really did play an innings boring to himself. In the Test match v. England at Old Trafford in 1926, he scored 109 in rather more than three hours. Fred Root bowled his legtrap inswingers. 'Wasting time', said Macartney; 'Rootie couldn't get me out, and I wasn't such a fool as to get myself out. So I watched the ball go past me . . . If it hadn't been a Test match I'd certainly have given my wicket away. I've no time for negative stuff'. He certainly hadn't; on or off the cricket field he was one of the most positive temperaments I have ever known, quick in all his reactions, alert always in mind and body.

He was square-shouldered and square chinned, of medium height, with forearms so strong that the power in them could be felt at a glance. His eyes were keen as a bird's. At the wicket, after he had taken guard, he would raise his bat high over his head, stretching himself. This action expressed, more eloquently than any spoken words, 'Now then — we're all ready. So here goes'. His confidence knew no bounds. But he was not at all boastful. One morning, the day of a Test match, he joined me at breakfast in the hotel. Macartney looked out of the window. The sun was shining full glory. He slapped his hands. 'Lovely day', he said, 'By cripes, I feel sorry for any poor cove who has to bowl to me today'. No, he wasn't boasting at all. He was sincerely saying that he was sympathising (in advance) for sweating and frustrated and wasted human hopes and energy.

He hated a maiden over bowled at him. 'When a batsman's in form he can get a single whenever he likes'. His quickness of footwork has never been excelled. 'If you get in position to the ball — to *any* ball — it's hard to miss it'. In style he was a sort of Bradman *de luxe*, Bradman plus wit and genius for improvisation. When Bradman was scoring at his fastest, his cricket seemed pre-organised, so to say, every stroke planned and perfectly executed accordingly. Macartney's batting gave the impression that it was perpetually creative throughout an innings, with several strokes for the same kind of ball. He was, like Sir Donald, a 'killer', ruthless in attack. But his style and presence told us that he was vastly enjoying himself, especially when, at the last split second, he changed an incipient off-drive into a late cut. Bradman's bat was like a broadsword, Macartney's like a rapier. But this 'rapier' metaphor won't quite do as a means of describing Macartney at the wicket. His drives had as much power as they had steely brilliance. It will be truer to his character and his cricket to say that he made his runs with broadsword and rapier alternatively. He batted with an extraordinary mingling of brain and impulse. He was fond of saying that a batsman should be able by rapidity of thought to know exactly at what point of its flight and momentum the curve of an outswinger should be 'sort of bisected'.

He scored a century before lunch for Australia at Leeds in July 1926, after A. W. Carr, England's captain, had won the toss on a soft slow pitch and put Australia in first (Charles Parker, best slow left-hand bowler extant at the time, was left out of the match and given the job of 'drinks waiter'). And Carr missed catching Macartney when Macartney was only two. A. W. Carr had good reason to remember Macartney, and of what he was capable in the way of assault and battery. For in 1921, as Trent Bridge, Macartney scored 345 against Nottinghamshire in just under four hours. And when he had made 9 George Gunn missed him in the slips ('They should have started a collection for me', said George.). This was one of the most dazzling exhibitions of strokeplay ever witnessed. Macartney simply trifled with a Notts. attack consisting of Fred Barratt, Richmond, Staples, Jack Gunn, with reserves of Lee, Whysall, Hardstaff and Carr himself. At one period of the afternoon the Notts. field was a shambles, running here, there and everywhere at the crack of Macartney's bat. Carr then decided to make a move. He changed his bowlers round. 'I did it just to let the high hats on the pavilion know that I hadn't lost grip on the situation. Nothing in it, of course — just a gesture'. And Carr also decided to bowl the over needed for a change of ends. 'I thought it would look well in the score-sheet — "A. W. Carr, 1 over 1 maiden, no runs, no wicket", because I was going to bowl wide, so that Charlie wouldn't be able to get at them'.

Wisden preserves what happened to Carr's one and only over:— 1-0-24-0. Macartney drove a ball clean out of Trent Bridge on that day of blinding sun and blinding batsmanship.

In 1912 England, Australia and South Africa played each other in this country — the 'Triangular Tests'. At Lord's, Australia batted first v. England. S. F. Barnes and Frank Foster opened England's attack, with Rhodes, Hearne and Dean to follow. Macartney, in first wicket down, was putting on his pads when a colleague, looking through the window down the wicket from the pavilion end, said, 'Cripes, Charlie Barnes looks pretty hot stuff today — cripes, that one went away like 'ell and missed the off stump by inches!' Macartney said nothing, but when he went out to bat, so I was told by a reliable witness, 'he was livid with rage'. Macartney scored 99, with thirteen fours, one from Barnes second bounce into the Mound Stand. 'The finest innings seen at Lord's during the season', records *Wisden*.

At the beginning of Warwick Armstrong's all-conquering invasion of our cricket fields in 1921, the Australians' first match was at Leicester. On a lovely day Leicestershire were shot out for 136 — McDonald, prince of fast bowlers took 8 for 41. Then, when Australia went in, Leicestershire's fast bowler W. E. Benskin, immediately clean-bowled Herbert Collins, amidst scenes of great local patriotism. I was sitting on the pavilion as Macartney, going out to bat, passed the defeated Collins coming in. 'I'll attend to the cove', said Macartney to Collins — meaning that he would attend to Benskin. He scored 50 in half an hour and 177 in all. I have seldom witnessed cricket as daring, as electric, as rapidly changeful as Macartney's that day. Cuts like the headsman's axe on the block, cuts from the middle stump, swinging drives glorious in rhythm, leg-glances so late that the wicket-keeper had to gape. Like an artist, Macartney sometimes tired of going through all his known and proven technical repertory; he would perform strokes hard to classify, yet every one of them sent the imagination and the aesthetic senses dancing. Old Australians maintain that Macartney as a stroke player approached closer than any other batsman to Victor Trumper . . . But I think there was a difference of style between them. Trumper was lithe, elegant, youthful. Macartney's batting, for all its glamour, was more obviously aggressive and blood-thirsty than

Victor's, who always scored with a kind of courtliness. Trumper really did 'play' with the bowlers; he enchanted them. Macartney pulverised them and put them to flight . . .

In Australia Macartney was called the 'Governor General'. But it was in this country that he found and sustained his finest ability. At first he was chosen for Test cricket as a useful all-rounder. During his first visit to England he went in to bat among the 'tail-enders'. In 1909, his batting performances against England on English turf were quite modest: 148 runs in 9 innings. When he came to England a second time, in 1912, he made runs so brilliantly and so masterfully in a wet season of 'sticky' wickets that he really did seem to be wearing the mantle of Victor Trumper. From May 9th to May 22nd he scored 127 v. Northamptonshire, 208 v. Essex, 123 v. Surrey and 74 v. M.C.C. The same summer of 1912 he scored 142 and 121 against Sussex in one and the same match. In each of these innings he batted not more than two and a half hours. For Australia in 1926, at Lord's, Leeds and Manchester, he passed a century on each occasion. Yet at the end of this season and rubber he told me he was disappointed with himself. It was at the Oval in 1926 that England, captained by A. P. F. Chapman, won back the 'Ashes'. When Australia went in a second time with 415 runs needed for victory in a deciding match, the wicket was not entirely trustworthy. There was moisture in it and Larwood made the ball rear menacingly at a great pace. Macartney, in first wicket down, dazzled everybody by a series of rapid strokes. He was marvellously caught in the slips by George Geary off Larwood for 15. 'I never in my life hit a ball harder — smack in the middle, one of my delayed square-cuts. A miraculous catch'. 'But', I said, 'you were not expecting to win the match?' 'Perhaps not', he replied, 'but I was determined the England bowlers should pay for it'. He was always of an independent mind, quietly but confidently aggressive. 'Any batsman worth his salt', he often said, 'should let the bowlers understand at once that he is the boss here today'. Conceit? I once asked him, 'How would you compare yourself with Victor Trumper'? Without hesitation came the answer: 'I'd always have been proud to carry his bag'. The parfit — but not very gentle — knight!

MY RIVAL
By Bert Oldfield
(FROM HIS *BEHIND THE WICKET*, 1938)

TOWARDS the end of the 1914–15 season I was promoted to the first-grade team and played in the last two matches, the first game being against Waverley Club in March on our home ground at Wentworth Park. It was a memorable occasion for me as my first victim was the famous Australian Test batsman Syd Gregory. He was caught behind after making three runs, and I felt that my baptism into senior cricket was more than satisfactory. Other internationals playing in that club match were Hanson Carter and Warren Bardsley. Alan Kippax, then a youth, also figured in the match.

There are other reasons why I shall never forget that game. As I arrived at the ground, 'Sammy' Carter drove up in a sulky — a two-wheeled vehicle — drawn by a small pony. It was amusing, but I was soon to learn that this was always his means of transport to his Saturday afternoon's cricket. 'Sammy' was ever like that, full of independence.

Carter was, of course, my rival wicket-keeper in this match. After watching him, I felt that I should like to model my style upon his: he was so quick at stumping, so neat in his work and so far ahead of any other wicket-keeper I had seen up to that time. Little did I then dream that within a few years I would be selected to visit England in the same team as this great international. Carter, as I lived to learn, possessed a unique style founded on unorthodox methods.

But the World War now was raging and I felt that a momentous decision had to be made. In September 1915 I enlisted . . .

Returning to Australia with the A.I.F. team in 1920 I once more met . . . Carter, whom I had not seen since our first brief acquaintance in my first senior game with the Glebe Club.

He was now captain of New South Wales against the touring side and once again he kept wicket in his inimitable style. This was my first realisation that he belonged to a school all his own. Carter would take up his stance at the wicket about four feet away from the stumps, no doubt having in mind that he would from this distance benefit by a longer view of the ball and therefore would be able to follow its flight more accurately. He would squat in the same manner that other small wicket-keepers do, and complete the movements with the same clever footwork and anticipation.

In stumping from this stance, as I reason, it would be necessary to make a step towards the wicket, which entails the loss of a certain amount of time. Possibly this has deprived him of victims which he would have claimed with a closer stance. Again, in making a catch at the wicket the angle of deflection of the ball becomes greater the farther it travels, and from this backward position Carter would be called upon to make more ground or reach farther for the ball. This, I contend, would have been avoided had he stood nearer to the wicket.

Personally I do not follow his technique and cannot, therefore, subscribe to his methods. Still, my great predecessor succeeded in spite of what I regard as a violation of orthodoxy, which goes to show that excellent results can be obtained by different methods. Except in the case of Carter, I have not seen or heard of any wicket-keeper adopting this somewhat distant stance.

In Carter's batting, too, he was just as unorthodox as compared with our other batsmen. Many deliveries pitched outside the off stump he would be just as likely to lift over his left shoulder as to play past mid-off. This he called his 'shovel shot'.

As a travelling-companion Carter was very entertaining, bringing an alert mind to his stories. He loved reminiscences. During our voyage to England in 1921, Carter passed on to me advice regarding the preparation of gloves. It was from him that I learned the wisdom of applying eucalyptus to the rubber palms of my gloves. In contrast to Strudwick's method of protection for his fingers, the Australian did not, as a general rule, believe in using leather stalls, though when injured he found comfort in so doing.

Having regard to this great wicket-keeper's unorthodox style, despite the success he achieved with it, I considered it would be unwise even to attempt to follow his methods, realising the success I had won by the orthodox movements, which to me seemed more natural.

Carter represented Australia in 21 Test Matches against England and claimed 51 victims, made up of 17 stumpings and 34 catches.

HERBY COLLINS
By Arthur Mailey
(FROM HIS *10 FOR 66 AND ALL THAT*, LONDON, 1958)

HERBY was an enigma, a paradox, a riddle, a parcel of sharp contrasts, a model of inconsistency, a collection of discords, which harmonized and made an interesting and likeable character.

At heart Collins was a gambler. His hunting grounds were the racecourse, the dog-track, Monte Carlo, 'The Den of Thieves' (near the Strand in 1921-6), a baccarat joint at King's Cross, a 'two-up' school in the Flanders trenches in World War I and anywhere a quiet game of poker was in operation. 'Mauldy' Collins gambled anywhere except on the cricket field, and on anything but cricket.

As a batsman Collins was a miser; as a left-arm bowler, like Charles Macartney and Wilfred Rhodes, he was an even greater miser.

To save the fourth Test match in 1921 at Old Trafford, he batted from 11 a.m. to 5 p.m. for forty runs — probably the most valuable innings he had ever played. It was this performance which illustrated his self-control and shrewdness on the field. Runs were of no value, time being the dominating factor, and Collins seldom attempted to score. Often he would play a very loose ball towards the outfield and stroll casually to the other wicket.

After the match I asked Collins why he hadn't tried to hit boundaries off the loose balls. 'Solomon' Collins replied:

'After lunch the fieldsmen, realizing that I wasn't going for runs, didn't hurry after the ball, merely trotted. This meant that there were fewer overs bowled during the day, which on the law of averages gave me a better chance of staying in, in addition to which I reserved my strength and concentration by not hurrying down the crease. The reason why I didn't try to hit boundaries was to waste time by allowing the fieldsman to dawdle almost to the boundary to recover the ball — and then again he was in no hurry to get the ball back to the bowler. If I'd hit a boundary, the spectators would have thrown the ball back like a shot and saved the time I was doing my best to lose!'

How different from the tactices shown in the Lord's Test in 1953 ... Trevor Bailey's valiant effort was in danger of being spoilt on at least three occasions when he was nearly run out trying to sneak a short single. Yet England's position was on a par with ours at Old Trafford in 1921. Runs were valueless and it was just a matter of how time should be dissipated.

Herby Collins' astute captaincy may have been a legacy from Alf Noble under whom he played most of his matches in his youth. As a captain his greatest achievement was undoubtedly the moulding of the famous A.I.F. into one of the strongest teams in the history of Australian cricket. After an early squabble which terminated with the disposal of a well-known player, Collins, a corporal, took the helm and steered the team through a most successful tour in South Africa and Australia (where, in addition to other victories, a meaty New South Wales side was well trounced).

The 'Little Corporal' and his team of non-commissioned and high-ranking officers ploughed the profits of the tour back into the A.I.F. Amenities Fund.

The value of the services of this A.I.F. team to Australian cricket generally is very difficult to estimate. Its fighting spirit and amazing camaraderie gave our cricket a badly needed shot in the arm and I feel that much of the success of Armstrong's 1920–1 side was due to the presence of Corporal Collins, Jack Gregory, Johnny Taylor, Bert Oldfield and 'Nip' Pellew. Of the remaining members of the A.I.F. team, Carl Willis, Charles Winning, Cyril Docker, Bill Trennery, Jack Murray, Allie Lampard, Eric Bull, Bill Stirling and Ted Long gave great support to their States.

And while we are on the subject, let's pay due credit to that great worker in the cause of cricket, 'Plum' Warner, for his untiring efforts to organize Empire cricket during the war and particularly the A.I.F. team of World War I.

It was no wonder that when the massive Warwick Armstrong shambled out of cricket after the 1921 tour, the 'Little Corporal' should take his place.

I was given an insight into Collins' shrewd cricket brain when we served together on State Selection Committees. I soon realized how the original A.I.F. players had been welded into such a match-winning team. In picking a team Collins was relentless. He strove for combination above all things, not for a collection of spare parts. Once we dropped a player who had scored a double century in the previous State match. Collins wouldn't have him.

'With Gregory in the side,' he said, 'we need another slip. Tom isn't a good "slipper". We have all the batsmen we want and we've got to build our team around two bowlers, you and Gregory. If Tom comes in, then a very essential part of the team's mechanism must be taken out.'

Result: England, who had beaten Western Australia, South Australia and Victoria to a frazzle with wickets and runs to spare, met their 'Waterloo' at Sydney.

In Melbourne at a later date England were in a favourable position at tea. Frank Woolley had tasted blood and threatened to annihilate the tired Australian attack before stumps that day. Collins took the ball and bowled yards outside Frank's stumps until close of play for very few runs. Next morning we came on fresh again. At the first interval people were pouring into the ground expecting to see an interesting day's play. At the same time the players were pouring out the exit turnstiles with the match over. Collins was right again. The caterer on the ground could have killed me — but it was really my captain's fault. It was his brain as much as my bowling that had schemed England out.

England never won a Test match on that tour.

Collins was one of the most undemonstrative yet one of the richest characters in Australian cricket, during my playing career at any rate. His faults to me were virtues. His so-called weaknesses faded away or were set in true perspective for me by the richness and fine quality of his nature.

Herby never complained, never moaned. His philosophy seemed to provide an antidote for bad luck. Indeed, frowning fortune to this little possum-eyed Australian was just another incident that would be of no account when a new day dawned.

A Short Note on Mailey
By Neville Cardus, 1963

ARTHUR Mailey was, and I hope still is, a man of humour and fantasy. He first came to England in 1921, one of Armstrong's invincible XI, which contained the terrible fast attack of Gregory and Macdonald, who on wickets not yet repaired after the 1914–18 war, and in a hot summer every day, were a perpetual danger to limb and thorax. Of this rough-riding Australian XI Cecil Parkin said; 'They've brought two killers with 'em, also a funeral director and a gravestone maker.' (H. Carter was in private life connected with 'funeral parlours', and T. J. E. Andrews with gravestones.) I could never fit Arthur into this company of unsmiling Ironsides. He was so casual, so apparently lazy. He never seemed to exert himself when he bowled in a few easy strides, and an almost negligent swing-over of the arm. But the left side of his body pointed classically down the wicket. It was a beautiful action, with a strong leverage of the wrist. He bowled any amount of full tosses. 'If ever I bowl a maiden,' he once said to me, 'it's the batsman's fault, not mine.' No bowler who loves the arts of leg-spin and 'googly' likes to send down a maiden. Some Australian wit — I think it was Ray Robinson — maintained that Mailey bowled leg-spin like a millionaire and Grimmett like a miser. Few leg-spinners have put onto a cricket ball a spin as tremendous as Mailey's. One morning in the nets at Perth, Western Australia, he bowled to me. A half-volley floated slowly towards me, hit the hard earth, then whipped away with an enormous acceleration of speed. I drove blindly at it, and the ball gyrated still faster over the back-net into the Australian bush. It was never recovered. 'That was a devil of a ball, Arthur,' I said. 'Yes,' he replied, 'it's the ball you criticize Patsy Hendren for not driving past cover for four.' Mailey bowled his gigantic leg-break at me on one other occasion. At midnight in London, on a lovely June night, along the pavement in Piccadilly. But it wasn't a cricket ball he bowled at me this time. It was an apple. And after pitching on the pavement it spun over Piccadilly to the rails of the Green Park — or thereabouts.

MAILEY IN TAILS
By *Denzil Batchelor*
(*PLAYFAIR CRICKET MONTHLY*, 1964)

THERE was Mailey himself, arriving for the final Test of the '26 tour still unchanged, in the white tie and tails he had worn to dance all night. As he emerged from his taxi, he bumped into his team's manager, who drew a deep breath. 'Not now,' pleaded Mailey, 'not till after stumps.' He then changed and prayed that Australia would lose the toss, and he would take six wickets. He wouldn't dare take only five: the manager might have had something to say — but there could be nothing to say to a man who'd taken six. He took six (including Hobbs') — and spent the following night dancing.

Aboriginal Cricketers

THE ABORIGINAL TEAM, 1868
Anon.

YOUR swarthy brows and raven locks
　　Must gratify your tonsors,
But by the name of Dick a Dick.
　　Who are your doughty sponsors?

Arrayed in skin of kangaroo
　　And decked with lanky feather,
How well you fling the fragile spear
　　Along the sunny heather.

And though you cannot hope to beat
　　The Britishers at cricket,
You have a batter, bold and brave
　　In Mullagh, at the wicket.

THE 1868 TOUR
By Donald MacDonald, c. 1917

THE death of that fine old cricketer of early international fame, Charles Lawrence, recalls one or two unusual incidents in the story of Australian cricket. Lawrence was not only a member of the first team of English cricketers that came to Australia, but fifty years ago was a member of the first Australian eleven that visited England. No team was ever better entitled to the term Australian, because, with the exception of Lawrence, who coached and afterwards captained them, they were wholly aborigines.

It was in 1865, I think, that the idea of taking a team of blacks to England was first mooted, and in 1866 they played a Victorian team — with the cracks of the days excluded — on the Melbourne Cricket Ground, but the English tour came off some 18 months later, in 1868. W. R. Hayman, of Edenhope, was the first to suggest it, and the team was chosen wholly from that area about the watershed of the Glenelg, which, after fifty years of development, is still largely pastoral country, with Edenhope, Harrow, Balmoral, Casterton, and Coleraine as its centres. Playing with local clubs, Mullagh and Cuzins had already won some distinction — this pair were in all-round capacity not only the backbone of the side, but some of the ribs as well.

... 'Mullagh', the Black 'W.G.' of the team, was a superior man in many ways. He had all-round capacity in cricket, with something of a personality to back it. He was remarkably abstemious ... never spoke pidgin English, and quietly professed not to understand it when someone sought to air his knowledge of the bush and the blacks using it. He has been not extravagantly described as one of nature's gentlemen ... The boundary hit had a special appeal to him, not so much in that it counted 4 as because he got the 4 without running for them. Yet one has only to glance at the results of the tour to see that for Mullagh and Cuzins especially the series of 47 matches played in England — of which 14 were won, 14 lost, and 19 drawn — must have been particularly tiring.

Had this black team been chosen from all Australia it would have been a stronger side, but originating in Edenhope it was largely local. The names suggest that its members had been much in association with white men. Mullagh took his name, I think, from Mullagh Station, owned by the Fitzgeralds, who were much interested in him, Cuzins got his name as well as much of his knowledge from a firm of Balmoral store-keepers. Charles Dumas no doubt came by his in much of the same way — the others were indebted to irregular baptism of a not very original kind, since it seems to be common to the black races, whatever part of the world they inhabit. On the names they might have been the original Georgia Minstrels. Such are King Cole, Bullocky, Jim Crow, Dick-a-dick, Mosquito, Tiger, Sundown, Tuppeny, Red Cap, Charlie, and Peter. As a rule most of the blacks took the surname of a family with whom they lived for any length of time.

They opened their English tour at Kennington Oval, where, amongst the team opposing them, were at least two notable names in those of Jupp — who afterwards came to Australia — and I. D. Walker. Mullagh struck his form in the first game, getting 73 in the aborigines' second hand; and the innings was described as being worth at least a hundred, for they at once noticed Johnnie's aversion to hard running. Amongst white players there have been notable examples of men who never took risks for the other fellow's hit, but got all that was going for their own. Mullagh was impartial and unselfish in this respect. He would run just as slowly for himself as for his partner. With 94 as his highest score in England, he averaged over 23 for 71 innings, while Cuzins had an average of 19 for 72 innings. All Mullagh's powers were in his wrists — he never seemed to use force in his strokes, but trusted to wrist work and exact timing. In style, Bullocky looked one of their best bats, but he had one failing — he liked to stay in for a long time whether he got runs or not; so Bullocky's average for the tour was only 9 per innings. Years afterwards I met Bullocky, or a black who professed to be Bullocky, and whose bulk answered the description — on the Murray, where he sometimes played with the Corowa team. It was a wet day — wet for Bullocky in more than one sense. The big black had fallen face forward on the road. Three dabs of mud, on forehead, nose and chin illuminated him as if for a corroboree. He passsed me obvious compliments upon my skill as a cricketer — compliments which the club score-sheet did not always confirm. The end and object came in the call of the wild all the world over — 'Chuck us a bob'.

As a bowler upon that tour Mullagh, who was medium pace, right arm, took 245 wickets at a cost of 10 runs a piece. Cuzins had 114 wickets at 11 runs a piece, and the third all-round star of the organization was the white captain, Lawrence, who in batting averaged 20 for 57 innings, and took 250 wickets at 12 runs a piece. Only two of the blacks averaged 10 or over with the bat. Tuppeny and Redcap did something in bowling — Tuppeny with 37 wickets at 7 runs a piece, Redcap with 54 at an average of 10 runs. Their fielding was always good. Mullagh at his best was almost as good a bowler as batsman, and on one occasion took five of the Warrnambool wickets for one run. In England the calibre of the side, apart from the few, was soon realized, and no very strong team was sent against them.

The progress of the games was a good deal interrupted by exhibitions, such as spear and boomerang throwing, a novelty to Englishmen, though Lawrence expressed the view afterwards that straight-out cricket would have served them best. One of the cleverest of their feats was that of Dick-a-dick with the aboriginal war shield, called a Kumnal in the West. The shape of the shield is pretty well known — oblong, concave, 3 ft. in length, perhaps 6 in. wide in the centre and tapering to points at either end. Stationed 15 or 20 yards off, and holding the shield forward with the one-handed centre grip, he allowed three or four of his opponents in each match to throw cricket balls at him as hard and fast as they pleased, stipulating only for a throw 'on the full' not a grounder.

Standing almost as still as a statue, and with a twitch or flick of the shield, he turned the ball off his body as a batsman would glance it to leg. It was a remarkable exhibition of eyesight, dexterity, and coolness, yet with it all Dick-a-dick was not a prominent batsman. He was evidently using the wrong implement in a bat. Not less remarkable than his skill in turning the straight throw was his judgment in picking the ball that would miss. Very often they almost brushed him. With provoking deliberation and coolness, leg, arm, or head were moved a few inches to one side to let the ball go whizzing by. A peculiarity of the whole team as batsmen was their helplessness with slow bowling, even the simplest of underhand lobs, such as W. H. Handfield sometimes bowled for the M.C.C. getting them out. It seemed to be a weakness peculiar, not only to this team, but to the whole aboriginal race, whose spearmen can, as a rule, hit a running mark better than a stationary one. On one occasion a pretty good Corranderrk eleven went to Warrnambool, and Frank Allan, who knows blacks well enough to bowl nothing at them but his famous slow 'googlers', took the ten wickets for 11 runs. In the second game Frank stood out, and the aborigines scored heavily against the Warrnambool fast bowlers, and won the match.

Years after this tour, when Lord Harris brought his English team to Australia, Mullagh played for Victoria against them and scored 33. The baleful off-theory had just been introduced, and when the black champion stood back to the first of them from Tom Emmett, the M.C.C. ground rang with laughter and cheers. The hat was sent round and for the innings Johnnie got £50. He is buried in Harrow cemetery, where the sportsmen of the West put a memorial over his grave.

To Lawrence, especially, the tour was not altogether a pleasure jaunt. Restraint was irksome to the blacks; the family somewhat difficult to manage. To save them from English hospitality they were sent to bed early, but it was often a case of in by the door and out by the window. Tiger, a convivial spirit, was arrested and fined for attacking a policeman. Public opinion in Victoria was rather against the undertaking. There was a feeling — which members of the Aborigines' Board shared — that it might prove a better thing for the promoters than for the blacks, and in the end they were practically smuggled out of Victoria. After a game played at Queenscliff they went out in a yacht, professedly on a fishing excursion, and were picked up by the *Rangitira* on her way to Sydney. Before the tour was long in progress, Sundown and Jim Crow were sent home ill, and King Cole died in England.

THE DEATH OF JOHNNY MULLAGH
(THE *SYDNEY MAIL*, AUGUST 22, 1891)

THE Victoria aboriginal cricketer, Johnny Mullagh, was found dead on the 14th instant at Harrow, in the Western district. Mullagh was the principal bat in the famous aboriginal team which visited England in 1868. He had been the mainstay of the Harrow Cricket Club for many years, and though of late he became weak and stiff from age and exposure he was a keen batsman and lover of the game. The Western district will regret his death. He had been ailing for some weeks, but nothing serious was anticipated. Mullagh had often refused overtures made to him to provide him with a suitable home in his old age, and he chose to live near his birthplace at Pine Hills, and to some extent after the custom of his forefathers. He was the last of his tribe. His funeral took place on Sunday, and representatives came from considerable distances to pay their token of respect to the deceased. On the veteran's coffin were placed the bat he used, and a set of stumps tied together with the Harrow colours, and surrounded by numerous wreaths. The Anglican clergyman read the burial service, and gave an address, pointing out that the world of cricket had lost a mighty man, and also dwelling on the virtues of the deceased, who was exemplary in his habits. He hoped that the cricketers of Victoria would erect a suitable monument to his memory. Much feeling was shown by all present.

MARSH IN SPLINTS

Arthur Gregory's account of the New South Wales XI v Colts XV
match in November, 1900
(THE *SYDNEY MAIL*)

DONNAN and Trumper opened for the Eleven, and both were out by the time 11 runs were hoisted. Marsh, the aboriginal, had Trumper in the pace, the ball breaking back just sufficiently to beat the bat, Trumper trying to place the ball to the on side of the wicket. At 11 Donnan was cleverly taken by Evers off Howard. Without further addition to the total Noble narrowly escaped being caught by Evers off Marsh, the snick travelling just beyond the wicket keeper's reach. Marsh was after this no-balled now and then by the square-leg umpire, W. Curran, the umpire at the bowler's end passing the delivery as legitimate. Three times the bowler was 'called' in the over, the first two overs being unchallenged. The effect of the umpire's action was to considerably reduce the pace of Marsh. There was some demonstration along the terrace against the 'no-balling', so that when Marsh cleaned bowled Iredale there was a hearty round of applause accorded the bowler. Iredale seeing that there was no one in the country essayed a big hit off a short ball, and his wicket required readjustment.

The first 'no-ball' was a vastly different delivery to any ball previously sent down, and even from my position in the pavilion I thought it was an unfair delivery; of course it is just possible that had I been at square leg I might have thought otherwise. The other couple of 'no-balls' to my eye were no different to many formerly sent down ...

Marsh, the aboriginal bowler, was much upset over his being no-balled. Undoubtedly his delivery is suspicious; still he was himself satisfied of the fairness of his delivery. Getting a few leading cricketers together he suggested a test to prove that he did not throw the ball, and the means adopted was to fasten a bit of wood tightly along the elbow in such a position as to absolutely prevent the joint being bent. The experiment was successful. Marsh bowled as fast as ever. An order was then placed with a maker of such things, and a split was prepared. There was, however, something in this arrangement which did not please the umpire, W. Curran, who declined to further officiate unless the bandage were discarded, or that he be allowed to tie the splint. But he proposed to cover up the wrist as well as the elbow, to which, of course, the darkie objected. Marsh wore the splint, the umpire stood on his dignity and refused to go out. Our old friend Sam Jones took the vacant wicket. In my opinion the umpire was right in 'calling' Marsh, but he was wrong, undoubtedly, in retiring from his post. Nothing beyond the mutual request of the captains or ill health of the umpire can justify the latter's retirement from his duty.

JACK MARSH
By J. C. Davis
(THE *REFEREE*, JUNE 9, 1916)

It has been established that the aboriginal whose death at Orange was referred to in last week's 'Referee' is Jack Marsh, the fast bowler and professional runner. The Coroner opened an inquest at Orange on Wednesday, and two men are charged with having feloniously slayed Marsh. The aboriginal was one of the steadiest men of his type I ever met. In his cricket days he did not drink to excess, and all who had anything to do with him spoke highly of him. He was a perfecly-built man, and a very fine athlete. In the days of the running boom he was one of the fastest of the aboriginal runners, some regarding him as second only to Samuels, when at his top. He was a much better-built man than his brother Larry Marsh.

In cricket, Marsh was very popular, and for a time filled the public eye in Sydney quite as much as Victor Trumper, for he was a fearsome bowler with the South Sydney and Sydney clubs, in his prime. Many held that he threw. I am sure he did so at times in his early career, but later, when he was even more deadly, his delivery struck me as being not against the laws. This, of course, is a matter of opinion, and with a man of his peculiar powers, there will always be some doubt on the point, especially among those who did not take the trouble to look closely into his action.

Marsh could make the ball do stranger things in the air than any other bowler I ever saw. Moreover, in making the ball swerve and drop he bowled at a faster pace than most men and at different paces. Like M. A. Noble, he was able to make the ball that swerved away from the bat to the off-side break back awkwardly after it pitched, with the difference that Marsh could do this on the best wickets, and often with the ball flicking at an awkward height off the pitch. In his own way he studied bowling, and was able to explain how he imparted the spin, which made the ball swerve. He held the ball in the palm of the hand, and got the spin with practically the whole of his fingers, in concert with a super-imposed action of the wrist. Marsh was always a pleasant fellow, very amusing when he discussed his powers as a batsman, for he took himself much more seriously as a batsman than bowler. His one weakness was dress, for he loved to be decked out well, not gaudily, like so many men of his colour, but neatly and stylishly. And few men filled their clothes better than he did. That Jack Marsh would have been one of the world's greatest bowlers if he had been a white man I have always believed. If he had been able to win a place in Test match cricket I believe his bowling would have established a fresh standard of hard-wicket excellence and created a new type, differing altogether from anything ever known before. But the fates decreed that his bowling should not come into Test matches. Archie MacLaren objected to playing against him at Bathurst, though the English captain did not have a leg to stand on, for if Marsh did not bowl fair it was a matter for the umpires to determine . . . He was held to be thoroughly honest and was well behaved, though he did not care to work at anything laborious.

THE OBLIVION OF EDDIE GILBERT

By David Frith

(THE *CRICKETER*, NOVEMBER, 1972)

THE Queenland aboriginal cricketer Eddie Gilbert, famed for his bursts of express bowling during the 1930s, had not been heard of for so long that I took it upon myself when in Brisbane to track him down.

An old-timer in the suburb of Red Hill, where Eddie was last seen, thought he had died about five years before. We checked in the general store run by a cricket fan of some sixty summers:

'I'd just about swear to it. Old Eddie went right out of circulation and we never heard nothin' of him for ages I reckon he must've died ten years back at least. They had him in Goodna for a while.'

I drove out to the psychiatric hospital along the Ipswich Road in the hope of establishing the truth of the matter. The superintendent, barely concealing his surprise at my questions, led me through to the records office, where he produced Eddie Gilbert's hospital history card.

'Eddie was admitted on December 8th, 1949. His age was shown as 37.'

I thought he would have been slightly older than that; perhaps the paperwork was completed hastily that sad day.

'If you're writing about him,' the superintendent volunteered, 'I can tell you a few things. He took six wickets in his last game for Queensland. Terrific bowler — only ran half a dozen steps. He got the knack from boomerang throwing. Some reckoned he chucked, but I never thought so. It was just his funny wrist action. Wish we had somebody like him right now.'

Some weeks earlier Bill Hunt, the pre-war New South Wales player, had been in no doubt about it:

'Eddie threw *me* out! By cripes, yeah! And later on I deliberately did the same to him. And d'you know what he said? . . . I'll tell you. He put his arm round my shoulder and said 'Well bowled, Bill. That was a beauty!' So you see, the little fellah couldn't tell a bowl from a chuck anyway! Nice chap, but.'

It was Hunt's contention that Stan McCabe, whose name will live for three classic Test innings, himself considered his best hand to have been a 229 not out against Queensland at Brisbane in 1931 after Eddie Gilbert had served Don Bradman with 'the luckiest duck I ever made.'

The lithe black man that day, bowling with horrifying hostility on an under-prepared pitch, had New South Wales in ribbons at 31 for three, with Alan Kippax in hospital after a dreadful blow on the temple from a mis-hook off Thurlow.

At that point McCabe took command.

So long ago. Now here was I seeking to trace the conclusion of a life story. The superintendent glanced up from the history card.

'He was married at the time he came here. Nobody's visited him for ages. He used to be violent occasionally, but he's all right now — no trouble. But he's bottled right up within himself. You won't get him to talk. We've tried everything. He'll never change. Just as well perhaps. If he went out again he'd be back among the plonkies down at the *Adelaide* in no time.'

'You're telling me he's here — alive?'

He nodded. 'As I say, he's completely withdrawn. It's impossible to get through to him. He walks the grounds all day — he's content in his own private world. We've tried to interest him in some kind of recreation: his reflexes are still sharp. But when we put a cricket ball in his hand he just stared at it.'

It came as a shock. Eddie — still ticking after all! Even the locals had seemed so certain. I had fallen into line with them and quietly and briefly mourned their popular hero of long ago, the fast bowler to whom they had bellowed encouragement to 'give Jardine a taste of his own bodyline medicine.'

In *That Barambah Mob*, David Forrest's amusing blend of fact and fantasy, Eddie has already been immortalised: on the top of Henry Stulpnagel's head was imprinted in reverse '. . . nufactured in Austra . . .', a living souvenir of a Gilbert bumper.

'When that ball hit the concrete,' he exclaimed, 'she'd smoke!'

Mr Stulpnagel also knew why Eddie never became a Test cricketer: 'He made an ape of Bradman, and he was black, and he was born in Queensland, and they didn't like the look o' that whippy wrist of his.'

I made my reverent plea to the superintendent: 'I'd like to see Eddie.'

'It's no use. He won't talk.'

I pressed him. I had to see the historic cricketer.

He picked up the phone and asked the attendant at the appropriate wing to 'find Eddie'.

We walked across the sunlit lawns, past slumbering patients, small-talk lost in the insistent buzz of insects. The coolness in the outer block was a relief.

Eddie was some time in coming. Sitting in the office, I scanned the grounds through the open window. Suddenly a male nurse was standing at the door, and behind him, reluctant to advance, was a thin man in a maroon T-shirt and black shorts. His hair was white and close-cropped, his skin glistening ebony. It was unmistakably Gilbert.

He shuffled into the room, head to one side, eyes averted, impossible to meet. His physique would have been insignificant beside Tom Richardson, Miller or Trueman, yet he was not the midget legend has depicted. Five feet eight, with long arms: the devastating catapult machine he must once have been was apparent.

'Shake hands, Eddie,' his attendant urged kindly.

The hand that had propelled the ball that had smashed so many stumps was raised slowly; it was as limp as a dislodged bail. He was muttering huskily and incoherently, gently rocking his head side to side.

'Want a fag, Eddie?' the nurse asked softly.

Eddie grunted, watched the cigarette begin to smoulder, and puffed at it. His legs, typically of his race, were thin. He turned on them restlessly. He was an outdoor man; a room was a cage.

When I asked the nurse if Eddie could write his name for me he coaxed him to pick up the ball-point.

At the end of an agonising minute Eddie backed away, leaving only a tortured 'E' on the paper. His squinting eyes, deep-set and bloodshot, flashed briefly across all of us.

I thought then of what Archie Jackson, Australia's batting genius, had written about Eddie Gilbert in 1933: 'The adulation he has received has not affected his mental equilibrium. Such a player is an ornament to the game; may he continue to prosper!'

Eddie walked off, still breathing his wheezy monotone; he wandered through the meal hall, and the last I saw of him was as he drifted, a desolate individual, across the parched grass.

OF LATTER
DAYS

WHEN SID BARNES PLAYED THE CLOWN
A press report, November, 1952

SID Barnes acted the buffoon before a big crowd at Adelaide Oval today.

After the foolery had fallen flat, he walked off in frigid silence. The whole sensational yet tragic scene lasted only eight minutes.

One of the most tense Sheffield Shield struggles for years was nearings its peak in Adelaide when the NSW 12th man, Barnes, went on to the field with drinks, with half an hour left for play.

On a treacherous wicket, NSW had scored 146 with Lindwall the batting hero.

As the wicket improved in the bright sunshine, NSW bowlers, spearheaded by Miller, who took five wickets, were trying desperately to get South Australia out.

Barnes had become 12th man at his own request, to give Flockton a chance to play.

When Barnes went out with the drinks at 5 p.m. he wore a double-breasted suit — not the cream flannels usual for a 12th man.

He had on a pair of dark glasses.

Walking ahead of a SA Cricket Association steward, Barnes carried a basket covered by a white towel in his left hand, and a portable radio, over which was draped a white towel, in his right.

The steward followed behind with a tray of drinks.

As Barnes reached the gate on to the field, the grandstand crowd recognised him and immediately began to cheer and whistle.

Barnes turned, laughed and waved.

Then, when he reached the New South Wales players, the SA batsmen and the two umpires grouped in the centre, he took the towels off his tray.

He produced a box of cigars and attempted to hand them around, including some to the umpires. The crowd laughed.

Then he took a big mirror and comb and tried to comb Keith Miller's hair.

He produced a clothes brush and went to three or four players and brushed them down.

He then turned on the radio which he had taken on to the field.

He also sprayed scent on one or two of the players, using a scent-spray he had brought with him.

The players, embarrassed, had moved away from Barnes, and he stood, uncertain, and alone.

The laughter faded and the crowd watched in silence.

Then people in the members' stand began to shout, 'Get off the field.'

Barnes walked off in silence, leaving the radio on the field.

A South Australian Cricket Association steward walked on to the field and collected the radio.

Interviewed last night in his Adelaide hotel, Barnes was light-hearted about the whole incident.

Asked the reason for his acts, Barnes said, 'Well, it was the first time I have ever been twelfth man.

'And it was a wonderful thrill to be twelfth man to such a fine team of sportsmen as the NSW players.

'The boys appreciated the little breaks and so did the crowd. The team voted me the best twelfth man they have ever had.'

COLIN McCOOL, A CREDITABLE PERFORMER
By Alan Gibson
(THE *CRICKETER INTERNATIONAL*, May, 1981)

I first saw Colin McCool play in 1948, when he was over here with the Australians. I had heard of him, as had every other cricketer, a couple of years before, when he had a successful season against Hammond's last England side. In the Tests of 1946-7, he had scored 272 runs in seven innings, which included a century and a 95, and with two not outs, gave him a batting average of 54. But this was not so important, because it was a fairly easy season for Australia to make runs, and he usually went in after Bradman, Barnes and Morris had trampled on the English bowling. What shook us was that he took 18 wickets, at just over 21, and this at a time when Lindwall and Miller, to say nothing of Johnson and Toshack and Dooland and Tribe, were about. Most of McCool's wickets were taken against the best English batsmen. He got Bill Edrich, upon whom he seems to have cast a spell, four times; Hammond twice; Yardley three times; Hutton, Washbrook, Fishlock and Ikin once each.

McCool was, it seemed, the coming Australian leg-spinner, the successor to O'Reilly, the man who would nicely complement the opening assault. Nobody suggested that he was so good as O'Reilly, but he had the advantage of being a batsman, and all seemed fair for him when he was chosen for the 1948 England tour.

It was a grievous disappointment to him. He had a sore spinning finger which would not heal. There were arguments about the best treatment — was it better to rest it, or try to harden it by regular use? Spinners and their captains have often faced this problem: and, as usually happens, neither course was thoroughly followed. Australia kept winning matches anyway. McCool did not play in a Test. It was not, however, the end of his Test career. He went to South Africa with the 1949–50 Australians, and did pretty well. With a match against New Zealand in 1945, and three against India in 1947, he finished his Test career with 36 wickets at 26.61, and 459 runs, average 35.30.

A creditable all-round performance, we thought, and forgot about him. I do not know who was responsible for fetching him from his Queesland milk-round to Somerset. (In case this should meet his eye, I must explain that a milk-roundsman in the remoter parts of Queensland is a very posh chap, selling a great many things besides milk: more like a bloated capitalist than your friendly morning milkman in Somerset.) But he still liked playing cricket, and was tempted back to England to play in the Lancashire League, and qualify for Somerset. There were no instant transfers for overseas players in those days; and while he was qualifying, the regulations were changed, unfavourably for him, so that he had to wait an extra year before he could play in championship matches. It was then 1955, when he was 40 years old, and though he had done well in the League, it was three years since he had played in a first-class match. There was much gloomy talk in the bars of Taunton and Bath about investing in an old man.

Nevertheless, he gave Somerset five seasons of splendid service, if not quite in the expected way. Maurice Tremlett, his captain, decided that he needed Colin's batting more than his bowling. He put him at No. 4, and told him to take no silly risks. McCool bore the burden of a frail batting side, and scored about 1,500 runs a year for them, taking nearly 50 wickets a year as well, and tolding about 140 catches, almost always in the slips. He felt, himself, that he was not put on to bowl enough — though he always got on well with Tremlett. What was happening, though we had hardly begun to realise it then, was the inexorable and tragic decline of the leg-spinner. When the pitch was thought likely to help spin, it was the finger-spinners who were given the first chance — and Somerset had a reliable one in Brian Langford (I believe he is still the only man to have bowled eight maiden overs in a Sunday League match).

Colin McCool, I am proud to say, became a warm friend of mine during his years in Somerset (and Devon, I must add, not forgetting the

Torquay Festival, and some evenings at the Cott Inn, Dartingdon). He did not quite come to terms with the West Country, as Sammy Woods had done, long before, or Bill Alley did, soon afterwards. Woods and Alley settled here. McCool, his five years up, went back to Australia. He missed the sunshine. 'There's no winter,' he said, 'and the beer's better; and the b . . . off-spinners don't turn.'

I think an additional reason was that he found some difficulty in accepting the conventions of English cricket, as it was then. There was a Somerset committee-member, who liked and admired him, and would greet him in the morning with 'Morning, McCool'. The committee-member was seeking to be courteous. He would have thought it pompous to say 'Mr McCool', and impertinent to say 'Colin'. But it infuriated Colin. He thought it was a reflection on his status. He would have preferred something like 'Hi, Col, you old bastard'. The worlds were too far apart.

But I remember him, both for his cricket and his character with deep affection; and so do a great many other people in the West of England.

UNCONVENTIONAL KEITH MILLER
By Alan Davidson
(FROM HIS *FIFTEEN PACES*, 1963)

MILLER was one of the game's great characters, full of whims and moods totally unpredictable but immensely gifted.

When Miller was in charge things really happened. The conventional held no place with him. He acted on impulse — a sudden bowling change here or a surprise closure there — but luck so often favours the bold and besides, he had his own freak genius to support any impulse.

He was the best natural cricketer I have ever seen, a crowd favourite and a player without limitation in any department of the game.

On the surface, he possessed a nonchalant, carefree nature. Yet there were times when his temper flared, much the same as we saw Ted Dexter ruffled on occasions on the 1962–63 MCC tour.

Once at the Sydney Cricket Ground nets I was bowling to Miller and slipped in a shortish, faster ball which caught him sharply in the ribs. He glared down the wicket and said: 'Have *you* had a bat yet?' I replied, 'Yes, thank goodness.'

I think my reply would have been the same had I not batted. Miller is no man to tangle with in that mood.

His greatest Test performances are familiar cricket history. His most remarkable Sheffield Shield performance surely occurred against South Australia in Sydney in 1955.

N.S.W. had declared a 8-215 and Miller had sent down just four balls before stumps. The next morning he completed his over then walked past me at slip and said: 'There's nothing in this wicket for me. I'll have just one more over, then you can take over.'

He took three wickets in the next over and finished with 7–12. I didn't get a bowl.

He was never punctual. Sometimes the umpires had visited the dressing room and were on their slow trek to the centre when he would burst into the room. Somehow, he always got out there on time, although once or twice he had to sit down to tie up his bootlaces before he could bowl.

I have always thought that Miller's casual approach left a marked impression on Richie Benaud who developed a habit, too, of making last minute arrivals at various grounds.

Rarely did a day's play under Miller pass without humorous incident. I recall the N.S.W. Shield side stopping over at Maitland for a one-day fixture on their way to Brisbane for the match against Queensland.

It was a big event in the town and the N.S.W. team was accorded a civic reception. Miller's mind was far away, however, when the Mayor delivered his speech of welcome. Came Miller's turn to reply and he said: 'Mr. Mayor, we're very pleased to be here in this town, er . . . this city . . . er . . . er where the bloody hell are we anyway?'

It was in this match that Miller overlooked nominating the 12th man for the day. So the whole team trooped out after him. The umpires scratched their heads then complained: 'You've got 12 men.' Miller looked back, shrugged his shoulders and said: 'Well one of you shoot through.'

He continued unconcerned on his way to the wicket. When next he looked around he was in solitary splendour. The other eleven players had all returned to the pavilion.

Miller, however, could be a down-to-earth realist when the occasion justified it. At Manchester, Jim Laker had placed England in an unassailable position. Australia was 375 runs behind on the first innings and the cause was lost. Ian Johnson, however, endeavoured to rally the team. He said with some feeling:

'We can fight our way back.

'We need guts and determination.

'We can still save the match.'

Miller, sitting in the corner of the room, lifted his head from a racing guide and commented indifferently: 'Bet you 6/4 we can't.'

RAY LINDWALL: THE COMPLETE FAST BOWLER
By Trevor Bailey
(FROM HIS *THE GREATEST OF MY TIME*, LONDON, 1968)

FAST bowlers are always more formidable when they can hunt in pairs, Gregory and McDonald, Larwood and Voce, Trueman and Statham, Hall and Griffith, Heine and Adcock, Lindwall and Miller. This makes certain that the unfortunate batsman cannot escape to peace and quiet at the other end. Of all these great combinations none was more menacing than Lindwall and Miller in their prime.

Ray was the most complete fast bowler I have ever faced. He had everything: speed, hostility, change of pace, swerve, stamina, and superb control. He was truly an artist in a trade that all too frequently relies on brute force.

How quick was Lindwall? The M.C.C. players who toured Australia in 1946-7 reckoned that he was at his fastest during that trip. Whether that was because they were encountering real speed for the first time since the war, or because bowlers are quicker in Australia than in this country (Frank Tyson provided a wonderful example of this), I do not know, but there is no doubt that Ray was unpleasantly, and often devastatingly, fast when he made his initial visit to England in 1948 under Sir Donald Bradman.

I first batted against him at Fenners during this tour. Until then, because there were no really fast bowlers in the country I still cherished the hope that I might become a bowler of genuine pace. Ray's speed compared with mine made the whole idea ridiculous and I realised that I had to develop along other lines if I were to trouble good players, so for the first and not the last time Ray was to have a direct bearing on my own career.

The fast bowler, like the heavyweight boxer, is one of the greatest attractions in the game. Spectators love to see real speed with the prospect of stumps somersaulting out of the ground, the odd delivery rearing past the batsman's nose, and the ball thudding into the 'keeper's gloves standing some twenty yards back. All these things become even more exciting when the bowler has such a perfect approach, body action, and follow through as Ray Lindwall.

The run up is a vital part of pace bowling. It should start slowly and be of sufficient length to enable the bowler to reach his crescendo at the moment of entering his body action and to fade gracefully away in the follow through. Ray more than fulfilled all these requirements and I always maintained that watching him bowl was one of the most satisfying spectacles the game has ever produced. He was indeed a classic bowler. The only one thing which might be criticised was the lowness of his bowling arm. This, combined with his drag, meant that he achieved rather less movement off the seam with the old ball and less lift than a bowler like Miller with a higher action.

Ray was the first of the great post-war 'draggers'. At the time this method had a number of practical advantages which outweighed the disadvantage of losing height at the moment of delivery. In particular the Australian umpires were satisfied if the bowler dropped behind the bowling crease and then dragged through. This meant that the 'dragger' could release the ball closer to the batsman than the orthodox bowler, and at real pace this made a considerable difference. The situation became really impossible when Rorke managed to break the batting crease with his back foot without being no-balled and this was eventually to lead to the later experimental Laws on what constitutes a fair delivery. In England after 1948 the umpires insisted, as they did with both Trueman and Tyson who also dragged, that Ray landed a foot or so behind the bowling crease. Such was his control that he overcame this handicap without any apparent difficulty.

I have never come across a genuinely fast bowler who moved the ball in the air as much and as late as Ray. In consequence he was a most devastating exponent with the new ball that I have encountered and I believe the game has never seen his equal.

It is a common complaint in all grades of cricket that bowlers tend to waste the new ball by not bowling at the stumps. The chief reason for this most justifiable criticism is the difficulty of controlling swing. Aim at the off stump and the ball is apt to swerve too early and too much to worry the batsman; switch to the leg stump and the ball refuses to move and the batsman can play it comfortably through the gaps on the leg side. This problem did not worry Ray and was one of the main reasons for his outstanding success. He possessed the ability to start to swing the ball *outside* the line of leg stump and hit the off. I shall never forget how he deceived Reg Simpson with just such a delivery at Lord's. Reg, besides being a particularly fine player of pace bowling, was very strong off his legs. He attempted to push a Lindwall delivery through the leg side only to find it swing so late that it took the outside of his bat and he was caught by Richie Benaud in the gully.

Ray's natural swing was away from the bat and in common with all great fast bowlers he made the odd ball come back off the seam. However, as a result of a spell in League Cricket he added the inswinger to his repertoire, something I learned to my cost while collecting one of my more lengthy 'ducks'. I was opening the innings with Sir Len Hutton and after a considerable period in which I had the utmost difficulty in making contact I decided it was time to get off the mark. There was only one fieldsman in front of the bat on the offside and Ray bowled almost a half volley outside the off stump. I attempted a push out into the open spaces only to find the ball had dipped in late, careered through an enormous 'gate', and carried my middle stump back to the 'keeper.

Although Ray was a cunning and almost Machiavellian exponent of his craft, as a person he was straightforward and down to earth; a completely uncomplex character who would never need a psychoanalyst. With his stamina, physique, and lust for life he would have made a magnificent pioneer in the early days of Australia, just the man to have around, providing he was on your side, when things were tough; indeed a true Australian.

Ray was such an outstanding bowler that it sometimes is forgotten that he was also a formidable attacking batsman, and the ideal person to take apart an attack which was beginning to wilt. He was an outstanding cutter and could hit with exceptional power. His defence was somewhat suspect, especially, like so many of his brotherhood, against real pace.

Ray's cricketing life and my own have intertwined more than most. He is the only bowler to put me out of action for any length of time. During my first to Australia he bowled a particularly fast delivery which rose chest high from just short of a length. My defensive shot was hurried and I tried to keep the ball down. I managed to achieve this, but used my thumb instead of the bat. Subsequently it proved to be broken and meant that I missed my one and only Test in five tours.

He is the only bowler to whom I have deliberately given my wicket in international cricket. There was nothing on the game and it was then thought that he was retiring from the Test scene and only needed one wicket to bring his total up to 200 victims.

Ironically enough two series later he was to end my own Test career by removing me for a 'pair' in our final encounter. In retrospect it seems to me that I was on the losing side of the deal, but that was a very small price to pay for having had the privilege of facing this great fast bowler on so many occasions. He was a hard but generous adversary who once paid me one of the nicest compliments I have ever received. This occurred after we had won the Ashes back in 1953 and the Australians invaded our dressing room. Ray then made some charming and unprintable comments about my own part in that particular operation.

If I was asked to sum up Ray's bowling in one word I would say 'control'. Control over the fundamentals and control over the finer arts. One of the big problems when batting against him was that as a result of that glorious approach and body action you never knew what to expect. With many bowlers you can pick the bouncer from the moment they commence their run up, but not with Ray; while his slower ball was an absolute masterpiece. When he was at the very height of his career he would bowl about four deliveries within himself, which were quick enough, and then really 'slip himself' for the other two. One of these was frequently a lethal yorker which he could produce without slinging in the odd half volley.

ALAN DAVIDSON
By Richie Benaud
(FROM HIS *WILLOW PATTERNS*, SYDNEY, 1969)

THEY called him 'Al Pal,' or the 'Mayor of Gosford,' and he was one of the finest all-round cricketers the world has seen. Few bowlers could match his late swing and awkward movement off the pitch and there weren't many better fieldsmen in any position in the world. As a batsman he more often than not turned the tide for Australia after the early batsmen had failed.

I first struck him in 1945 when he was playing for Gosford High School and represented Northern High Schools against Combined Metropolitan High Schools in a match at the end of the schools season. In those days he was a hard hitting left-hand batsman and, as always, a brilliant fieldsman, but he bowled left-arm unorthodox over the wrist deliveries rather than the ones that later made him famous. We went on our first tour together to England in 1953 and thereafter Davidson never missed a match other than through injury, nor an overseas tour. I played against him for a couple of years in this Combined School cricket and then suddenly he came from Gosford to play with Northern Districts and was an immediate success. So much so that he played his first Sheffield Shield match in 1949, only three years after leaving school cricket.

There are great cricketers in every era and Davidson was one of the greatest Australia has produced, particularly in the period from 1957 to 1963. This was after Miller and Lindwall had left the scene — Lindwall temporarily — thus allowing Davidson full scope with the new ball rather than condemning him to come on when the shine had all but disappeared.

He was injury prone — sometimes real, sometimes imaginary — but he never left the field or stopped bowling for any other than a very real reason. I caught Johnny Waite off him one day in Cape Town in one of those dismissals where fieldsmen and captain work on a certain plan and it happens to come off. Alan had been limping back to bowl and then boring in at the batsmen and moving the ball late, either into or away from them. Then he would limp back and Craig would ask him if he were all right — he would say 'no' and get a sympathetic pat on the shoulder and then bore in again and yet another magnificent delivery.

The Cape Town pitch was very slow and I asked Craig if I could come up three yards at gully for the one that flew off the thick edge and wouldn't normally carry. Davo limped back for the next ball and Waite square drove it like a bullet. I caught the red blur, body parallel to the ground, and was just rolling over for the second time when Davo arrived alongside me, saying excitedly, 'It was the old trap, you know. The old trap.' It had taken him just two seconds to get down and the boys thought it was the quickest he had moved all day.

This was the match where, so much was he on the massage table, that we had a copper plaque engraved and nailed on to the message table and inscribed 'The A. K. Davidson Autograph Massage Table.'

I saw Waite in South Africa some time later and he recalled this particular incident in the context of Davidson's Test performances and bowling skill. Waite contended that Alan was at his best when not feeling 100 per cent fit. He said the real danger time was when you could see him limping back or looking sorry for himself.

I have never played with or against a more penetrative opening bowler, possibly because of the particular angle in which he came at the batsman, bowling from wide of the return crease to a point just outside the off stump and then swinging late to round about middle stump or middle and leg. He wasn't big swinger of the ball but he certainly moved it as late as anyone I have seen, and this was one of the prime reasons that he was so successful. He only needed to hold the ball across the seam for variety and deliver it with the same action as for the in-swinger and I will defy any batsman in the world to pick the fact that the ball will continue straight on instead of swinging in.

He used to do this sometimes and at other times he would cut the ball away from the right-hander in a fashion that made him the joy of wicket-keeper Wally Grout and his slip fieldsmen. He and Grout used to refer jocularly to the fact that they had 'made' one another, each pointing out that the other would never have done as well without the benefit of either the bowling or wicket-keeping of the other. There was a lot in this for Grout took some magnificent catches off Davidson, both on the off and leg side, and developed a great understanding with him, as well as the ability to pick the way the ball was going to slant.

I think Grout was one of the finest wicket-keepers of all time, fit to be ranked level with Tallon and Langley in my time, but in many ways he was lucky that he played in the same era as a great fast bowler who could find the edge of the bat as often as did Davidson.

I don't think I ever saw a bowler beat the bat as much as Davidson and this was probably because there are more right than left-handers in the world and once the shine had gone from the ball he was constantly coming at them from such an angle that even if they played straight it was still possible for them to be beaten. Some said that he didn't like bowling against left-handers but this was fallacy and they went the same way at their right-hand counterparts unless they were really great players.

For the five years after 1957–58 whenever the side was in trouble the captain, whether it was Craig, Harvey, or myself, always looked for Davidson and rarely did he fail. There was always the thought that at some stage he might break down but the times when he left the field could be counted on the fingers of one hand and he bowled a lot of overs for Australia and New South Wales. In the Fourth Test in Adelaide in 1962–63 he badly tore a hamstring muscle but still played in the Fifth, and in the first Test I ever captained in high temperature in Brisbane he left the field with heat exhaustion in the first session. There were one or two other occasions when he wasn't feeling too well but it was no wonder, considering the amount of work he was given.

I used him unmercifully because he was the best bowler I had and, in fact, the best bowler in the world at that time, constantly worrying the batsmen and thinking them out even if the pitch were unsympathetic to his type of bowling. He bowled well all over the world, irrespective of conditions, sometimes slowing his pace and cutting the ball and sometimes concentrating on bowling as fast as he could in the initial overs and then bowling within himself with the occasional quick delivery to unsettle the batsmen. And he could be quick too!

He is always listed as a fast-medium bowler, and indeed I think of him as such, but he could be really slippery at times and his bumper lifted at the batsman from a spot on the pitch farther up than most. He rarely wasted a bouncer and generally had it about shoulder height at the batsman, and there weren't a great number of bowlers who provided more difficulty with this ball than Davidson. One day in Melbourne, in the second Test in which I captained him he had three for none in his second over, Richardson caught by Grout, Graveney lbw and Watson bowled, in an astonishing display of swing bowling. Graveney played no stroke at the ball that dismissed him and it came back so late and so quickly that he had only just begun to shuffle across when the ball hit him.

In England in 1961 he was uncertain of being fit for the Second Test at Lord's the day before the match, when Harvey, McDonald and I were settling down to choose the side. He called me across to the massage table and said that he didn't think he'd be able to play, a statement that was a crushing blow in view of the fact that I had just declared myself unavailable to the co-selectors. I said to him that he would have to play as Neil was captaining the side and he'd need every bit of support he could get. Davidson has a great regard for Harvey and immediately said that he'd try for 'the little bloke,' and he went out the next day and took five for 42, a magnificent display of fast bowling.

Marvellous character Davo! Two of the things I'll always remember him for are when I took the fluke catch off him at Western Province that day — and how he changed from an invalid to an athletic broad jumper in two seconds to pump my hand and clap me on the back — and the day I felled him with a 'clever' throw. Wes Hall was the batsman at the S.C.G. and he had been playing his shot and running a few yards up the pitch to try and force a throw. I was at mid-wicket and decided to pick the ball up with my back to Wes and throw the stumps down at the batting end next time he tried it. Unfortunately I forgot to tell Davo. The ball hit him in the throat and he went down like a felled steer — gave a final convulsive twitch and we thought he had left us. Up and about 50 seconds later he bored in at West and the next delivery was just about the quickest he bowled all day.

Those two performances live in the memory but they were just two of many that set him apart from the ordinary run-of-the-mill fast bowler. In Sydney in 1962–63 he took five for 25 in England's second innings, routing them with an almost unplayable series of in-swingers and away cutters. But I suppose my fondest memory of him is at Manchester in 1961 when he and McKenzie added 98 priceless runs for the last wicket and then Davo shattered Statham's stumps to win the match late on the last day.

WALKING TALL WITH BENT KNEES
By Peter McFarline
(FROM *THE BEST OF 'THE AGE' 1980–81*, MELBOURNE, 1981)

KEN Mackay bent my knees 23 years ago. They have stayed that way ever since, to the horror of parents, posture experts and the Australian Army.

Adulation of a sport hero has scarcely taken a more personal form. Or a more inexplicable one to those who couldn't comprehend the admiration of a man who carried Queensland cricket through good times and mostly bad. And did it on knees that were bent permanently and shoulders that drooped alarmingly.

There probably has never been a less athletic-looking creature to make it to the top in Australian cricket. Certainly there hasn't been one who built up such a fanatical following in his home town.

I wasn't the only fanatical teenager to mimic his gait and that bovine dedication with which he attacked his chewing gum. In fact, 'Slasher' Mackay put Stimorol gum on the store shelves in Queensland and thus became one of the first sportsmen to be associated in advertising a non-sporting product.

To those raised in Queensland in the 1950s, he deserved far more than he got from the game. After all, Mackay — bent knees and all — stopped Queensland from being the laughing stock of the Sheffield Shield.

And eventually, when the national selectors overcame their bias, he did the same in 37 Test matches. Richie Benaud, who captained him in most of those appearances, insists he was the best team man possible. Despite Benaud's affection for the kind word, we who idolised Mackay knew he was right.

Some said the stooped walk, the loose arms, the general air of debilitation stemmed from a childhood bout of polio. But that was not true. As a schoolboy, Mackay set records for high scoring and never lost the taste. But his determination to occupy the crease at a higher level gained him notoriety rather than acclaim. The nickname 'Slasher' came from his refusal to take risks, at a time when Queenslanders absolutely loved taking risks. The phlegmatic Mackay refused to be drawn from the game he thought should be played. After a double century against New South Wales in Sydney in the 1955–56 season, he was finally recognised.

And didn't he give his detractors some joy in his first Test match against England at Lord's in 1956. Thirty-one runs came in 264 minutes, enough for an entry high up in the Wisden section 'Slowest Individual Test batting'. In that match also Mackay sent down his right-arm medium-pace. Colin Cowdrey drove fiercely. Benaud in the gully put up a hand to take one of cricket's great catches and noted English writer Denzil Batchelor said: 'A cricketing sprat had been used to catch a whale'. I wasn't too happy about that.

Like most of his team-mates, Mackay fell victim to Jim Laker in that series and was left out of the Australian team to tour South Africa in 1957. Queensland all-rounder Ron Archer failed a fitness tests on the eve of the tour, Mackay went as a replacement and averaged 125 runs per innings in the five-Test series. My enduring ache was that he never hit a Test century, although three times he reached the 80s. In the first Test of the 1962–63 series, Mackay was 68 not out when play resumed on the second day. He saw four partners depart and was stranded on 86 not out.

Despite the slow batting tag he always wore, Mackay could score with the best of them — even better. In the Queensland–MCC match before the 1962–63 Brisbane Test, he hit 105 not out between lunch and tea. And that included 20 boundaries.

That season saw his Test demise. He had not been selected until he was 30 and lasted seven years in an Australian cap, scoring, with that neat little prod in front of point, 1,507 runs at 33.48. And he took 50 wickets at 34.42.

These figures scarcely matter. His great achievement was that he succeeded facing up to the world's best bowlers in a manner rather reminiscent of W. C. Fields wielding a croquet mallet.

COLIN EGAR'S BIGGEST DECISION
By Colin Egar
(THE *BRISBANE COURIER MAIL*, c. 1969)

IT was the biggest decision I had to make in cricket of any kind. But if I had not made it, I would have been less than fair and honest to myself, to Ian Meckiff, and to cricket in general.

This was on a Saturday afternoon in November, 1963, in the first Test at Brisbane of the South Africa-Australia series.

Let's face it. Something had to be done about 'chuckers' in cricket. At the time, with nine Tests behind me, I was the senior umpire in Australia. Someone had to bell the cat. It fell to me. It needn't have, but a decision by Australia's captain, Richie Benaud, put me in the hot seat.

Let's look at the background first. The Meckiff business actually had its beginning in the second Test in Sydney in 1959 when Australia beat England by eight wickets.

In England's second innings, Meckiff — whose nickname was 'The Count' — and Alan Davidson ran through the Englishmen as if they didn't exist.

England made only 87, and 'The Count' took six wickets for 38 off 15 overs. Immediately, many English cricket writers branded him a 'chucker.' I had not umpired Test cricket then. But apart from Meckiff, there was growing unease among cricket administrators about the prevalence of illegal actions among some bowlers, mainly those who were quick . . .

By the 1962-3 season, Meckiff had changed his action, but could not find form for a while, and did not play in any of the Tests against England.

I umpired four of the five Tests of this series, but missed the Sydney one while a new umpire was being tried out.

While the Sydney Test was on, Meckiff came to Adelaide with the Victorian Sheffield Shield team for the game against South Australia. I umpired it. This was the only time in that season I officiated in a match in which Meckiff played. Then why didn't I call him, in view of the current agitation? I don't know whether I would have, but I didn't have a chance to, anyway.

In two innings, Meckiff bowled only from my end, and it is not the bowler's end umpire's responsibility to call for throwing. That is the square leg umpire's role. And in fact, he was called. Jack Kierse, at square leg, called Meckiff, but only once.

The Count just muttered, 'Ah, hell ...' but took it very well otherwise and went on bowling. He reeled off about 40 overs for the game. At this time, Meckiff was not bowling with the same demonic pace as in 1958-9. He found form towards the end of 1962-3 season, and finished high on the State's bowling averages and aggregates.

Meckiff's selection in Australia's team for the first Test against South Africa inevitably sparked Australia-wide conjecture.

I went to Brisbane with no pre-conceived ideas about Meckiff or anyone else. [He] was the hot topic. The night before the game, the Count and I were in a room at Lennon's Hotel, talking cricket. Ian said to me, 'If you think my action is illegal, it will embarrass me more than you if you call me. Don't worry' (or something like that).

Australia did not take the field against South Africa until after lunch on the second day, Saturday. Lou Rowan, a detective in the Queensland Police Force, was my umpiring mate for this game. This was only one of 19 Tests which we umpired together.

I took up station at square leg, at the southern (or scoreboard) end. It was expected Australia's captain Richie Benaud would open the bowling with Graham McKenzie bowling with the breeze. But when he got out on the field, Richie made the decision which put me in the hot seat. He decided to open with McKenzie bowling INTO the breeze, with me at the bowlers' end.

For the second over, he brought on Meckiff, and I went to square leg. If it had not been for Benaud's change of mind, Ian Meckiff might have gone through the match. I don't know. I don't know how Lou Rowan would have viewed him.

The first ball he bowled, I thought was suspect. I took the plunge on the next, and called him. I think I heard a pin drop in the outer. It was that electric. Then I called him again ... and again ... and again. Altogether I called him four times. Were they the only balls I considered illegal? No. Meckiff bowled 12 balls, and I would rate eight of them as illegal.

But if I kept calling him, when would he ever finish his over? At tea ... at stumps ... or when he broke down from exhaustion?

The Brisbane crowd was very conscious that the first trouble over Meckiff four years before had been set alight by English cricket writers. [They] made their views pointedly clear that I was on the side of the Englishmen in absentia.

After McKenzie's second over, Meckiff moved up to take the ball again, to bowl his second over. But Benaud called for the ball, had a brief word with Meckiff, then called for Alan Connolly. Why didn't Benaud bowl Meckiff from the other end, where I would have been bowler's umpire? I didn't ask Benaud why, and he said nothing.

None of the Australian team showed any outward reaction to my calling Meckiff. I knew, and they knew, that this would end his cricket career. Deep down, it was impossible for me not to feel regret. But it had to be done if I was to square off with my own conscience. I think the Australia team was expecting it.

Barry Shepherd, from Western Australia, was twelfth man for the game. That night he said to me, 'You know, the 11 of us are right behind you, Colin.'

I said, 'No, 12 of you.' I'd been talking to Meckiff.

But while the reaction of the Australian team — and of the South Africans later — was very comforting to me, the Brisbane crowd had me 'set.'

As we came off at stumps, a mob of about 20 or 30 young chaps rushed on to the ground. They made straight for Meckiff to take him off shoulder high. They carried him to the stand gates, then turned and saw me walking across the field. They rushed up to me, and spat at me, all over my white coat. I am accustomed to hotheaded football fans — I umpired 100 Australian Rules league games, also grand finals — but I never in my life thought this sort of despicable thing could happen in cricket.

As soon as I got into the dressing room, I took off the coat in disgust and distaste and threw it into a corner. I said to Meckiff later, pointing to my coat on the floor in a corner, 'How do you like that? They spat all over me.' He replied, 'What are you grizzling about? What about me? As soon as they saw you coming, they diced me on the concrete terrace.'

As I walked off the ground at tea, I had been given the silent treatment by men and women in the members' stand. I was pretty cheesed off about it. When play was resumed on the Tuesday, when we came off for the lunch break, Lou Rowan recognised two of his plainclothes police officer mates. They were standing by the gate leading from the field.

Then they told us they had been detailed to keep watch over us. Some crank in Melbourne had rung police headquarters there, and told them, 'We're going to do a Kennedy on Egar.' Lou Rowan and I kept this pretty quiet. But you can't keep much quiet for long in cricket.

After lunch, when play resumed, I was at square leg, dead square on to Australia's wicketkeeper Wally Grout, a Queenslander.

After a couple of balls, he signalled to me to move sideways a couple of paces. I did so. But after the next ball, I moved in close to him. I called, 'What's all this about?' He called back. 'There's a chap right behind you in the stand with a camera to his eye and he's got a gun in it. If he missed you, he'd get me.'

Irrepressible Wally had heard of the 'assassination story,' and couldn't resist having a dig. It was one of the few laughs I had during that Test.

THREE CAPTAINS

By Bob Simpson

(FROM HIS *CAPTAIN'S STORY*, LONDON, 1966)

WHEN I made the Shield team at the age of sixteen my first captain was the mighty Keith Miller. I will never forget my first match with him. He had always been a boyhood hero of mine and I was delighted at the prospect of playing under him. As we walked onto the field I stuck close to him thinking, 'Well, here I am beside a great man.' I followed him to the centre and waited to be sent to my position. He stood by the pitch surrounded by the crowd of players. Suddenly he looked around. I thought, 'Now he'll really show me what to do as a captain and set the field.' He said just one word — 'Scatter'. And that's what the fieldsmen did — they scattered to their positions.

I didn't realise at the time, but in those days the N.S.W. team virtually ran itself. The team was so powerful and had so many great names — Miller, Morris, Lindwall, Benaud, Davidson — that it needed little captaincy.

The outlook then for a young player was completely different to now. As the youngster of the team I did not quite move in the same circles as Miller, who was much older and more experienced. I felt Keith did not pay enough attention to the young players. On the field he was a dynamic character and, in many ways, a great captain. I was probably a bit young to appreciate the best of Miller's captaincy, but I know Richie Benaud holds him in very high regard. Benaud considers him one of the greatest captains he has played with.

Miller's greatest asset as a captain was his ability to inspire his team by his own performances. Benaud could do this too, but Richie's greatest attribute was the way in which he could inspire confidence in the players themselves. Miller, on the other hand, could take complete charge of a game either batting or bowling. In many games we played he would be loafing around the field when suddenly he would realise we needed wickets desperately. He would grab the ball, knock over a couple of wickets and we would be back in the game ...

Ian Craig was my first Australian captain. Craig's service as captain of Australia had never been fully recognised. I'm sure that much of the success that followed with Benaud can be attributed to the good start Craig gave the team. Cricket was at its lowest ebb when Craig took over as captain. Australia had been thrashed in England in 1956 and beaten by Pakistan on the way home. Craig was named as captain of the New Zealand tour in 1957 and took with him the youngest team ever to leave Australian shores. Ian got the job ahead of Neil Harvey and Richie Benaud, one or the other of whom had seemed certainties. Both these great players got right behind Craig and helped to mould the team into a happy and competent bunch. Harvey 'did a Grout,' declaring in front of the team that Craig had his full support.

Craig did such a good job as captain that he was again appointed for the South African tour in 1957–58. We started the tour as complete underdogs. Australia had just lost to England and South Africa only eighteen months before had drawn a series with England. When we landed we found the Springboks being quoted as 4–1 favourites. This probably did us more good than harm. It made us even more determined to show the South Africans Australia could still play cricket.

In this tour Craig really blossomed as a captain. His handling of the team of the field was remarkable for one so young. He was only twenty-two, yet he had the team working as an efficient unit. His captaincy on the field was equally magnificent. He had the team 100 per cent with him and did a wonderful job with Alan Davidson and Richie Benaud who suddenly came to the fore as the world's greatest all-rounders.

Craig's career as a captain was cut short when he picked up hepatitis after returning to Australia. He was unavailable for the 1958–59 series and Richie Benaud stepped into the breach. Richie was a surprise choice because Neil Harvey had been Craig's deputy in New Zealand and South Africa. On top of that, many people doubted if Benaud had the temperament to do the job. I can understand why this was so. Benaud, especially before 1956, had seemed to many to be a bit standoffish. Most of those who played against him did not like him at all. They found him unapproachable, aloof — not at all the type who appealed as a likely captain. On his appointment, however, he seemed to change completely. From a man who was very unpopular in Australian cricket he became one of the most popular captains we have ever had.

To a man his team admired and respected him and was willing to follow him to the end.

The secret behind Benaud's success was Richie's tremendous enthusiasm. Whatever Benaud lacked in ability he made up with enthusiasm and zest for the game. He practised harder than anyone I have ever seen. At practice Richie would have a hit first. Then, at 3.30 or four o'clock he would pick up the ball and not put it down again until six o'clock when practice was called off. In South Africa, when he was not happy with his form, he would stay at the ground when the rest of us had gone home and for an hour or more would bowl at a handkerchief laid on a good length. A couple of native boys would retrieve the ball for him until he was satisfied with his bowling.

Benaud carried this enthusiasm through into captaincy. His first act as captain was to arrange a team dinner before the First Test in Brisbane. A dinner before every Test match is now standard practice for Australian sides. At these dinners anyone is free to take the floor. We all put up our ideas, our observations on players from the other team, we talk about our own form and the methods we think would work best against certain opposing batsmen. Even the most junior player can put forward his ideas and sometimes he comes up with one that might prove a match-winner.

The 1958–59 series was a triumph for Benaud as a bowler as well as a captain. His bowling seemed to improve with the responsibility of captaincy and this probably helped to build up the blind faith his team had in his ability. We followed Richie through anything. If he felt we could do it, then we knew we could do it — and we did . . .

Nobody whinged when they got out playing the Benaud brand of cricket. Richie was easily the best captain I have ever played under. Every man in the Shield team and every man in his Test and touring teams was made to feel an important cog in the wheel.

Benaud was the greatest bluffer in cricket. All the time he would be trying to outwit the opposing players and if he could not outwit them he would outbluff them. In the Commonwealth team tour at Hong Kong, Richie had been fiddling with the game in his usual fashion until it got to the stage where we had to get six batsmen out for six runs or lose the match. Richie slipped the word to Neil Adcock to get stuck into them. Sure enough Neil bowled over the six wickets for five runs and we won the match.

The finish prompted the English bowler Howard Rhodes to explode, 'There's no doubt about you, Benaud, if you put your head in a bucketful of garbage you'd come out with a mouthful of diamonds.'

When I was elected captain, Benaud sent me a telegram: 'Congratulations. Remember — diamonds are a skip's best friends.'

Benaud's greatest contribution to Australian cricket has been the establishment in the players' minds that the game is played to entertain the public. When I got my start in big cricket the players did not really care about the public. They used to think, 'Let the cricket and the public take care of themselves.'

Benaud took over when cricket was not at its highest ebb and quickly instilled into the players that the public must be entertained. He quickened the tempo of the game. He made the bowlers get through their overs quickly and kept the idea in the batsmen's minds that they must score quickly. Yet he never really drove the players. He used to give me instructions before I went out to bat. Get on with the game, get runs, and get them in the shortest and safest time.

DOUG WALTERS'S SECOND VISIT TO A TEST MATCH
By Ian Wooldridge
(*THE CRICKETER*, 1966)

THE frustrated poets who write newspaper headlines sweated blood to have him neatly and alliteratively labelled for life by the morning-after, but the best they could do was the Dungog Dasher and I doubt if it will stick.

For one thing Kevin Douglas Walters does not come from Dungog. For another, while 'dashing' vividly describes his first blistering scoring stroke in Test cricket, it evokes an image of a latter-day Miller destroying an attack between games of poker. Walters will never play his cricket like that.

The first physical feature that strikes one about him is a quite un-Australian paleness. The second is a baffling agelessnes of face. You might guess at 25 or even 30 but at Brisbane you would have questioned or even suspected, as some actually did, his 19 years 11 months and 23 days. The effect, then, is less of a supreme athlete with a glowing Olympian presence than of an old head on young shoulders. If you glanced twice as he passed you in Regent Street you might take him for a youngish family man recently promoted to head office from Portsmouth.

You could certainly complete a long conversation with him without knowing that he had recently been promoted to the exclusive brethren of ten Australian batsmen in 100 years who have made centuries against England on their first appearance.

His speaking voice is an octave lower than Sir Donald Bradman's but he wastes about as few words. He talks in neatly rounded sentences. The same economy applies to his cricket. He stands motionless in the crease, bowls medium pace off the shortest effective run.

His apparent slightness is deceptive. He is 5 ft. 9½ in. and slender. But he weighs 11½ stone and has great physical strength. At 19 and 2 months he scored 253 for New South Wales in Adelaide and went straight back to take 7 for 63. He enjoys bowling as much as batting which perhaps, after all, is an admission of innocent youth. Otherwise, at Brisbane, there were only 48 minutes in which he looked anything less than totally calm, totally mature, totally in command of his destiny.

Those 48 minutes came as he edged his way along the precipice of the 90s. It was an unforgettable passage of cricket, played out in the rich, stained-glass hues of a lowering sub-tropical sun. Few writers of even the most lurid schoolboy fiction would have dared manufacture such an implausible climax. The interruption for drinks, the distraction of the runaway mongrel, the remorselessly tight bowling of Titmus and Allen stretching his nerve to snapping point, the near run-out at 98 . . .

It was rightly recorded in some of the most colourful writing of the tour, but it would have been less colourful had one known what was passing through his mind. 'It never occurred to me at that stage,' he said later, 'that I couldn't get the 100. I was careful because they were bowling so well.'

He took the ovation and the acclaim of a nation as calmly as he had advanced to 90. He has made 100 on his first appearance at each new level of cricket except for the New South Wales state side. This, quite amazingly, was only his twentieth first-class match yet failure seemed barely to have occurred to him.

He knows precisely where he is going. There was, for example, no press of businessmen at his door the following morning, out-bidding one another for the exclusive rights to endorse their bats with the Douglas Walters autograph. Those arrangements had been completed a year before. It is a strangely sophisticated picture for a boy whose background is authentically provincial and unprivileged. The Dungog of the headlines is merely the nearest railhead, some 130 miles north-west of Sydney. Walters's home is at Marshdale, still deeper in the sticks. It is claimed that the entire population of 112 listened to every ball of his innings.

He is the third of four children born to Ted and Fay Walters on their 13,000 acre property. By Australian, let alone Texan, standards it was prosperous enough to have supported a son at Timbertop. But Walters read the three r's at a rural school, left at 15 and milked the cows. It is perhaps this parallel, more than any other, that will burden him with comparison with Bradman. Yet the lines veer sharply apart when you probe his cricketing education.

By 16 he was a prodigy, being slipped into the New South Wales Country Districts side to make 0 and 17 against Ted Dexter's team at Tamworth. But he cannot recall when he first held a bat and denies any compulsive urge to play cricket at all. 'I was probably about nine,' he said. 'I remember we rolled out a pitch on the farm and some of the lads used to come in. It's as vague as that, I'm afraid.'

Even while his name was spreading through school and junior cricket there were few privileges. His first visit to a Test match was to watch Goddard's South Africans for a single day in Sydney. His second visit was to score 155 in Brisbane. By then, however, the talent net had caught him. He landed in safe and experienced hands, moved to Sydney to work in a sports store and play grade cricket with Cumberland and Richie Benaud.

Despite eye-catching feats in his first full Sheffield Shield season he was left home when Simpson led Australia's 1965 side to West Indies. His next chance came against M.C.C. for New South Wales. He took it with a century and a fortnight later was opening 93 telegrams on the occasion of his maiden Test 100. The one he valued most came from Norman O'Neill who, having made 31 runs in four innings at the start of the season, was home in Sydney. Another came from a Canberra opportunist who had rushed from the maternity home to wire: 'It's a boy and we're naming him Douglas.'

Back home in Marshdale, Bill Hudson lost 100 schooners of beer when he bet that Kevin Douglas Walters could not make 100 first time out against the Poms. Only when you have seen him bat and tested his self-possession do you realise how rash that wager really was.

CONSIDER THE LILLEES
By Ronald Mason
(*JOURNAL OF THE CRICKET SOCIETY*)

THERE can be no doubt that the chief abiding memory of the 1972 season must be, for most of those who saw it, Dennis Lillee's run-up and action. This tall and graceful character, you will remember, moved meditatively back from the region of the bowler's umpire (polishing the ball, meanwhile, in the uninviting contemporary manner, on the tenderer reaches of his upper thigh) until at about the forty-sixth pace it occurred to him that if he was ever going to get the ball actually delivered he might as well turn back; the which he then frighteningly did, tearing flat out as if the hounds of hell were after him, with the wind whistling through his hair and moustache, until he rose in the last half-dozen yards of his sprint into a glorious rhythmic liberation of shoulder and elbow and free-flowing swing of release, which loosed upon the batsman a scarifying thunder-bolt that I was always surprised that any one of them ever saw at all. What happened after that was the batsman's affair, not mine, thank goodness; it was the glory of the action that entranced me, entranced, I am sure, everybody on the ground, with the probable exception of the man whose business it was to cope with the ball when it arrived, very shortly after.

THOMSON MADE THE DIFFERENCE
By Henry Blofeld
(THE *GUARDIAN*, JANUARY, 1975)

AFTER England's first innings in the first Test at Brisbane it was likely that either Thomson would have to break down or one or two of England's batsmen would have to discover unknown powers if England were to salvage anything from the series. Among the arguments about the morality of bouncers, about the inadequacy of the umpires, and about the Machiavellian appearance of Lillee on the field, not to mention the technical shortcomings of England's batsmen, the true ability of Thomson may have been lost to sight.

To the Englishmen he has appeared from nowhere as a nightmarish figure. When the batsmen sleep at night their rest must be disturbed by that change of step just before delivery, those enormous heaving shoulders, and the agony of trying to pick up the line of the ball and lay a bat on it before the ball strikes a thigh or a rib a painful blow. There have been moments when one has felt, too optimistically perhaps, that Thomson could be played, and that all it required was a mixture of guts, technique, and inward composure. But in fact it needed a great batsman to play him. Cowdrey has given a glimpse of how he would have succeeded 20 years ago as he did against Lindwall and Miller; but he had genius which transcends and combines the mixture of guts, technique, and composure.

Thomson is extremely fast. Only players who have been involved can make true comparisons, but once a bowler is as fast as that, it does not matter if he is half a yard quicker or slower than Tyson or Larwood. It was Frank Tyson himself who said to me at Brisbane that he thought Thomson was about Statham's pace of 1954/55 out here; but he has had to revise that opinion since. When Thomson first appeared, many were not quite able to believe it and put his achievements down to the pitch or to bowling in front of his home crowd.

When bowlers are as quick as that — and there are seldom more than two or perhaps three in a decade — they win Test matches on their own. Thomson is fortunate to have Lillee to partner him, for Lillee has since his return to cricket developed into probably a more formidable bowler than before, and into one who, when his blood is up as it seems to be almost all the time, is only a little slower than he was in 1972.

Combinations of fast bowlers are even more irresistible when it comes to winning matches. Perhaps the only time a formidable fast bowling combination near its best has lost a Test series was in Australia in 1958/59 when England had Trueman, Statham, and Tyson and lost 4-0. But the methods of the Australian bowlers in that series were, to say the least, questionable. Meckiff, Rorke, Slater, and Burke had a combination of crooked elbows and drags that had never before been seen on a Test ground at the same time. In these last weeks Lillee has clearly helped Thomson and taken some of his wickets for him, but a bowler who is able to make the ball lift so frighteningly into the batsman's ribs from just short of a length does not need all that help.

Thomson is an erratic bowler who has turned Marsh, his wicket-keeper, into a fairly considerable athlete. He has a slinging action which makes him a sort of Les Jackson of Derbyshire to the power of two and a half — but without the same control. To start with the balls go down the legside, down to the right of first slip, over the wicket-keeper's head for four byes; there is a wide, followed by a no-ball, but then that vicious ball short of a length which the batsman thinks he has covered. He does too, only to find that instead of coming on to the middle of the blade the ball is lifting at a vicious pace towards his gloves and his chest. It needs genius and luck to play those for any length of time.

Like all great fast bowlers Thomson has an extra yard of pace in reserve. All of a sudden a batsman may feel that he has settled in and worked Thomson out when along comes a ball a yard quicker which prompts a hasty reflex and an edged catch.

Cowdrey — and there cannot be many better judges — felt that Thomson's worth as a fast bowler was perfectly illustrated by the last three balls he bowled to him in England's first innings in Sydney. Cowdrey's technique against the really fast stuff has been happier than anyone's although he has not yet made a big score. The first ball now was the one short of a length. As always, Cowdrey moved behind the line, but the ball took off and hit the bat handle, going over the slips for four. The next was short again, and Cowdrey aimed to turn it to leg; but it rose and hit him on the left arm, for this time Cowdrey was able to pull his bat away. The next ball was the quicker one on middle and leg. He played back, tried to take his bat away, but could not and was caught at short leg off the glove.

Cowdrey said he could not remember facing three such nasty ones in a row. None was really short, and they showed the tremendous strength of the man. Batsmen who can play this type of bowling grow: they are not produced. England do not have them at the moment, and after four Test matches Thomson incredibly has taken thirty wickets. If he had not been there, England's batsmen would probably have been comparable to Australia's. If England had had a similarly devastating bowler who could have generated equal confidence in the side, England's slips and gullies would in all probability have themselves been holding remarkable catches. England may not have a Ross Edwards to field in the covers, but if things had gone well, whoever had found himself there would have fielded a notch or two above himself in accordance with the spirit of a successful side. It really can be said that this is a series won and the Ashes regained by the efforts of one man.

There were other lesser reasons too. Ian Chappell is a tough and an astute captain; there was Lillee to combine with Thomson; and then there were the tall, cheerful, mustachioed figure of Walker able to cut and swing the ball into or away from the batsman at will; a wonderful fielding side; and an off-spinner in Mallett, tall, thin, and fair-haired, who in spite of his nick name "Rowdy" was as silent and taciturn as ever and who in the end spun the ball accurately enough to make sure the Ashes came back to Australia yesterday evening. Take away Thomson, and the equation would not have been the same at all.

GREG CHAPPELL, EFFORTLESSLY UPRIGHT
By Kate Fitzpatrick
(THE *SYDNEY MORNING HERALD*, FEBRUARY 26, 1983)

FROM 11 am Friday morning until sixish on Monday evening I watched the Sheffield Shield Match between Queensland and NSW. I was supposed to be interviewing Greg Chappell when he wasn't fielding or batting.

But, as Mum says, "the road to hell is paved with good intentions." All we did was reminisce. I went into a four-day trance; watching cricket is as near as I'll ever get to meditating; and was swamped by waves of nostalgia.

I guess it had something to do with being the same age as Greg and coming from South Australia.

Greg Chappell's old school, Prince Alfred College, had the same maroon colours as Queensland. It was strange last weekend, a time warp back to school matches between PAC and the blue and white boys from St Peter's.

When I was at school, PAC boys were considered a bit fast — glamorous Protestants who were not forced to confess experimenting with the 1, 2 and 3 minor mating league steps out of a possible (but unthinkable) 10. SAC (my old school) girls were considered a bit fast themselves, but anything more than 3 (or 4ish) was beyond the pale and *we* had to confess.

I was safe. Apart from never getting any offers, I was far too busy chaperoning my friend Viv to muck around. She had a crush on a tall, blond, handsome PAC football star with a red MGA. Simon was *very* glamorous. At Victor Harbour over Christmas he took us for 100 mph car rides with the roof off. This was before breath tests, seat belts and kilometres. Wherever he went, Viv went and so did I.

The "Gidget goes sporty" romance lasted for two years. We watched all the PAC cricket and football matches and attended every dance. I don't remember seeing Greg Chappell. I know he was there. We probably even danced together . . . but made absolutely no impression on each other.

I can't imagine why, he's pretty impressive these days. Tall, lean, erect, proud, dark, strong and silent. He looks broody and mysterious. He has an absolutely wonderful back, completely straight without being rigid and no wings. Ray Robinson described him as a poplar, upright in growth with little spread. Effortlessly upright, he gets taller as you watch him.

It's hard to imagine him ever joining the rest of us as we curl, curve and collapse back to the all fours of our beginnings. He bends in all directions, even falls backwards, and instantly returns, springs back to an absolute centre. Even leaning on his bat he is perfectly balanced.

The hand on his hip corresponds with the leg crossed in front. The straight leg echoes his stiff arm, with its bat extension. Exactly half of him is either side of a plumb line. And he's resting!

He was probably carried, and then walked, never crawled. He has thick dark very curly hair, and big deep blue eyes that miss nothing. "I have an American friend who is amazed when I can tell him what time he arrived at the ground and where he was sitting. You can see a lot out there. You get used to it."

He can tell you if (and when) you nodded off, or wrote something or cracked a joke. "I don't miss much — just the odd ball . . ." He thinks he's pretty good at reading people and situations.

He has long legs, arms, small wrists, and very beautiful long-fingered hands, which he uses economically, deftly, like a good mime artist. They are very strong and quite tough looking. One has a permanent scab that he keeps worrying and knocking. And the other a bone broken taking an amazing catch to dismiss David Gower. Occasionally they become side flippers which he raises to acknowledge a "Hey Greg" or "Good on you Chappell". Nothing else moves, just his hands — from pointing down to parallel to the ground, wrists still attached to his thighs.

It's great fun trying to work out his field placing signals. To watch him and Allan Border practising what seems to be fly casting or elegant tennis forehands, and wonder if it's a trap. On the opposing team his brother Trevor seems to turn away as if he doesn't want to see them and feel obliged to tip off Dirk Wellham at the other end.

His mood on the field changed from day to day . . . lean boyish jumping around, head butting the ball, one day . . . still, severe, tougher, older, meaner looking the next.

Going to a Shield match is a bit like attending a school play or sports day. Most of the audience are players' friends, or family on comps. Waiting for guest tickets to be brought down to the Members' gate, you can pass the time by trying to guess which cricketer and what relation. "I bet that's Dirk Wellham's brother."

On the third day, huge white clouds behind the empty Hill looked like snow-covered mountains, and the idle, suspended, cable cars like a ski-lift ... Cricket in Switzerland ... Edelweiss, Leiderhorn, the Matterhorn, cow bells and red balls. As my mind wandered off, my companions joked about feeling like cricket groupies and discussed the other regulars there permanently positioned under the players' window, and the 16-year-old down the front today featuring a plunging white bathing suit top, and modest skirt ensemble.

Suddenly he's with us again, jumper on, towel around his neck like a thick scarf, and would not be drawn into a conversation about cricket bats.

We start on childhood again. "I didn't grow much until I was 16. I was very short, then all of a sudden, over the Christmas holidays. It probably has to do with the fact that I never ate much. Not much at breakfast, still don't. And I never ate lunch. I used to throw my Vegemite sandwiches away behind the shed. Mum'll kill me when she reads this.

"It was a waste of time. I was too excited to eat. I wanted to play cricket. You had to stay in the shelter, *sitting down* for 15 minutes! I couldn't stand it. I was exhausted at the end of the day. I'd ride my bike home and on the way stop off at a friend's place to do a bit of boxing. I was fine, until he hit me in the stomach. Then I was history."

Half joking, he says: "I sometimes think I started to grow when I started eating lunch." His son, Stephen, is the same. "Only not, sneaky like me, he brings his home untouched".

He says he doesn't hold grudges, but remembers *every* mean thing ever done to him, from the age of three, in the most astonishing detail. Mrs Boxer, a grade three teacher, hated smelly little boys, and accused him of passing a rude note. "I was at cricket practice, not even there."

He was supposed to tell his mother, didn't and sweated for 10 days waiting for a parental show-down after the PTA meeting. Nothing happened. Either Mrs B forgot, or his Mum ignored it. "Anyway, none of us were very smelly."

Another teacher, Mrs Thompson, kept him in after school and forgot him. His worried parents arrived at the school and found him still sitting, alone, in the dark classroom.

He was "pushed" off a fence at seven, by someone he remembers, but won't name, and hurt his arm. His mother said it looked all right and to stop wingeing . . . just the way my Mum did to my sister after a game of Rockets to the Moon.

After three days of little weeps under the tankstand, and less sleep, a doctor announced he had a greenstick fracture. Momentary triumph that something really was wrong with him changed to frustrated boredom when he wasn't allowed to bat. "It drove me crazy. I kept arguing that it'd make things better, like wearing an arm pad. But my coach wouldn't wear it."

Queensland declared at 405. I glanced back at him behind the glass and never found out what he meant. The pitch is being flattened by a dear little motorised roller, squeaking slowly up and down, missing the stumps. Two other groundsmen with buckets, spades, and brooms come out to fix the pot-holes. They look like the grave diggers in *Hamlet* . . . rough, very casually dressed, leaning on their spades, cracking jokes.

He didn't like school. Never read a play or finished a book, and still passed. "It wasn't hard. The teachers relied on a few of us getting through to keep their jobs. They usually gave you the questions, went over and over the main points until something sank in. I'm not proud of it but I didn't want to be a doctor or lawyer. I just wanted to play cricket. Anyway, after cricket practice I was too bloody tired to read."

He reads a lot these days, novels, autobiographies, golf magazines. Currently *A Retreat From Radiance* by Ian Moffitt. "I thought he was showing off to start, but as I get more towards the climax I'm loving it." Before that, *An Indecent Obsession* by Colleen McCullough. "Didn't bother with *The Thorn Birds* . . . everyone else had. Didn't go for the Beatles much either. I never wanted to do or like anything just because everyone else did. It put me off. I'm still the same. I liked the Dave Clark Five and the Hollies."

The men in green coats seem at a loss — powerless to stop guests sitting in front of the Members' Stand. They give up finally and decide to join their families, cushions and Thermoses, and watch. Very shiny, clean men with red faces, and brilliantly-oiled short back and sides, with a perfectly-combined breaker wave in the front. They are much nicer on slow Shield days. It's a bit Hitler's Dad's Army during Tests or the Benson and Hedges games.

Allan Border comes to the door, baulks when he sees someone, backs off inside, has a *good* look, and then comes out with a cup of tea. Greg's back. He says he's not demonstrative, overtly affectionate or emotional. Wasn't encouraged to be. "We were told to win and lose gracefully — that's it really. Ian's the most volatile. Says what he thinks. Trevor's had the advantage of learning from both of us."

Warm hands, cold heart. "I try not to hurt people. I'm amazed how people can hurt others. I'm sure I've done it. Mine'd be acts of omission more than anything else. I think of sending my wife or my mother flowers when they're ill, for example, and remember late at night, or on a plane. I've got a great memory, but forgot my shoes on my wedding day, had to borrow my brother-in-law's. They hurt."

He loves his family, his brothers, his wife, *all* children, especially *his*; cricket and Dennis Lillee. He was very upset by a newspaper report about a two-year-old girl drowning in a backyard pool. He lives with the natural parental fear of something happening to his kids.

The only time he remembers crying (described as "near to tears") was the day his first child, Stephen, was born. He was at Lord's in England, batting. His wife was in Australia. When drinks were brought on the twelfth man handed him a wire service photograph of his wife, Judy, and his brand new son. It made me teary hearing the story.

Cheating? "I cheated a little bit at school, but I was dumb — only from kids who knew less than me — or were wrong. And I was usually found out."

Cricket? "If you call appealing for an LBW or a caught behind when you aren't sure, but hope you'll get away with it, cheating . . . I've done a bit of that, everyone does."

He is adamant that money or a "win at all costs" attitude had nothing to do with the Melbourne underarm incident. He was frustrated and annoyed. It was a protest about bad conditions. The administration was taking no notice: "Nothing's wrong."

"Would actors go on with holes in the stage and a leaking roof? There was no consideration for players. We had no right to an opinion. Look, six off the last ball was a one in one million chance . . . a three or a four wouldn't have helped them. Winning for us meant a couple of days off, a luxury, that's all.

"It *was* wrong. I regret it. I wouldn't do it again. I was shattered at the outrage and screaming chaos that follows. I'm stuck with it . . . but it wasn't illegal." So he went to New Zealand the following year and was voted man of the series.

He is very pleased that his children are musical and artistic like his wife. "The only thing I regret is not learning to play the piano." When he has finished playing cricket he intends taking it up full-time and playing golf. He says his son is the best seven-year-old cricketer in the world. "He's had a bat in his hand since he was born. If that's what he want I'll help him — but I won't force him. I'm happy he's learning the piano."

On the afternoon of the fourth day while NSW batted, an old man had a heart attack — the Members filled up with police, doctors, paramedics and ambulance men with respirators, injections and little flat-iron, heart-starter jumper leads. Elderly spectators moved away and looked steadfastly ahead, cricket wiping out fears of mortality. The players turned every now and then to check progress.

When I announced that I was interviewing Greg Chappell I dimly remember various people saying, "He's difficult, taciturn, secretive, humourless or hard." He must have hated those people or been bored witless.

"I feel I'm quite misunderstood — that's OK." Somehow I didn't believe him. He admits to being determined, ambitious, going after and getting most things he wants. He says he's not much of a businessman, just good at picking partners.

He likes writing but thinks too fast and gets frustrated. On the other hand he can't stand being ghosted. He does have a phenomenal memory — long and short-term — quotes conversation verbatim and remembers in detail what happened and what everyone wore. He'd be a great witness.

He is very grateful for the encouragement, help and sacrifice of his parents and refutes the story of his grandfather's (Victor Richardson) apparent lack of interest. "That's rubbish — he was very keen on us playing and doing well — I remember playing with him once on a turf wicket behind his house. It must have been when Trevor was born."

The only time Sir Don Bradman ever spoke to him was to tell him to change his grip. "I was strong on the leg side — not the off. Sir Don was a SA selector — he didn't speak to anyone really except Ashley Mallett, the best spinner I've seen. Anyway he walked through as usual. I said, 'Good morning, Sir Donald.'

"He stopped, turned and said, 'You'll never be a good player with a grip like that.' I asked if he had any suggestions. He did and showed me and said it'd feel uncomfortable at first but it would be easier with practice.

"He then walked off, stopped at the door, turned and said, 'I've only given this bit of advice to one other player. He didn't take it. He's no longer in the team.'

"I rushed to the nets. It *was* uncomfortable but it got easier. It's the grip I use now. I've used it ever since."

He has ears that join without lobes — like mine. It's supposed to indicate criminal tendencies. "I think I would have been a criminal if I hadn't been a cricketer."

Yeah I bet — a hit and run merchant no doubt.

He is warm, friendly, charming, well-mannered, humorous, sensitive, devoted to his wife and family, earthy, honest and a lot older and younger than 34.

He's a very Aussie hero, a bargain whatever way you look at it. Mrs Chappell is a lucky woman. I didn't ask about the ducks. May he never have another.

ACKNOWLEDGEMENTS

WE are extremely indebted to the following publishers, authors, executors and family representatives, who have granted permission to reprint copyrighted material:

Keith Dunstan for several of his articles which appeared in his book *The Paddock that Grew* (Cassell, Melbourne, 1962) and for his definition of 'cricket' from his *A Cricket Dictionary* (Sun Books/Macmillan, Melbourne, 1983)

To the literary executors of the late A.B. (Banjo) Paterson and RETUSA Pty Ltd, for permission to use extracts from the several articles which appeared either in *Songs of the Pen* (Lansdowne, Sydney, 1983) or in the *Sydney Mail* (1932)

John Woodcock, editor of *Wisden Cricketers' Almanack*, for Sir Robert Menzies' court story

David Frith, the editor of *Wisden Cricket Monthly*, for 'The Oblivion of Eddie Gilbert' and for his article on Leo O'Brien.

Christopher Martin-Jenkins for permission to use several articles from *The Cricketer*

Mr A. McCleary, the son of the late G.F. McCleary, for 'The Match that made the Ashes', from his book *Cricket with the Kangaroo*, reprinted by permission of the Bodley Head Ltd for the publisher Hollis & Carter

Malcolm Gemmell, executor of the estate of the late Jack Fingleton, for several articles by Fingleton

The editor, Mr Jim Coldham, for the several articles which appeared in the *Journal of the Cricket Society*

Margaret Hughes for 'Lightning Perfection' from her book, *All on a Summer's Day* (Stanley Paul, London, 1953)

Margaret Hughes, as literary executor of the late Sir Neville Cardus, for 'Leeds' 1930, which appeared in the *Field*; for 'Bradman 1948' from *The 1948 Australians*; for the articles on C.G. Macartney, A.A. Mailey and W.J. O'Reilly which appeared in *Playfair Cricket Monthly*

Collins Publishers and Dr Brian Robinson, son of the late Ray Robinson, for 'Yabba', which appeared in *From the Boundary* (Collins, 1951)

Irving Rosenwater for 'Fireworks at Blackheath', from *Sir Donald Bradman: a Biography* (Batsford, London, 1978) and for his poem, 'GSC, In Tribute'

Mr R.J.L. Altham, son of the late H.S. Altham, for 'Destiny in His Hands'

Walter Mailey, the son of Arthur, for the several articles by his late father

Bill O'Reilly for his 'First Duel with Don Bradman'

Bob Ellis for 'Fatty Finn's Prayer' from his *The Adventures of Fatty Finn* (Angus & Robertson, Sydney, 1981)

David Denholm (Forrest) for his *That Barambah Mob*

Lothian Publishing Co. Pty Ltd for *A Cricket Match at Hogan's* by the late Edward S. Sorensen

The Bulletin, formerly *Sydney Bulletin*, for the poem, 'A Boy's Cricket Dream', and certain other articles

Jeff Clores for his poem 'Lillee', which appeared in *The Cricketer*

The Herald and Weekly Times, Melbourne, for the C.J. Dennis poem, 'Oh to Be in England', from *The World of the Sentimental Bloke*, and for 'Dad On the Test'

The Hon. Mr Justice Gibney for the poems by his late father, J.T. Gibney

The literary executors of the late John Masefield, for the poem 'Eighty-Five to Win' which was published in *Blue Bells and Other Verse* (Heinemann, London, 1961)

Richard Stilgoe for his poem 'Lilian Thomson', and for his song 'Two Hundred Years of Cricket', and to its publishers Noel Gay Music Company Limited (a subsidiary of Noel Gay Organisation Ltd)

Blanche d'Alpuget for 'Bob Hawke in Form' from her *Robert J. Hawke: A Biography* (Schwartz/Lansdowne, Sydney, 1982)

The Hon. Joh Bjelke-Petersen for his contribution

Kate Fitzpatrick for her article which appeared in the *Sydney Morning Herald*

Gordon Ross, former Editor of *Playfair Cricket Monthly* and now of *Cricketer Quarterly Facts and Figures*, for the Denzil Batchelor pieces which appeared in the former publication

Michael Parkinson for his 'Fingleton, the Cricket Writer' and 'The Coming of the Aussies' from his *Sporting Fever* (Stanley Paul, London, 1974)

The Richardson and Chappell families for the article by the late V.Y. Richardson

Adrian McGregor for his article which appeared in the *National Times*

Mrs Ruth Oldfield, wife of the late Bert Oldfield, for the pieces on Gregory, McDonald and Carter, from his *Behind the Wicket*, Hutchinson, 1938

Peter McFarline for his 'Walking Tall With Bent Knees' originally published in the *Age*

Alan Gibson for his article about Colin McCool

Keith Miller for his explanation of the origin of the 87 superstition

Alan Davidson for his recollections of Keith Miller, from his *Fifteen Paces* (Souvenir Press, 1963)

Richie Benaud for his tribute to Alan Davidson

Bob Simpson for his appraisal of three captains, from his *Captain's Story* (Stanley Paul, London, 1966)

Ian Wooldridge for his article about Doug Walters

Colin Egar for his account of the Meckiff no-balling

Ronald Mason for his description of Lillee

Mr Christopher Milne for permission to use the letter to the *Times* on bodyline, by his father, A.A. Milne

Henry Blofeld for his report on Thomson

Trevor Bailey for his profile of Lindwall, from his *The Greatest of My Time* (Eyre & Spottiswoode, London, 1968)

Michael Page for his quote on Bradman, from his *Bradman: The Illustrated Biography* (Macmillan, Melbourne, 1983)

Robert Radford for Blue's account of Cotter's death

Air Vice-Marshal Rod Noble for two articles by his father, M.A. Noble (the Trumper profile is from M.A. Noble's *The Game's the Thing*, Cassell, 1926)

The Fairfax newspaper group for permission to use various articles

In a few instances, we have not been able to contact the owners of the copyrights. We ask their indulgence and request that they contact us. Similarly, we shall also be grateful to receive information for those items whose author, source or date we have not been able to establish.

Index of Authors